T. Buchanan Price

Snap. The ox-train era. Early troubles of border trade

T. Buchanan Price

Snap. The ox-train era. Early troubles of border trade

ISBN/EAN: 9783743351738

Manufactured in Europe, USA, Canada, Australia, Japa

Cover: Foto ©ninafisch / pixelio.de

Manufactured and distributed by brebook publishing software (www.brebook.com)

T. Buchanan Price

Snap. The ox-train era. Early troubles of border trade

CONTENTS.

			PAGE.
CHAPTER	I.	IN THE SNAP O' THE WHIP,	11
CHAPTER	II.	THE LITTLE MOUND,	27
CHAPTER	III.	A BARBACUE — THE HAUNTED CABIN — GONE!	41
CHAPTER	IV.	THE PIRATE'S CAPTURE,	55
CHAPTER	V.	THE SCOUT'S RESCUE,	72
CHAPTER	VI.	SUSPENSE — THE RALLY,	88
CHAPTER	VII.	THE LONG JOURNEY — THE REAR-PORCH,	104
CHAPTER	VIII.	TIM'S RIDE — NEARING THE END — CATO'S HOLIDAY,	120
CHAPTER	IX.	THE CONSPIRACY,	138
CHAPTER	X.	THE WAY-WORN RIDER — ROLL OUT!	151
CHAPTER	XI.	THE PIRATES — THE ROAD-SIDE CAMP — YARNS,	164
CHAPTER	XII.	THE BAZOUKS — THE BLACK BRIGADE — THE SPIDER'S NEST,	181
CHAPTER	XIII.	TO THE FORT — THE ROUGH-RIDERS,	195
CHAPTER	XIV.	"STRUCK HARD" — "WIPED OUT,"	209
CHAPTER	XV.	REBUKED BUT NOT REBUFFED,	223
CHAPTER	XVI.	IN THE WING,	238
CHAPTER	XVII.	THE OUTBREAK,	252
CHAPTER	XVIII.	THE ATTACK — THE BUGLE-NOTE,	265
CHAPTER	XIX.	TWO DEATHS — BECK'S DUTY,	279
CHAPTER	XX.	THE MAHOGANY CASE,	293
CHAPTER	XXI.	THE STRONG MAN'S TROUBLE — HIS REWARD,	306

SNAP.

CHAPTER I.

IN THE SNAP O' THE WHIP.

On the high bank of a western river, far out among savage haunts, stood a cabin post, the lonely mart of a rude trade.

In an outlook raised on the roof, not unlike the pilot-house of a steamboat, sat the trader, who suddenly spoke aloud.

"Hello! that's Beck," he said.

With a shout he hailed the rower, who neared the foot of the bluff, but his voice was lost in the whirl of the current, or spent upon the radiance of a sun-bronzed plain.

Beck in his canoe was but a few strokes from the landing; one dash more, with a few strides up the road, brought him to the cabin door.

"Back soon, pardner," the sentinel said.

"Yes; a short, tough scout, I tell *you*, Peter; I'm fagged, too, and hungry as a cayote." Thereupon the two men locked arms, taking the path to the abode near by. A word only was spoken by the elder, and that, the simple welcome:

"Come in."

The plain, weather-boarded white dwelling, under a high roof, with eaves sheltering a porch on either side, looked cosily clean in the mild, clear light of the early spring. The doors and shutters were of heavy timbers, crossed and cleated; above the front door a bison's head held in its teeth a horse-shoe; bunches of rose-bush grew by the porch rail; the fibrous creepers, not yet green, clung to the lapping board-work; cone-shaped evergreens and poplar spires sprang from the sward near the entrance. A wide hall led out to a kitchen yard, and a vine-clad lath frame, closing in a patch where summer blooms would spring, set apart the quarters, poultry-coops and well-shed. Within, there was a quaint sort of outfit; here and there a rough bench, a rustic seat and a deal table, took shyly to their betters. The trader had bought his furniture less for use and ornament than from some capricious notion of its former service. It was altogether a snug, far-west domicile; a highway charm to the traveler who saw the sun-flare on the garret windows. The grove and chimney tops were known in camps beyond the plains.

"Thar's a good farwell to it," said Beck, smacking his lips as he put his glass down on the sideboard.

"An heah's a set-out, to take the sharp edge off." said the other, pointing to a bowl of hot coffee, a pone, spare-ribs and hominy on the table, while he continued speaking:

"So you keep yer arms outer sight, John?"

John's long, dark beard fell upon his blouse of butternut jeans and his under-garments were belted, without weapons. From the knees to the feet he wore fawn-skin leggins, buttoned.

"Yes; you see, Peter, killin ain't the thing; all I do is to keep others from killin me, or you. I never shoot less I'm 'bleeged to; it tain't the best sign to see the tools in sight; they're handy, though, I reckon, if you'll look heah at my blouse-waist, inside."

"You say right; they offen make a fight or spile a bargain. Well, what you got to tell, John?"

"Lots; but let me off now." John was enjoying himself.

The pause gives a good opportunity to take their pictures; none better to touch upon their antecedents.

Cheviteau's face was a good one; every feature did its part kindly, in frankness; not less the gray hairs in grace, to the descendant of a *voyageur*. Toil is unpoetic; toil and strife, alike, cruelly prosaic. The splendor of a sunset marvel, the fleeting, airy grandeur of the dawn, had been cold and colorless, when as a barefoot boy he viewed them, leaning upon his whip. With his strong, virile faith, he had no fancy, no sentiment; a kindly nature unwarmed, for the poor are chilled, stood sternly to its duty. He was illiterate, superstitious; the phantom fires threw back to where he stood a lingering gleam on waves of gold-tipped verdure. He saw the omen, only. In the track of the sun, lying straight before him across the danger-haunted waste, he saw the path to success; he saw besides, all its lurking terrors, trials and mishaps, but with a snap of his whip he resolved to follow it. From the spot where the sun had bid him go forth he made his start, and there in after years he pitched his camp. At the foot of the bluff the river formed a wide plateau; there he built his wharf, — a steamboat landing.

First, as a cattle-driver, he held his way full well. Soon he owned a team; in the snap of the whip he earned enough to buy another, for he was shrewd, almost to cunning. He was self-reliant; all his earnings were turned into cattle, and experience, as it came to him, stood in the place of book-learning. He raised stock on shares with a cattle dealer; his teams increased to a train, and he became a freighter of goods to distant forts. He was brave, though prudence was his best virtue. Betwixt these little epochs of a lowly life, came all the changing hazards of the border; the wearied, footsore tramps, the sleepless nights; he was chased, hunted, driven back, robbed and cheated, but through all he strode into manhood with a round sum laid up. Then he married the dealer's daughter; a comely helpmate, who shared his cabin, shaped his habits, bore him a child, taught him to read and write. When death divided them, he felt a strong man's sorrow, deep, tender, lasting, but moved on, facing danger. The steamboat found his cove and linked his future with good fortune; he held it well, as to him seemed best. The place was known as CHEVITEAU'S LANDING; his men called him Colonel.

"Peter, when's that boy of yours coming?"

"In the nex boat."

"Can he load a wagon, or yoke a lead-team?"

"As good as any man."

"Does he know the peach-color; can he bring 'em wo-hawr on the run, in a short turn?"

"He knows an ox, John, from hoof to hawn, throws a lash pooty as a streamer, an on a trade he's keen as a briar."

"I never saw him on the road; what's his pluck?"

"Bes kind o' grit; you ken supple his jints if you need him."

The youth spoken of, an orphan, had been left in childhood a charge to the trader; had been trained in camp, sent off to school, thence to a city counting-room, and was purchase agent in buying the supplies for the post.

"He'll do, I reckon, Peter."

Beck's face, usually grave, was a little careworn. Years before he had enlisted at a far-away fort, and after winning, through merit, a sergeant's chevron, he set up for himself as a scout. His talk was careless, never boastful; his habits steady, and his sense of duty true to the old man's friendship, to the value of a name for good qualities; his past was a closed book, never opened or touched; his manner was calm, almost gentle, the fineness of true courage. In height and port he was a giant.

Mary, the trader's daughter, fresh from the field, looked in at the door.

"Anything wanted?" she asked.

A round, rosy face, in the summer hue of health, was seen under her rye-straw hat; the large, soft eyes were the light of a winning look, and the brown hair, caught up in clusters, coiled trimly above her neck. There was something ever so neat in the dark dress of the young woman, with its broad, white collar, and a scrap of red at the throat. Mary, too, had been sent from home; she, to motherly hands that reared her, and Christian hearts that loved her; she came back, and the goodness she had dwelt with came as a part of her; she took up each care with ease, her duties with a quiet good-will. Sometimes she paused, as if to think upon her exile, or to counsel with her courage, and her face saddened.

"So you've got back safe, Mister John, with a whole scalp," she said, using a common phrase.

"Did you think I'd leave it behind me?"

"No, truly, not you, if Kit can see the way."

"And you're fixed to stay out here for good, Mary?"

"I give her her liking, John, to live with her friends or come to me," her father answered for her, pleased with her choice.

"What would you all have thought of me if I stayed away?" the while she fluttered about like a bee; she dusted the pedlar-clock on the fireplace shelf, turned a chair in place, closing the sideboard door; "and you see, Mister John, I'm better off where there's plenty to do, with the will to do it; little by little, bimeby much may come to pass: a church, maybe; then a school-house, you know, and, maybe, — a good Christian out of you." She laughed at the thought of making a saint out of the sturdy scout.

"S'pose an Injin ketches you before all that."

"And wouldn't you catch the Indian, Mister John?" she asked, in her charming, childlike way.

Going out into the hall, she stopped at the door of one of the rooms.

"I've sent for the milk, Doctor Tom."

"Thanks, little sweetheart," answered a voice, as Mary hastened on to the porch, where she took up her knitting.

Over the lattice, not far from the knitter's seat, Chloe, the cook, handled the loaves and pies at the oven. She was a trusty old domestic, short, fat, and black. Her face, in eclipse, held on ever through the darkness of servitude to the good that was in it; its humor and content. She had served for long years in the trader's family, and had been Mary's nurse. Standing near her was a boy, a blacker mortal, and a cross betwixt the monkey and Jim Crow. He tapped with his heels the time of a tune, singing: —

> I'se got no time ter terry,
> I'se got no time ter terry;
> I'se got no time to stay wid-ee you,
> O—h, good fokes, pity me.

"Dar, now!" cried the old woman, suddenly; "what I tole yer, eh? He's gwyne an dun it, sho!"

"Who dat?" asked the imp, stock-still, his eyes and mouth wide open.

"Sumpin's gwyne to happin; dus yer h'yar me, Cato?"

"What fur?" The jet of the boy's face grew smoky.

"What is it, Chloe?" asked Mary.

"De chicken, honey; free times he clumb de fence an crow'd, chile."

This alone was the dire mishap; but the resemblance to the cock-crowing of the Scriptures, to her a sacred mystery, was quite enough as a portent of evil, from which she believed there was no escape.

"Let's have a smoke, Beck."

The two men passed out of the house, while the darkies fell to work, wondering.

The dwelling stood in the center of a group of storehouses; and from the path where the men were standing there was a good view of the post and its surroundings. With their faces to the prairie, on their left, partly within the circle, was a dense grove, a relic spared by the axe in clearing a larger wood. On the right was the cabin post, surmounted by the outlook, from which an unbroken vista reached to the horizon, and below it, far and near, could be seen the bend and sweep of the river. From the house-front, the eye fell upon the outlying plain; the kitchen-yard extended to the storehouses in the rear; a short distance further on was the bluff's edge. A deep road was cut into the bluff ascending from the landing into the enclosure, at the door of the post. Within bugle-call, on the right, was the camp; in the far distance a forest, and nearer a picturesque ruin. A creek ran across the plateau, near by this crumbling landmark.

"The post and camp, Peter, look about the same."

At their feet a grassy slope fell away to a lowland plain, hedged in by thickets.

"It has cost a heap o' trubel, John, to scrape all that together."

"I reckon," he replied, listening to the workshop anvils and the whip-snaps mingling with the sounds of a busy scene. A small army was quartered in the little valley. There, in sight, was the corral; lines of wagons, double-filed and parked; a settlement of cabins; further on, the grazing-ground, and cattle everywhere; to the right of it, the hayfields. And later in the season, the mowers' blades would be seen flashing in the sunlight.

There was good management of men, in the discipline of the post and camp, under train-leaders and a train-boss; a man, the latter had need to be, of many turns, fore-handed, firm, experienced; a jockey, a veterinary, a cattle-driver, knowing road-craft, savage customs and savage manners. Such men were hard to find, when found were seldom honest. The scout's calling differed from this, and included higher qualities as a leader, a guide. His employer was a freighter of goods, called a trader, as a purchaser of supplies, under contract. The period was that in which the narrow trails of the Indian and trapper widened to the highways of commerce. The scout was a leader of the caravan; he planned expeditions; he saw that the roads were clear, or fought his way through; he knew every stream and ford, every tribe, friendly or hostile; he must of needs be fearless, cool-headed, prompt, prudent, of sound common sense, a good rider, a sure marksman. And Beck was all of these.

"How's your stock of goods?" he asked.

"Pooty nigh chock-full; what Charley has bought will fill them houses."

The log store-rooms encircled the dwelling in a wide, round cluster of many buildings, separated to ensure less loss from the accident of a fire. Such was not generally the arrangement at out-posts, but seemed to be an idea of the trader, caught from the manner of parking his wagons on the road. There were assortments stored therein, with arms and ammunition, in readiness to supply a fort upon order of the government. In the way of drill an armed teamster stood guard, pacing the muniment, at night, crying the hours, while the trader snored like a patriarch.

The room they entered, called an office, held a high-desk, a table, an iron-box, a few chairs behind a rough, plank counter; on the wall a pen-traced map of North America hung from a spike near the roof.

"You ken go, Harry," was said to the young book-keeper, Harry Carver, a clever fellow and sharp, as the word goes, who seized his hat and went out.

They found Jack McQuain,—an old weather-worn trapper, just in from the mountains with his peltries, and ready to depart for Santa Fé,—seated there. A queer relic was this gaunt figure, whose broad jaws, ever in motion, ground the morsel of comfort.

"Hello! life everlasting," said Beck to the veteran, who drew forth his bladder wallet.

"It's forty year sence, I reckon, Beck —"

Happily, a distant sound checked what would have been a long recital; a sound much like the mellow-voiced harvest horn's over a meadow. Mary had heard it, and as the men listened, she called to them:

"Father, they're coming; it's the boat."

The trader rose, and taking down a battered Kent-bugle, he blew three blasts to summon his bull-whackers to the wharf. The boat's commander, after blowing the stop-whistle, was, in good faith and morals bound to wet his own, at his friend's sideboard.

Those who came in the boat were Charley Marshall, the adopted; Louisa Sommers, Mary's schoolmate; Judge Smith, and a loquacious old woman named Garrulson. Mary, at once, disposed her friends agreeably, except the aged stranger, who stayed behind in quest of a feather bed, the making and care of which had cost her hours of anguish. In good time she came along with her burden.

"May I never!" she exclaimed, "ef that ain't a breather."

"Wait, Chloe will help you," Mary said to her kindly.

"Jes tell me whar to put it, chile;" and presently she was toiling up the garret steps with the servant's help, rattling on, catching breath as best she could.

"Et's full six foot, nigh onto it, an no skimp mezure nyther, an Sue Fax's boy, the wus I ever seed, afore I had onct throw'd my akin bones acrass it, drapped a coal o' fire right in the middle on it —"

"Dar now, ole Miss, yuse safe," said Chloe, grasping the chance to put in a stopper.

Lu Sommers, Mary's friend, the pet of an aunt, and at her own home the favorite of a coterie of country girls, light-hearted, lovable and of sweet, plain manners, was pretty. She had an income in her own right. Lu was a childish, affectionate girl, but a riddle to her friends, in her simple, uncertain ways; just such an enigma as the truthful friendship of Mary could find out. Both were of good size, in the vigor of health, but they were as midgets in the company of the sturdy men about them.

There was little in the appearance of Judge Smith to modify prejudice, for he was not a popular man, though a politician. He was too much of a busy-body, with too little merit or grace; pompous, with no learning, an intermeddler where he was generally mischievous, and was called "Jedge" because somebody said he was a lawyer. In meaner parlance, he was spoken of as "a shark." The man was leanly tall, slovenly in dress, wearing his locks long, for effect, behind his ears; the few hairs below his nose were ill at ease, under the stare of his cold, gray eyes.

Beck was alone when the trader returned, but when he and his friend were seated, he said, promptly:

"I told you, Peter, I had lots to tell; now to

bisnis. How long has this train-boss been with you?"

"Oh, a long time; an he's a feller what knows all about oxen; knows too, every tribe twix h'yar an the Pacific."

"Don't he give you trouble?"

"Heap of it; he war a drunken slouch wen I bought out his teams; I took him kase it war safest, for he might set a tribe agin me; he has lived among em all, an he speaks Mexan, you know. I dragged him outen many a scrape, onct for the ruination of a family, an I've heerd wus things about him."

"Ain't his looks enough?"

"He ain't a pooty man, John; them eyes of hisen is like a thirsty steer's a day's pull from water; but wat ken I do; trade mus go on an we can't git good men fur his place; I do believe he'd yoke hisself with the devil, to bus me up, ef I turned him off."

"Your trains were robbed before I come to you; is that so?"

"Yes; an men, good men, war shot down at their teams."

"When was that?"

"Well, I know it war jes four days arter a full moon; the yeah I disremember."

Beck smiled, but went on:

"Peter," he said, almost sternly, "your train-boss worked that job."

"Oh sho; no — no; how could he?"

"He's a land-pirate; don't I know; he's in cahoot

with Injins an Mexans; he's chief of a gang of train-robbers."

"You shure, Beck?"

"Shure! why man, the nex thing will be to murder you."

"Tell me quick, John, how you know it."

"Know it! I know him like a book, an heah's a leaf out of it; see."

Beck drew from his blouse a piece of elm bark, on the inner side smooth as paper, upon which had been burned, with a hot point, certain hieroglyphics. Placed before the trader, in the upper left-hand corner was seen a circle; thence, diagonally, were four smaller circles; then two lines crossed, and a figure like the stem and branches of a tree. In the lower right-hand corner was a rough profile face, marked by a deep line drawn at an angle across it.

"That's a signal, Peter."

"Ken you read it?"

"Yes; see heah; that first circle is a full moon; that shows the day when the hound sent it out to the Injins; well, the four little ones are four moons, or days, don't you see now?"

"No, not zacly."

"Why, four days after a full moon you were robbed; how's that?"

"Go on, go on."

"Well, now see; the cross-lines and figger means the cross-roads and the lone tree on the forty-mile stretch; that's zacly the spot; thar your train was struck."

"Thunder!" cried the trader, as if suddenly stricken himself.

"Hold on, heah's more: that face you orter know by the mark on it; that's the slash cross the mug of your train-boss. That's the way he does bisnis; that's a letter to some Injin who led the raid on your train, and it was plain enough to him; they fought at the lone tree; the men fell back an give up, the Injins plundered an arterwards divided with the boss. D'you see?"

"Whar did you git this, Beck?"

"Never mind now; drop this pirate right off or your men'll think you're fraid of a thief."

"Fraid of him! don't you know better nor that, John Beck?" The old man's lips trembled; in truth, he saw all the old, old troubles fresh and fearful before him; an enemy vicious, devilish, step out on his path; an enemy to fight down through danger and death. But he got up from his seat quickly, bustled about with his books, and said:

"He'll go or hang, now mind, John."

The boss was sent for and soon he came shuffling through the gate of the counter, sneakingly. It was a hard, evil face he turned on the scout; a heavy brow, scowling and black, and there was a scar from the mouth to the temple.

"Mornin, kurnel."

"Hyar, take yer money an go; you hound, now go an no words about it."

"Yer all-fired scrumpshus; what's up?"

"Go, will yer go?" screamed the trader in rage, breaking the fellow's whip-stock, which he snatched from his grasp, throwing the pieces in his face.

Jack McQuain stepped in.

"Heah, Jack, quick," called Beck, laying his hand heavily on the train-boss's shoulder, "don't you know this thief?"

McQuain faced the man, staring hard at the cut on his face growing purple.

"Bill Cartwright, the cribber!" but the wretch had freed himself, howling curses as he broke away.

CHAPTER II.

THE LITTLE MOUND.

Before the sun was up, old Jack set out on his journey and was seen far away, a figure dwindling to a speck, as the day grew brighter.

"Come here quick, Jump; bring the rifles, and don't be as slow as your figures."

"In a minit, Whack. What's it?"

"A good shot at a squirrel. Come on."

Whack and Jump are not strangers, for Charley Marshall and Harry Carver had fallen by these nicknames in the most naturally boyish way. One called the other "a bull-whacker;" the "follow-suit" of the chum was "counter-jumper," and, boy-like, cutting these by-words short, they were known as Whack and Jump.

Whack was of good size, a plain, open-faced stripling, neither coarse nor comely; strongly built, wide shoulders, well-shaped hands and feet. He was the son of a Kentucky farmer, of good stock, who died poor. In his ways, the youth borrowed a little from the fresh manners of Western lads, and from the muscular form and freedom of a border-man. His mouth pleasantly held the cheery wrinkle of a half-formed smile.

Jump was very much like his friend in form and face, but the taller of the two, about the same weight, of the same mould; he stooped slightly from the habit of the desk. An air of conceit gave to his face a marked cast, not bold but complacent.

He was soon at the side of Whack, not far from the office-door, under a branching maple.

"Here, take your pet," he said, handing to his companion a Kentucky rifle,—the favorite border gun of those days: "let's load."

"Give me a greased patch; you can take your charge from my horn-point."

"It's my shot, Whack; where's your game?"

"Do you see that knot near the crotch of the big limb yonder?"

"Yes."

"Well, it's a squirrel."

"You don't mean that knot's not a knot?"

"Don't be funny, Jump; see here." Whack raised his rifle and fired, cutting the bark under the ambush, and the squirrel moved.

"Stand aside, Whipstock; give me a chance." The speaker was a good shot, but slow of aim, and while bringing his piece to a "dead level," Whack tried to flurry him.

"Your hind sight's raised, Jump."

"So is my gun;" but just as his sight in steady range covered the mark, a sharp, clear shot rang out behind them, and the game fell.

"Scalped him, by Jingo," cried Beck, lowering his

piece; "you're too slow, Jumper; an Injin would have spotted you before you shouldered. Come, Whack, the old man orders me to boss the camp, and you're my sargent. That's a clean, off-hand shot twixt his yehs," he said, as he threw down the dead squirrel.

"You may have it, Book-keeper; I told you your hind sight flickered," said he of the whip, laughing, as he strode off with the scout. His felt hat sat jauntily, and at every stride he flirted the skirt of his brown linen blouse,—the blouse of the plains, with its pleated front and rolling collar.

The report of the rifle summoned Doctor Tom from the ease of his arm-chair to the porch outside, and seeing the cloudlet of smoke, like so many of his hopes, resolved into air, he turned back, walking slowly.

This world-worn recluse was the son of a rich planter, in childhood a parent's darling, humored in the petty fancies of wealth, and taught to lean upon a family name and a feeble self. At college the boy studied and excelled, not from a love of knowledge, but spurred by a hate of those who tried to excel him; the only useful turn of his pride during life. He won honors in the profession of medicine, but his riches tempted him to ease, and sooner than be chagrined by a loss of practice, he quitted the practice altogether. The man was accomplished, but in little matters his vanity grew to be so puerile it was ever playing at cross-purpose with his better parts; a pride that urged the evil of his nature to war with the good and raised the strife of a dual self. He was ignorant of his infinite weakness; failure met him more than half-way, disgrace at every rash step, catching his morals in the meshes of a passion, ungodly, unmanly. His mind became morose, his nerves unstrung, and so he blindly went his way; he quarrelled with best friends, fought a duel, and went down through easy stages to the weaker vices of the gaming-table.

With what was left of his means he bought a steamboat. It had passed and re-passed Cheviteau's landing, and Doctor Tom and the Colonel were sworn friends. On one of the trips the Doctor, in a freak of high frenzy, being bantered at cards by a noted player, lost his steamer on the throw of a card. The furniture and outfit were exempt from the chance, and these, with a small stipend from land rents, were the remnants of a large fortune.

The throw of the card was a miracle, for nothing less could bring such a man suddenly to his senses; his better nature, his better self, upheld him in the crisis, his true pride was touched and quickened. He rose from the table indifferently, lighted his cigar with a bank-bill, bowed to the company and found his stateroom. There, in the silence, in his conscience, as in a mirror, he saw his dual self reflected; a poor, tortured, trembling spirit, helpless, almost hopeless, spoke to him feebly but gently. He fell asleep; the voice in his ear and tears on his pillow.

He was another man when he stepped ashore at the landing and made the formal transfer of his steamer to the winner, in the Colonel's presence. What passed between him and the trader afterwards was known only to themselves, but the Doctor, after choosing a part of the outfit, sold what was left of it, and became an inmate of the house. And so it was that therein the long oaken table, covered with green cloth, became the dining-board, the leather-seated arm-chairs ranged with coarser fellows, the carved side-board gave out an odor like a Turkish cabinet's, the little elegancies of Mary's room were tokens of the Doctor's regard. She was to him the seraph in the desert of his misfortune.

"What yer doing man?" cried Chloe from her doorstep. A teamster stood near her quarters about to fire upon a bird on her roof-tree, "is yer gwyne ter bring de jegment?"

"No, I'se gwyne ter bring down a bird."

"Doan yer do it, please; dar now don't; kase yer see mister thar's gwyne to be truble; its a comin sho; in de bang o' de rifle dar's blood, I tell ye, ony you keep on."

While she talked the bird flew away.

"Good-by, Doctor Tom;" it was Mary's voice, as she looked in at the porch-door.

"Good-by, little run-about," he replied, walking faster to see her off, and kissing his hand, with a bow, as she left the steps.

"Good-by, aunt Chloe!"

"Good-by, honey, is yer gwyne? de laws, Cato," she said, dropping her voice, "all dat little one wants is fedders fer to fly."

"Fedders!" the boy's mouth once opened, it burst into song, as his heels flew up:

"In der mornin, in der mornin."

"Oh, hesh, boy, yus allus a tryin fer to frow yer legs away; do hesh."

"She's cut out jes like my sester Ann, and she was the pootiest piece of gal-flesh —" here Mrs. Garrulson stopped short as Chloe left her "to min de stobe."

Mary started out on her love-lighted path, catching the glow and the glory of the bright summer morning; in her hand a quaker-basket filled with nic-naes for the sick, and the little rye-straw hat. Her daily stroll, and many times daily when needed, was to the white hamlet of cabins, close by the green cattle pasture. Around her steps a flowery wilderness threw its perfume on the air. Her influence was felt in all the little matters of the post and camp. In the cabins she was an oracle; to the simple folk she was as one inspired, working wonders through the perfect sway of love; her own sympathies so tender, she felt suffering as keenly as the sufferer, chaining each one to her happy self, each link a blessing from other hearts.

As she neared the camp she heard the cheer of the men, a welcome to Beck; she saw her father tending the cattle-drove; she heard the sound of the anvil, and the snap of the whip: nor did she fail to note the Judge in a shady spot hedged about by a group of off-duty hands. His acquaintance with each had ripened in ten minutes, in ten more he spoke as one who had known them all their lives. Some of the men had families, and the log-huts were held by them rent-free on conditions which enforced order and cleanliness, Mary's own terms. Nor was she loath to reprove or warn them.

"I heard of you, Mister Tim," she said, to a rollicking Irishman.

"An did ye, indade, mavourneen? I' faith, its little good o' me, that same, ochone. Bys will be bys," all the while squinting a mischievous eye, for he had been on a spree, and he knew that she knew it.

A step further she asked a Scotchman:

"How's the baby, Mister Sandy?"

"Bad, bad, mi lassie, it war a skittish night along wid the sic 'un."

A little beyond she met Jane Potts, a buxom damsel, wearing a downcast, timid look, who spoke in whispers.

"Good mornin," the girl said, as she edged away.

"Well, Jane, has your ship come in with the beau you wait for?"

"Not much of a ship jes yet."

At the cabins crowds of urchins followed her; she passed in and out of each hut dispensing her basket's freight, striving to make some one happier, or something better, in the delightful drudgery of doing good. She looked in upon the sick child asleep, whispered a caution, and hastened back.

To vary her walk a little, Mary took a path skirting the camp, and as she moved along briskly, she was suddenly confronted by Bill Cartwright. He eyed her thievishly and boldly advanced a step, then shuffled off, as if by a glance he had been warned to move on; a step further in the grass stood a mounted Indian. At an angle of the path some distance beyond, in an interspace of foliage lighted by the flickering sunshine, she heard a woman's voice and saw the form of one; no longer the demure Jane, but Jane as a hoyden taunting Whack. She passed by, and where the path entered the camp she saw Beck awaiting her.

"Don't take that cut-off any more, Mary; tisn't safe."

"If you think so, Mister John, I'll take the other."

"That's right; didn't you see my rifle leveled on that hound; he saw me, and the boys have gone to warn him off. Now I'll see you home."

"Well, come along, if you will; won't you carry the basket?" She tossed it to him.

Had he grown dear to her, this son of Anak, this boyish giant? Was she trying his wits by her winning ways, or teasing his shyness? She knew calmly his worth, his kindly heart, its truthfulness, his bold, brave manhood, but there was much in his life ajar with her conscience.

"Thar's some bad men about, and that's why I said what I did, Mary."

"That's kind of you; if evil meets us or dogs our steps, Mister John, can't we find a little fresh good, for every new evil; that's the right way, ain't it?"

"Right enough," he answered, looking down on the midget of his admiration, as if she had read to him the law; then straightening, he drew closer, from an instinctive right to guard her.

In height, and in the power of his massive limbs, the latent strength of his sweeping stride, the swing of his arms, in presence and purpose, Beck was a leader; but the manner of the man, at his ease, was almost boyish; there were moods also into which his spirits fell suddenly, from gay to grave, and sometimes abruptly into a show of temper, or a transition to a sober strain that seemed despondent. His old friend thought all this came from some cross in life, and Mary hoped it was a dislike of his calling or a distrust of it. He was delighted in her company; to what she said to him in playful humor or in the many and varied ways in which her conversation was set to catch his thoughts, his consciousness, he was a kind and ready listener; but his past was always forbidden ground; if invaded, he rose confused, with a shade of pain on his face, and walked away.

" What a splendid day this is; I wish I was a barefoot girl again."

" You."

" Yes, me; don't you know I once run barefooted?"

" You! — well — Mary!" The scout gave voice to surprise, or showed his respect in this concrete form.

" Well, what, Mister John?"

" Nothin, only thinking of a little, white foot, on the big green earth; didn't it hurt you?"

" No, of course not," she said, laughing.

They had reached the porch where the Doctor was

talking with Lu, and Beck moved on towards the office.

"Why didn't you take me with you?" asked Lu.

"Take a day's rest, write to your Aunty, then I'll show you everything."

"How's the baby?" asked the Doctor.

"It was asleep."

"That's better than physic."

An hour later she was seated in her room, stitching an infant's dress.

"Mary, here's a friend would like to see you," called Lu; and laying aside her sewing, Mary came out to meet Sandy, the teamster, at the door.

"Will ye come, lassie? the bairn is takin bad, an the mither is sore worrit."

"I'll come right away, Mister Sandy."

"An I'll gae to the cabin wid the word, bless ye."

As the teamster hurriedly left the house, she called Chloe into counsel, handing her the tiny dress, which she looked at, as she parted with it, with gentle regret.

"Do it up, nicely, Chloe; will you? Make it white, Chloe; just as white as snow."

"Chile, dat baby'll neber put it on."

"Maybe not; but fold it prettily for me; won't you?"

"To be sartin, honey; sho, I will."

In another moment, after placing the house in Lu's charge, she started off, tripping over the same sunny path. She paused, looked back and said to her friend:

"Lu, don't forget, father likes three lumps of sugar in his tea." In the gleam of the summer day, still and golden, she sped along, and Beck seeing her pass, followed at a distance, with his rifle over his shoulder.

Sandy's cabin, just over a roll in the prairie through the camp, was soon reached. It stood in the shade of a sycamore; a window on either side gave it the semblance of comfort, and a bush of sweet-briar scented the air about the door. Mary entered the front room of the two; from the rafters hung yellow gourds, onion-ropes, dry herbs; there was a pile of walnuts in a corner; a jar of apple butter and a row of pale, blue-rimmed plates, a burnished knife or two, on a shelf.

Taking up, at once, the duties of nurse:

"Come mother," she said to Sandy's wife, who sat on a stool by a trundle-bed, fanning, "take some rest now, I'll call you if baby's no better."

"Ah, chiel," moaned the woman, looking up, "ye've come to see the last o' the puir thing."

"As God wills, as God wills, mother; but I'll wake you, and maybe baby will mend: go now."

"I'll rest the body a bit, for it's mony a night it's needed it."

As the nurse opened her budget, the weary wife stretched herself on the larger bed, and was soon asleep.

Taking the stool, Mary glanced down tenderly at the sick child. There was pain on the thin, haggard face, the hollow cheeks were bloodless, nor could the light of its golden hair, which she raised and let fall with a pang, lend warmth to the pale, cold form.

She rose, as the infant with a low, sobbing cry,

waked from its troubled sleep. Sandy was sent off for Chloe to hasten her to the cabin, for in all sudden emergencies she came at Mary's call.

"Say, Mister Sandy, that the child can't swallow, and leave word at the house, please, that I'll sit up all night."

It was not long to wait, for Chloe came in haste.

"It's no yuse, honey," she said, "nuttin kin help it, cep de Great Marster."

"Shall I wake the mother, Chloe?"

"It hasn't long to go on dis a way."

When Sandy joined his wife at the bedside, a feeble flutter of the baby's breath wafted the spirit into the evening's calm. All still, in its snowy robe, the little one lay, the pale face whiter in its nest of curls, and Mary placed in its tiny hand a sprig of the fragrant briar.

Silence, moved only by murmuring whispers, chastened the solemn watch. All was still in the heart of the solitude. Clouds, warm with the flush of sunset across the wide, white radiance of the moon, sailed by, and beams of light streamed in upon the nurse, and fell upon the cold little image. Out of the night came consoling voices to the ear of Mary; but suddenly there seemed to rise above the sweet-briar bush at the window, a dark and forbidding shadow; it changed to a hideous fright; and, as it grew upon her sight, she saw the dark, bad face of Cartwright. He leaned upon the window-sill, reaching towards her, and about to speak. Then, the luminance grew intense; she heard and felt the wafting of pinions, and saw a descending Azrael, whose sword was like a glint of the lightning, as the shadow vanished. Again, she heard the waves of distant winds, and the air was filled with a perfume not of earth. A flitting sprite, winged with the fragments of a shattered star, gazed in upon her, — greeted her with the smile of a cherub, — the face was the baby's.

As Mary rose in the transports of her dream, Lu caught her in her arms. The sun had risen, and the girls hastened home, stopping but a moment on the way to give directions for the funeral. The trader met his daughter at the door.

"You will come with us, father, this evening, when we bury the child, won't you?"

"Yes, we must all go," he answered.

In the twilight, they came together from household and camp. Cheviteau was the first at the cabin, and he said to Sandy in his plain, honest way:

"I'll take up the child, Sandy, my man, jes the same as my own, — jes the same, Sandy." Then raising the little painted box under his arm, and removing his hat, his men followed him in line to a knoll, where, among the flowers, the grave was opened. The scout, with friendly care, covered the coffin.

> "I wish that His hands had been placed on my head,
> That His arms had been thrown around me,
> And that I might have seen His kind look, when He said
> Let the little ones come unto Me."

It was Mary's voice, singing a sacred melody. Its

sweetness, trembling with emotion, rolled forth on the green prairie waves, dying out in pathetic pathos. It waked a thrill in the stern hearts around her, and left on the manly faces a happier look.

CHAPTER III.

A BARBACUE. — THE HAUNTED CABIN. — GONE!

A FLOWERING spread of daisies and buttercups overlaid the little grave, when the day of the barbacue came round.

The earnest request of the Judge to be permitted to address Cheviteau's men, in a formal way, had received kind attention. The old man was stoutly set in his own political notions, and never stinted those under him in the freedom of their own faith. So it was that when he gave leave to hold a public meeting in his camp, he determined to make the day set apart a holiday, and with liberal good feeling, a barbacue was allowed. Through the day, there would be feasting and sports, and in the evening the Judge would hold forth in a speech.

All had gone early from the house to the camp to join in the merry-making. Beck had led Kitty, his coal-black mare, to the family group, seated in the shade of a small grove, and having placed a side-saddle on the little pacer, held her so that the girls might have a ride.

"Come, Miss Lu, I'll help you up."

"Me! oh, no, please, let me off;" she hesitated, in a timid way.

"Yes, you will, Lu," Mary insisted, "for I know you're a good rider."

"I can set you in the saddle, if you say so;" an offer of the officious Whack.

"No, I'd rather not. I don't know the horse."

"I'll hold her head," Jump said, not to be outdone.

"Why, thar's nothing kinder on this yar arth than this little beast; she can do anything but talk; jes see heah: Down, Kit,— down, pet,— down." Beck touched the mare's knee with his foot as he spoke, and she swayed down so low he could almost stride over her.

"Is that a self-made hoss, Beck?" asked Cheviteau.

"She'll do anything I tell her."

"Come now, Lu,— for me."

"No, no, Mary dear; I don't like to, and all these men about the camp."

"Oh, pshaw, they're a kind, good sort of people,— home folks,— rough as they look. I go among them every day, Lu, and there's never an unkind word to me; they're a long ways off, too." Mary was a little piqued.

"Get up, Miss Lu; I'll ride behind and hold you on," Whack added.

"Give me sitting room on the tail, and we'll all go;" this was Jump's attempt to help out.

But Lu held back, while Mary, impatient, and more than all, not to let her friend think that her father's people would be rude, she asked, coaxingly:

"Won't you, Lu?"

"Not now."

"Well, help me up, Mister John." She measured the stirrup, and placing her foot in the scout's hand, she leaped into the saddle. "Break me a thorn or two, Charley, to pin on my hat; now, the whip." Then catching the bridle short, she turned away briskly.

"Well,—Mary!" exclaimed Beck, rubbing his hands like a happy boy.

"Hold hard, child, when you speed her; she's a pacer, mind," cautioned her father, as she passed him.

It was a balmy and serene day, all freshly bright in the youth of the season, and the little mare bore her mount far away in the white breadth of the sunlight. Not for a moment did the scout drop his eyes from the receding figures. He looked at them fixedly with an earnest, pleased look. The rider kept on in a steady pace to a wide, open mead, flecked by rolls of the prairie, and as she gracefully swept around it, changed her course to ride back. Beck's lingering sight saw her seat herself down in the saddle, shorten the rein, raise the whip, and he felt a sudden thrill caught from the spirit of the girl in the distance.

"Here she comes; here she comes," he kept repeating loudly, "here she comes, boys, like a prairie-fire,—look at that!" His wild manner was noticed at last by the crowd, and all came forward, looking on.

"Stand back," cried Doctor Tom, "make way—I'll bet—"

"Hoopee! look thar, — see that!" was heard, in the scout's wordy glee, while **Whack** and **Jump** kept a track clear for the speeding horse.

"Hold her hard, girl — steady!" called out the trader long before the rider neared him; repeating his heed at intervals.

Bending low on the mare's neck, her stray hair weighted down and afloat, like a loose lonely fleck of cloud, she plied the whip as her horse, now in a run, leaped over the stretch of meadow. On she came, charmed with the sport, and as she neared the camp she raised her hat.

"You, Kit!" she screamed, while under the whip and voice, the little, lithe thorough-sped swept through the lines of cheering men.

Beck seized the bridle, and without aid, Mary leaped to the ground. "There, Lu," she said, "you see how we ride out here; I am none the worse for it."

"Well — Mary!" said Beck, "it beats a circus;" he went on, as though the happiest day of his life was but half over; "and Kit, did you ever do it like that before?" patting the mare's face for an answer.

It was now high noon. At dawn the men had stirred the low fires of the roast-pit, where cords of wood burned through the night, and the huts of the hamlet turned out on the green, their household goods and gods. Men and women, their babes and brats, barelegged, barefooted children, round and plump, were there, the young ones running wild. The big, fat ox was spitted whole, then turned on chains with hayforks, and carved on a platform, with cleavers. Then, there was a set-out of loaves and pies on rows of plank-tables, loaded down.

The custom was, in the trader's primitive notion of a feast, to open it in person, standing with his family about him, at the head of the board, and as the men filed by, to exchange with each the homely good-wishes of the day. In this way came Tim Murphy, the rollicking Irishman, Heinrich, the Dutchman, Sandy, the Scotchman, the Mexican vaqueros — cow-boys — their ponchos, glazed sombreros, and jingling spurs a little at odds with the dress of others. Then came the border-boys, bull-whackers, all, — yahoos, suckers, corn-crackers, — and one, a lad from a local Egypt, called Legs, by his fellows, was set up well for a deep swallow. He halted, raising his tin above his head, and in a loud voice, saluted:

"Heah's to Miss Mary, boys, hooray!"

Cheer on cheer rang out, for the boy had spoken well, and had flattered adroitly. No good word of the day came nearer the trader's heart, and even in praise so boisterous, what he said was to Mary a touching reminder of the men's good will. Quickly taking a ribbon from her hair she tied it on the boy's whip-stock, saying simply,

"I thank you." Then they all cheered again.

And so the barbacue began while the family and friends drew off to their own pic-nic, that the people might the better enjoy themselves, left to their own fashion. The men enjoyed the treat heartily.

Standing by, old Chloe fixed herself and smiled, in

doubt of her senses; the pies and bread were no longer in sight, a whole ox had vanished, and her labor of a fortnight dwindled away in a twinkling.

"Gib 'em half a chance, dey'd breed a famine, sho;" she said to herself, as she turned away.

The meal broke up and the men betook themselves to their favorite sports, running, jumping, tilting, quoit-pitching, feats of strength; and above the flux of human voices, the crisp, sharp snap of the whip* was heard, till Mary rode her race. Some of the men were practising "the double-snap," others, trying to chip a plank with the cracker, or to make "the fur fly" from a dry hide. A good-humored set seized the giggling Cato and stood him upon the tail-board of a wagon, like a puppet. A threat was enough, and as the whips cracked, he danced and sang:

   Oh-ho — ah-ha,
    Toota, toota ta;
   De heel an de guffin
   A pattin an a puffin,
   Oh, watch dis little niggah
   As quick es eny triggah,
   A pattin an a puffin,
   Yer tink he's good fer nuffin.
    O-ho — ah-ha,
    Toota, toota ta.

Before the earliest bird that morning, Mrs. Garrulson had cause to make known to all under the trader's shel-

---

* This incessant sound was the music of the trade, but the ox-whip of the plains is a torture when used cruelly; the stock is a hoop-pole about five feet in length, the lash of twisted ox-hide of double length, of double-twist mid-length, and is whirled and thrown with both hands. The snap, in the recoil, is as loud as a rifle's crack; it bruises and scalps where it strikes.

ter, that she, at least, was awake, and in healthful vigor. A crashing sound, varied by an occasional scream, hastened Cheviteau from his quarters to the attic.

"What ails you, ole woman?" he asked, doubtingly.

"Ails, is't?" she shouted back, catching for breath, as she dropped the remnants of a chair, "ef half yer life had a bin spent a savin' penny arter penny; then all ther truble of a raisin geese, goose arter goose; then the pickin an a sortin of de feders, feder arter feder, ter make a bed fer yer ole man to stretch his akin bones acrass; to tote it roun from helifex to kingum cum, and to hev a darn-sarned, dog-gone rat a nibbling at it;" here she cast about her for the chair-leg, "I tell yer Mister, I'se boun to slay that ar varmint, ef I beat yer house down."

With the sympathetic feeling of an old man, the Colonel retreated.

Now she was seated on the green, the center of a crowd of women, and sun-browned curious urchins, forming an outer circle. She had talked to them in a tireless strain; the pedigrees of each she questioned closely, rattling on to scraps of gossip, to frantic romance, the dire and vengeful raids of Indians, to fables of spookes and blood-sucking vampires, to whip around to cures for cattle-murrain, rot in sheep and baby-colic.

"An ken you cure the heart-ache?" asked a malicious girl, eyeing Jane Potts, who stood up with shaded eyes bent upon the distant Mister Whack.

"Ar it bad sot; for ef it ar it's a death-stroke," she replied, gravely.

"Not so bad as that comes to, I hope," the other said, giggling.

"Hope; jes what I sed to John — an he ar my second and war slow to take on — John, ses I, ef it wasn't fur hope the heart would bust, — he tuk."

"An wat's good fer the rhumatiz?" queried a crippled neighbor.

"May I never! rhumatiz — why honey, I ken cure it; jes try a little frog's-fat."

"Frog's fat!" exclaimed Jane, in a loud, contemptuous laugh, "where'd you ever see a frog with any fat on it?"

In truth the old woman had never seen the marvel, but to be silenced in a flow of wisdom:

"What!" she said, springing up, "its jes as easy to find that ar, as ter find a young man's heart; gal, you don't know how ter find it;" turning the laugh on Jane she walked off in triumph.

Lu and Jump had drawn away, leaving the Judge and the Doctor, the trader and Mary chattily passing the time, in the shade, while Beek, looking after the stock, sent Legs out on the prairie to drive in stray cattle.

"Oh, such lots of fun as we had, such nice young fellows to ride about with us; how aunty would scold and fret;" warbled Lu, in little fits and starts, in high and low key, varied by the melody of her rich laugh. She spoke of her home, its many and lovely attractions, of a farm they had, its stock; of her pet cows and horses and almost everything connected therewith, until the plodding Jump, a business young man and from force of habit, soon resolved mentally the net value of these lands and tenements; what the income of the pretty girl might be, even to the simple and compound interest.

"I told them," she went on, "that I was coming back when I could bring a scalp to my apron-string, and not before," using a border phrase.

Jump whistled low, and said, after a pause:

"Did you?" rubbing his head, an intimation that he was ready to submit to her gentle cruelty. Lu prattled on.

The family party was broken up, when Mary and Whack took a stroll; the former holding back her consent until upon a quick change of thought she joined him in the walk. Her father had observed in Mary's manner throughout the day, a quiet, if not a sad turn to its usual mirth; even her ride had seemed to others than himself a feverish excitement, which some unknown cause had warmed.

"Yonder's a place I'd like to own, Colonel."

"Spec you would suh, but you can't squat thar, Jedge."

At a distance less than a mile, a picturesque ruin partly hidden in a clump of evergreens and wild, blooming berry bushes, caught the speculator's envious eye. It was a tumbledown, deserted cabin; birds made their nests in the crumbling chimney, the scarlet-leafed vine crept between the rolling logs, the rocks about it were weather-browned, capped with ivy or with moss. Perched on the crest of a hillock among shrubs, the ground fell away in slopes of verdure, greenest where the brook leapt laughing down the gorge. From the trees near by the lengthened shadows crept, color-crossed with sunshine, at one, around, about it, with the garish plain. It was a rare, poetic touch of nature.

"A beauty-spot, Colonel, that's a fac."

"It's a lanmark, Jedge, for forty miles to the trains comin in." Set in the round, broad, gilded space, it seemed to rise in the azure air like a tropic island from the sea.

"It's a squatter's site, ain't it?"

THE STORY OF THE HAUNTED CABIN.

"Yes; an the mos misfortunit set I ever seed, Jedge. Some yehs ago, a man an wife an chile came along an squatted thar. They lived sorter content like, till the man war took down with the agur, an from that out, things went crooked with em, — the crookedest sort. I give em a lift now an then, an Mary she took kindly to em, little as she was, but the man he went from bad to wus, and broke squar down in the fust rut. He war as crazy as a june-bug, Jedge, and then this sarpint Bill Cartwright crept over the doorstep. If I had a known it in time, I'd a made his flesh creep afore he went too far. Howsomever, I liked Tobias, for he war a hard-working, honest feller, I mus say that, an as fur scripsher, he know'd it, Jedge, from Genesis to Reverlations, varse by varse, clean through. I've seen him at the plow, the cattle pulling outer furrow, the sweat a pourin down his face, an he a talkin holy-writ. Things went wrong in course; his wife got tired an mopish like, an she took sick an died. Ole Chloe, she sot up long nights along with her, but it war no use. Then thar was the darter, a woman mos grown, the foolishest, mos stubborn, simple kinder critter I ever seed, but to her father,—why, Jedge, he thought she war jes an angel. I've seed em settin at ther door-step yander, at sundown, many a time, her head in his lap, an he a playin with her curls. She war a likely-looking piece too, an I've heerd him tell her them stories from the bible — better nor preachin, Jedge, — an I sot thar with em offen, an many a story took holt on me, an has hilt its holt ever sence. But the gal went off with Cartwright — an thar's no countin for a woman's notion --- he treated her like a dag, they say, an she died too. Wen her father heerd it, he went a ravin, an a stavin mad, madder than a bald-hornet, an he's bin wanderin about from that time out. It war a long time arter Bill come inter my service that I heerd about the thing, and then he mended like, but Tobias, some say he ar dead, some that he ar alive, but Cartwright allers swore he had seen his ghost out thar, an the men say the place ar hanted. But I got it from his people; it's a pooty place, too; jes see the sweep from the hill to the ravine, thar. No, Jedge, it can't be had."

"I'd like to have a mortgage on it," he said in a disappointed way, and the two separated. The trader sought out the nook where Jump was still paying the most courteous attention to Lu, and the Judge joined the crowd.

As Beck rode off on Kitty to picket her near the cabin till sundown, when Lu would ride, two mounted Indians rode into the camp. They were often seen there and no heed was taken of their coming, — a common imprudence on the border was to rely too much upon the Indian's show of friendship. Settlers and traders were generally careless until some catastrophe awakened their caution.

Bill Cartwright was not far away. The fellow, boy and man, had served his turn at every vice; his were the coarser qualities of the bully, though not without a certain boldness in crime; a blood-reckless audacity, a flurry of passion, which won him admiration among the worst of his kind. He consorted with thieves, a low gambler in the cribs of the south-west, the go-between of the debauched savage and ferocious white; he the prime cause of race antipathies and rankling hates.

Mary and Whack returned to their starting-place, talking fast, he protesting, and she with a warning finger.

"I have a right, Charley, to speak to you as a sister; such I've been to you and such I hope to be ever. Take care, don't trifle; she's not the girl for you; she's artful, and when too late you might find that something had changed your nature in a minute, and you'd be lost."

"But, Mary," he said, "you're too fast."

"Don't let that be said of you; now I'm going to the cabin alone, for some flowers."

"I'll go with you; it's a long tramp from here."

"No, never mind; I've been there often alone." She feared what might be thought of their going together, as too close an intimacy. Had Beck been there he would have followed her with his rifle ready, but Mary felt safe in the love of all who knew her.

And, as she tripped away, the two Indians, unseen, rode off on their ponies.

On the path she had taken, the ruin lay sleepily quiet; the fitful shade around it fell away in graceful curves. All forms of delicious color, from the scarlet hues of a low, western sun, to the far-off specs of beauty, one by one were singled out; the emerald and the ruby, plumes of crimson, the feathery and winged floss, waved in myriad sprays of light. And Whack watched every step of the gentle girl, as she sped along, swinging her little straw hat. Then he turned slowly toward the camp, as her form, in a flood of sunshine, disappeared.

Beck had sauntered into camp again, and the Judge, ever alert upon the chances of a politician, and in accordance with the day's arrangements, had now drawn the crowd around him. In the ancient form of a stump speech he made hay while the sun lasted, and he was near the close of his harangue, when, nearing the camp, the teamster, Legs, was heard hailing at the top of his voice.

The trader and the scout were standing on the edge of the crowd, and on the instant Beck's muscular form seemed knotted to spring beyond its common height.

"Sumpin's happened," he said in a husky voice; "where's Mary?"

"Where's Mary?" was repeated.

"Gone to the cabin," said Whack.

By this, the lad, running an almost breathless race, drew near.

"Gone! gone!" he shouted.

"Gone!" The word was taken up and retold, while Cheviteau drew the exhausted boy into the crowd.

"Speak quick," he said, trembling in the white heat of fear and suspense.

Again the ominous syllable, — "Gone!"

"Can't you talk straight. Who's gone!"

A moment's silence for breath, then the lad's pale face looked up and he answered : —

"Bill Cartwright an yer darter!"

CHAPTER IV.

THE PIRATE'S CAPTURE.

Out of the golden light into the shadow, out of the shadow into utter darkness, so danger followed Mary, enfolding her like night, as she bent above the violets and bluebells; a swift, black frown of fate seen in the faces of the flowers; a cloud-like, dismal ill, closing in her life, on the instant, to a narrow span of pain; a clutch like the vulture's, deep and vital.

"Open yer mouth," hissed Cartwright, as he threw a blanket over her head and his arms held her fast, "I'll brain ye with my pistol."

Through all her border-life she feared that some mischance might bend her spirit to a rigid test, but her native, air-fed strength, and that stronger trust besides in will to bear and suffer and be brave, had like an armor girded her. She felt the cold steel touch her shoulder; it waked her latent courage, and dashing the blanket aside, she stood alone, defiant.

"How dare you! how dare you!" she repeated with crimson cheek and quivering lip.

Springing out of the man's grasp with a sudden wrench, the brute was amazed.

"H'yar now," he snarled, "give in, you'd better,"

fearful to lay hands on the calm, steel-nerved young Spartan facing him — "you'd better, or it mought be wus for ye; I'se got nothink agin ye gal, mind that; wen yer ole man comes down to make us squar, I'll give ye up an not afore."

"It's worth your life to hold me," hinting that he would be slain if he did not yield, or was caught, "do you count on that?" she asked, folding her arms.

"I allus take that chence."

"What's your price?" She ventured the question to gain time, casting about her in a thousand flash-like schemes.

"Price! well, a cool thousand or two, I reckon; dus ye mean bisnis?"

"Is that what you want?"

"Yes, that ar all I'se arter; money ar the thing, gal."

During this brief, shrewd parley — and it brought her a world of comfort — she saw the one sordid motive of the wretch. From her kindness to him in her father's service, and from his manner now, she gleaned the belief that her capture, bad as it was, was the worst of his wicked design.

"If that is what you want, Bill Cartwright, listen to me; I'll pay the money. Let me go, and I will promise it."

"You!" he exclaimed, the scowl clearing away for an instant as he looked at her steadily; "gal, I'd trust ye fer a milyun, but you kent; don't I know, so don't tek on, an dry up."

He whistled thrice through his fingers, when two Indians on their ponies rode out of the hollow near by,—the same redskins who left the camp and who had been often fed from her father's bounty. They led the mustang of their leader and the scout's mare, stolen while grazing where he had fastened her picket-pin but an hour before. By signs they made known how they came by the catch.

"Luck," said the pirate, grinning coarsely with a lively faith in Chance, as a deity to be worshipped.

Mary now saw that to submit was the one sole alternative, in which the airiness of her disposition began to fade. Still, she held patiently to the belief that no other harm than a cruel captivity, how long she knew not, was in store. She tried hard to keep back the teeming fancies of fear and hope, the trooping thoughts of her home and friends, the ever wakeful doubts that she might the better plan an escape from the peril. Could she give a signal? What if she screamed or ran? Would he shoot her down? What if when mounted she dashed off at the risk of her life? She weighed and turned each thought, for there is no faint or spasm in the bravery of a border-bred girl, but in her captor's look she saw a purpose not to be trifled with; she was completely in the power of a brute and savages, he worse than they; nor was she allowed to dwell upon her miserable mischance. Cartwright motioned for the mare to be brought.

"Now, gal, mount; thar's no time fer foolin, an throw this round ye, fer we'se gwyne ter ride all night." He handed a blanket to Mary and was about to raise her to the saddle, when she sprang from him.

"I've warned you, Cartwright, not to touch me; if you do, I'll call the ghosts from the cabin to protect me." She had spoken hastily, girl-like, in a weak threat, but it struck deeper than she knew. A superstitious awe seemed to blanch the villain's face. He looked over his shoulder, as though he feared she had seen some specter in the ruin behind him.

"Ain't thar a hoss all saddled fer ye; wat makes wimmin so tickler, anyway?" He seemed willing enough not to provoke what charm her purity might have with unseen spirits, and permitted her to lead the mare to a stump and seat herself in the saddle. Waving his hand, one Indian took the lead, the other the rear, placing their captive in line between them. Cartwright, with a leap, crossed his mustang, and after a glance at his rifle, he looked up.

"Git!" he growled; and as they moved off he followed.

Just then the young teamster, Legs, made his way through the shrubbery. Hearing the voice of his former boss, and shrinking with fright at what he saw, he crawled behind a stump to rest his rifle. It was a sight to have unnerved the bravest heart in camp. The surprising boldness of the kidnapper, and the danger of the girl, so well-beloved, would have flurried the best among them. Legs raised his gun and leveled it, but as he ranged on the thief, the sight-line led to Mary further on; he changed place for better aim, but Cartwright in a rambling gait, seemed to shift his form so as to expose her to an unsteady shot. The boy's wits forsook him, his hands trembled, and the distance from his mark rapidly widened. Down the ravine, over a path leading to the river growing wider and smoother, the thief and his party quickened pace. The teamster sprang to his feet, fled to the camp, shouting his shrill alarm.

In the grasp of Cheviteau the boy dealt a hard, fell blow in the words he uttered. The old man staggered back; there was frantic haste in talk of the men around him, and the women circled about the form of Lu, who had fainted. Chloe went about clapping her hands, frenzied at the fault of having prophesied truly, and the crowd began, one and all, to wear the look of desperate men.

"Mount, boys; I'll give a thousand to the one —" said the trader, gaining strength and voice. For this little moment Beck stood apart, stung to the quick of his free, unfettered nature, and with pained impatience in his face, he strode into the group.

"Stop!" It was a stern command, and there was silence; "don't budge an inch; not a man."

"What fer, John Beck?" hurriedly asked Cheviteau, flushed with anger.

"Leave it to me; I'll bring her back. Don't you see what the hell-cat is after? He'd draw the whole camp out, to steal in and burn down the settlement. Don't you see his dodge? A crowd will make him hide. If I ain't back in three days, follow me along the

Divide. Double your guards and hold the camp; here, Whack and Jump, get ready; I want the big sorrel for the trip."

The boys had been silenced, for the wit's-end in youth is in facing sudden fright. Beck's forte was to do the right thing at the right time and place; he knew what to seek, what to avoid; there was scarcely anything he could not endure.

"Which horse for me?" asked Whack.

"The roan; give Jump the grey; both have bottom and speed; arm yourselves; thar'll be lively times, I reckon. Heah," he went on, motioning to the teamster who brought the news; "which way did Cartwright head?"

"Down the crick to the river."

"To the river," he muttered, walking fast; "then he'll hide."

At the house, Lu was attended by Chloe and Mrs. Garrulson, and the stories of the latter of similar trials, distorted from a supple memory, had in a measure composed her; but on seeing Beck she ran to him tearfully, wringing her little white hands.

"Will they kill her, Mister Beck? Oh, my, what will we all do? Now she's gone we all know what it is to be without her! Oh, Mollie, Mollie!"

"Keep heart, chile; thar'll be no killin of her, I reckon. Somebody else mought get hurt, if he keeps on a foolin."

"Will you bring her back safe? Will you, Mister Beck, do tell me?"

"Yes," he said, stamping the ground heavily, "heah, to the old porch again, — cep, maybe, — well, never mind." He was reflecting that it might cost his own life, as he made his way to the office, in haste.

None who stood in the startled crowd when the boy's cries brought all to their feet, felt the force of what the lad said like Doctor Tom; stab-like, piercing, it struck his heart, and he it was who jumped to the trader's help, with a brotherly impulse, in kindred sympathy; he it was who held that the scout was right, who stilled the rising rage to reason; for he felt that the cool, sturdy sense of Beck was the surety of Mary's rescue.

"Save your advice, it's out of place here," he replied, snappishly, to the Judge, and turned about to aid the men in mounting.

The scout was ready; he caught up his rifle, strapped it over his shoulder, with his powder-horn and pouch; then belting his blouse he spoke to the boys who had joined him.

"Sling your pieces; the nags must be let out, and you'll want both hands; get blankets; we'll be off."

The Colonel galloped up with the horses. Then came the order to mount, as Beck threw himself into the saddle, drawing a strong check on his sorrel.

"Let out, lads." There was a rasping sound of hoofs, then each sprang forward.

"Give 'em head, and spur deep till daybreak," called out the old man, as he stood straining his sight on the fading forms speeding away over the prairie, his heart gleamless as the blackness coming on. As the darkness deepened, the voice of the guard was heard:

"Nine-o'-gluck; ull-ish-rycht!"---"All is right,"— it mocked him, painfully.

The kidnapper signed to the dusky thief in the lead to take a shadow-covered trail along the river bank under the bluff, and pursuing it, they soon came upon a drift-wood barrier at the foot of a beetling cliff. Here he broke his way through the stubble, and they entered a dark, water-drenched cave and dismounted. Cartwright left them huddled together in the gloom, warned to silence, and hastily turning back to where the debris had been upturned and thrown aside, he reclosed the passage so as to deceive the best practised eye. It was the trick of a fox, but the visage of the man was that of a wolf, as he stretched himself at the cave-mouth, peering through the brush. There he awaited the later moon-lit hours, hoping to wear away the pry of a search.

On his horse, Beck, in the full liberty of action, — a recklessness of freedom, — fed the strongest passion of his nature. If not at times, genial as a companion, he was always a spirited guide, and to return Mary safely, upon the bond of his word, lent a glorious frenzy to his ride. As he and his comrades dashed on through the perfumed shade, the hoof-strokes stirring the odors of the sod, he spoke to them often.

"Lean forward, boys, and set easy for a long run." At the haunted cabin they drew up.

"Whack," he said, as they were about to separate, "you and Jump keep right on,— hipitisplit. Mind what I've told you, boy. I'll strike back to the river-line—the wolf thinks we've opened on a wrong scent— and I'll drive him out, and follow, while you must cross him. So long." Speaking sharply to his horse, he was soon out of sight.

The scout felt sure that Cartwright did not dare to take a straight course, to be seen from the post on the wide open prairie, and that he had dodged; that his round-about circuit would be by the river, thence to the Divide by another road, and his own plan was to hang close on the other's heels, trail him, follow him out of the valley to where the boys would confront him at the cross-road, on the ridge. He dashed out of the darkness of the ravine, rode to the bluff-line, and drew rein. He had drawn up above the hiding-place of the thief.

Mary stood in the narrow prison, watched and warned by the fierce, furtive glances of the redskins, and hardly dared to breathe. The stillness was unbroken, save by the seething of the pools or the buzz of the gnats. Now, in the light of the rising moon she saw the distant outlook, the outstretched arms of the grove-trees, but she closed her eyes and pressed her hands hard upon her heart.

In his ambush, holding his horse's head, Beck kept a long, silent watch. At last, in his steady search, he saw below him on the river-brink, forms moving stealthily in the shadow; he saw them mount and steal away. On sight he knew them. Beck had once seen the cave, and his instinct led him to it; now he counted the riders as they took the trail. He was astride his thoroughbred in a bound, and with the speed of the wind vanished from the bluff.

The Indians turned often to look back, but not a word was spoken; the thief merely motioned and they pressed on for hours. Riding into a clearing or park, in the river-bend, he signed to them to dismount. The place was a deserted post; a few rotting sheds marked the spot where the fortunes of some trader had been wrecked in a night, the treachery of the swift current forming a sand-bar, and cutting off approach to the landing. Here a grass-grown road diverged towards the Divide.

Mary permitted the ruffian's shoulder to support her as she jumped down; not that she was less resolute nor he less repulsive to her, but from a hard ride weariness, needing aid; and as her hand fell listlessly, it touched the handle of his sheath-knife; there was a quick movement, and the blade unnoticed slipped into her dress pocket.

The animals were allowed a drink and a roll, and the thief stretched himself likewise on the hard gravel. He sprang up to lave his face at the river's brink, and wetting his throat from a flask, he gave his pals a bite of hard bread and jerky, then ordered them off.

Kit swayed down to receive Mary in the saddle.

Folding the blanket about her head and shoulders she rode to her place between the Indians; on a sign they turned into a road. Mary had listened for a cheering sound, for she knew that Beck would throw his very soul into the pursuit. But the silence gave no token.

They had ridden far and fast, through the night, when another halt was gruffly ordered at a spring by the wayside; it gushed forth from a thick growth of tangled weeds and briars, upon which the moonlight streamed.

"Ef yer want a drink, cold as ice, thar it is," said the pirate, and he bade Mary get down and wait till he filled a horn-flask. He was groping among the brambles to the fountain-head, when suddenly a loud, wierd scream rang out on the still bright air; a scream as of some fiend in the caves of earth, shrieking to forbid the wretch's touch upon its waters. All at once there rose in the light a tall, gaunt, spectral form, almost fleshless; a ghastly, ghostly figure madly threw up its naked arms, and its white locks and beard, matted and snarled, fell about it like a vesture. Springing to full height, its shape, clad in patches of cloth and blanket, the long bony fingers tugged at a girdle for a weapon, and finding none, tore its hair in frenzy.

"Back, back, you lip-lapping cayote; hell's curses on you, go back!" then the nightmare vanished, creeping in the brush like a beast of prey.

One Indian touched his forehead and both were silent, and as Mary glanced down at her feet she saw Cartwright crouching there, a frightened animal. She had heard of the wild man, and knew the fear of him which many held.

"It ar the dead, the dead," the pirate whispered in a coarse voice, large drops of sweat standing on his face as he covered it with his hands. "I kent shake it; its har is like windin-sheet, and its eyes like Texas cattle's."

Wrapped in the same bright beams, wherein the hideous shade had risen, Mary's form and face like a fair spirit's seemed to guard the peace of the night.

"Vengeance is on your track, Bill Cartwright; will you hear me? You can be better, braver, bad as you are."

A drink from a liquor-flask had called back his courage.

"Don't yer preach; that I hates the wus kind; ef I are a bad man kent yer keep shet about it? Mount," he called out, savagely.

And Beck had seen it all not a fathom's length away from Mary; he stared at her with an earnest, loyal look from his shelter behind a rock.

The kidnappers rode on under the far-reaching sight of the scout, who saw them at a long distance disappear in a grove. Never before was the contrast stronger between the man's power and patience, his ease and vigilance, as when he loosed his horse, and in the love of his wild life, he was off like a flash. His course was at an angle from the road to the lower outskirt of the little wood, in which the thief's party disappeared. Where the thicket-growth hid him, he rode fiercely, or when screened by the high, moss-grown rocks, he held his horse hard, in a furious quest, yet noiselessly, and only the birds and r the leaves knew of his presence. He got down, tied up, threw a blanket over his nag's head, then crawled near enough to search the grove. What he saw in the faint light of the dawn made, his brave heart for once stand still.

Meantime the young aides of the scout were rising from the springy soil of the valley, and nearing the top of a ridge. Known as the Great Divide, by some called the Big Backbone, it ran obliquely across the plateau of the prairie, contrived to serve the needs of traffic. From its hard gravel the hoof-clatter echoed back upon the silent lowland, as they sped along, leaving behind landmarks that noted their speed.

"You see," said Whack, "they've got water handy to freshen up on," he spurred his horse and the two increased their speed.

"What road has Bill taken?" asked Jumper, not knowing the course laid down for them to follow.

"He's taken the river road, we reckon, but will turn sharp for the west, and on this trail, further on, we'll cross him, while Beck comes up in the rear. They're three, and we're three, the best must win; can you count that up, old pen-scratcher? Draw up, Jump, we'll let 'em champ the grass a minit;" the boys got down and stripped their animals.

Jump pointed to a rock jutting out from the hillside, "there's water there, let's get behind it."

"You see right well, for a bookkeeper, in the dark; if water was at the root of the grass, it would be high as your shoulder, but —" he stopped short, grasping his companion's arm; "listen," he whispered.

Above the hum of the mites, the drone of the beetle, a sound, at first far off, seemed to draw nearer, quickly. Loud voices were heard, broken by laughter and the jingle of spurs.

"Look to your horse and traps, Jump;" in another moment they were hidden behind the rock; "stand close in, take a turn of your lariat round your horse's nose; are you ready?"

"Yes," answered the other.

"Throw your blanket over his head; take care — easy; hold tight, lay your left hand near his nose; — right."

Now, close at hand, the tramp of hoofs and jingling of spurs were heard, and a voice, high above all, cried loudly:

"Hi, mula! vamo, carajo!" as a pack-train was driven furiously past their retreat.

"H-sh," cautioned Whack; after a while he added, aloud, "they've gone down to the valley on the other side."

"How do you know?"

"Can't you foot up that; oh, you're a jumper; if they were scratching gravel on the road wouldn't you hear 'em; well, as you don't hear 'em on the road, they must be off it; that's the sum total, rooster;" the sounds grew fainter and fainter.

"What kind of gang is it, anyway, Whack?"

"Land-pirates, certain; some train has been robbed since nightfall; Injins do the stealing and these cusses buy from them; they must have a crib not far off, and what puzzles me is, these Mexicans so far from their bee-line along the Divide, and so far east; but let's mount; we've got no time for cyphering."

"Why did you blindfold the horses?"

"Blindfold 'em!" Whack laughed outright; "that'll do for a pen-plower; they were muzzled, gummy; you see, Jump, if one horse sees another in the night, he'll whinny, sure; well, the blanket stops all that, if you hold it tight about his nose; and, if he can't see, he's got sense enough to stand still. Cover your rifle-cock from the damp; if it misses, somebody at the other end of it mightn't miss you; it makes a big difference, Jump."

Once more upon the hard, white road they spurred on, and crossing a creek, they again ascended to the highway, and held their pace till daylight.

"Here's the cross road, at last, Jump; see, it comes up out of the valley; we'll tie up here, till Beck is heard from."

On the lower side of a briar-wood clump they found water, and there unsaddled. As Whack turned to regain the ridge, looking up he saw in the dim, morning light, the lean ghost which had crossed the path of Cartwright. He whispered to his companion:

"It's the wild man of the wilderness, and I'll speak to him."

"Has he any sense?" asked Jump, very naturally.

"Sometimes plenty of it; he's mad on one thing only; and hangs about the trains praying like a beggar for a knife or gun; he never gets one. Wait."

With hands uplifted, the poor distraught inveighed against the vipers of the earth, the wolves in sheep's clothing. Again he spoke in altered voice, tenderly, as one in sane mood would to a wife or child, and he, to some dear vision of his memory. Whack laid his hand upon the creature's shoulder, speaking kindly, in the vein of his mania.

"Be strong to fight your enemies; come man, and eat;" the lunatic followed him without a word. At the spring the boys gave him bread, and Whack, in the same strain, to denote that he shared the wretch's sorrows in his own, spoke again, slowly.

"My sister has been stolen, and our home is broken up."

On the instant the wild man threw away his bread and sprang to his feet; staring hard, he seized the speaker's arm.

"Come here! come here!" he screamed, dragging Whack at his heels. On the highway, shading his eyes with trembling hands, he at last pointed to the valley.

"See the smoke, yonder away?"

The other, straining his gaze as the morning mist like a curtain rolled up in the distance, was able to trace a curl of blue vapor, rising slowly.

"I see it."

"It's the smoke from hell's hot-house," roared the tramp; "there the serpents writhe in and out, — in and out; go there, you'll find her; I saw her in the night; he took her there."

"Who took her there?" exclaimed the young man excitedly.

"The fiend, the robber; the lion which devours; the tiger with his prey; the devil and his whelps, Bill Cartwright; go there, you'll find the gal; give me a gun, I'll go."

"I have no gun to give you, my good friend, but, — " before he answered the vagrant was gone, running wildly; his arms cleaving the air, his voice that of loud supplication.

"Smite! smite! oh, ye hosts. Let down the vengeance held in wrath; vengeance, vengeance!"

"Come quick, Jump," and when they stood together, Whack said:

"Mary Cheviteau is yonder, in that grove, down in the valley."

"There's where the pirates headed for, I reckon."

"True enough; they crossed lower down, but bore away for that crib; poor Mary!"

"What will you do?"

"Wait for Beck, if we wait till doomsday; come here."

Whack pointed to a rock-mound near by, hidden and shaded, and there the boys, leveling their pieces ranged on the valley road, stretched themselves, waiting and watching.

CHAPTER V.

THE SCOUT'S RESCUE.

The Mexican packers who rode the fierce scamper over the Divide, were, as Whack believed, a gang of train-robbers fresh from the haunts of plunder. They were bearing its fruits to their crib, from whence the smoke ascended. This den, built of heavy, squared logs, circled by a brushwood shelter, was hidden in a close, thick-set brush-growth. A boundary of rocks, overgrown with the high grass of summer, enclosed the grove. The place was made to serve as a storehouse for stolen goods, bought up by train-robbers from thieving Indians.* The captain of this bold gang, from the far south-west — a young, saffron-colored cut-throat, was a rogue of the Spanish type; a crafty but trifling chief, and was obeyed by his gang as best suited their moods. Not so his slave-wife Josefina, ordered to hasten breakfast, who heeded his command, at once.

The pirates unloaded their packs while their leader,

---

* Collusion with Indians in the nefarious business of ox-train robbery by bands of desperate thieves, is well known. The use of a pack-train for such a purpose was not common, but several well authenticated stories are told of their use in this way.

caressing his mule, made a singular show of affection and malice, which the Mexican contrives to heap upon his beast.

"Companion of mine, friend of my soul," he said, kissing the shaggy face of the ugly hybrid.

"Beautiful as a girl, my heart;" still patting the neck and the dark cruciform on the spine and shoulders.

"You little, little mouse." This he meant for its size and color, also the wide difference from the American breed, in lighter and swifter limbs, and a playfulness less rash in the rear foot.

While he talked, his manner changed from a mild rebuke to tragic blasphemy; wherein the backbones and toenails of all the saints in the calendar were invoked with fearful oaths, and the pet of the moment before became the pitiful victim of the lash.

Suddenly the crowd sent up a loud, lewd noise of jabber and shout, laughter and jest, when Cartwright, his pals and the captive rode into their camp. It was a welcome out of joint, for without a word the kidnapper dismounted. He had no thought of meeting the gang at such a time; the theft of Mary was not a crime in common, and he was quite proud to feel that it was his own, of his own peculiar dash, and for his own pockets, only. Sullenly he gave his horse in charge of the Indians, and held Kit as Mary alighted.

Glancing at the swarm of cut-throats who eyed her keenly, her spirits wavered, almost hopelessly. Brave as she was, she felt deeply the wrench of fate; looks were set upon her that she feared less than she abhorred, and it was a pitiful strait for so good, so true a nature. Trial sharpened every emotion; the face of her mother was an ever-present vision; the voice of her father rang in her ears, and the manly form of Beck was remembered as of one among the dead.

Little she knew or thought, as with an effort of the will she turned her face sternly to defy the worst, that the eyes of him whose shadow seemed to fade away, were bent upon her with a glaring gaze. He stared in upon the scene that for an instant stilled every pulse of his being. Prone, at full length, peering along the barrel of his rifle through a rocky crevice, he felt his muscles twitch and spring; his hand tightened as he saw the tears, in a brief outburst, course the beauty-lines of Mary's cheek; he thrilled, strained, bit his lip deeply, but still he watched and waited.

Josefina, the round-faced, copper-hued woman, in the forties of her frail years, whose saucy mouth and fine teeth gave a generous touch to a happy look, sat near by. She was coaxing the damp chips to blaze, and the smoke therefrom was the far-away sign pointed out to Whack by the wild man. Now and then she turned to scan the sad features of the girl before her, a little jealously, for with a toss of her turban she as much as said:

"As the looks of me,— no, no; — me of the fandango, she of the whiter kind, the Mother's child,— no —

no;" if piqued for the instant, she curbed the feeling smilingly as she sang:

> "Las niñas del Durango,
> Conmigo bailandos
> Al cielo saltandas
> En el fandango — en el fandang."

While Cartwright, having led the mare off, was pinning her picket rope in a park near the skirt of the wood, the Mexicans had drawn round the cook and her companion. It was well that the ears of Mary were dumb to the loose words that fell from their lips, when the dandy captain strode up to where she sat, and without warning, touched her cheek. So bold an insult in effect was as fire to powder. Springing to her feet, her burning face aglow, she drew the knife and held it raised:

"Stop!" The one word only, spoken loudly, calmly, coldly, and the ruffian drew back.

Beck was on his feet ready to fire; his form erect, quivering. He took deadly aim at the villain's head; prudence to the winds, he was ready for the grapple hand to hand, but the voice of Cartwright stayed him. In the pause of the instant, Mary's conscience stirred, and all womanly, she trembled like a leaf.

Casting off his coat, with pistol drawn, she saw the fellow nearing them.

"Don't fire, don't fire," she had but time to say. He came on with a bound, his weapon down, to deal a blow that might have felled an ox. He struck the insulter down.

"Ahind my back to crowd a little gal like that, you pepper-fed sneak," he railed, with fearful oaths.

And Beck dropped his gun as he drew back, muttering:

"Good enough; so Mary's safe, and now you're cock of that heap, Bill; I know you."

"Don't you be afeerd, gal," said the boss, as kindly as he knew how; and then he beckoned to his redskins. Very soon thereafter they rode away on their ponies, and the Mexicans, forewarned, feared the man. They knew, should they slay him, before the day was done a tribe would hound them to a bloodier fate. And the knave went among them fearlessly, talked of plunder and passed round his flask; nor was it long before the stricken bully swallowed his wrath on easy terms, and played the dog for a drink.

Cartwright was surprised on meeting the pack-train at the crib, and more so the scout, with a sharp and strange alarm. The riddle worked out was this. The boss had sent to the south-west border for the Mexicans to come to him at a rendezvous named. He had conspired with the tribe whose lands were in sight of the post, and had led it on thieving raids. The spoil of many bloody forays was in its keeping.

The gang had bought Cartwright's share, and the Indians received their portion of the loot, and when the trade was over he warned the packers to retreat out of danger by the most direct route. But word came to him of the next day barbacue at Cheviteau's; he left the Indians hurriedly in quest of a chance to serve his bitter hate. The Mexicans, lazily resting, held up their departure till the following night, and then, directed by the tribe, drove their train to the crib.

The affront to Mary softened the heart of Josefina; it melted in the warmth of her rancor towards the brute, who mastered her and who was cowardly to the girl. In trouble, women are more helpful one to another than men, and she prevailed upon Mary to be seated near her, as she piled up the tortillas or stirred the pot-mess, reddened with pods of pepper. All the while, in the musical flow of the Spanish, so richly expressive, she prattled, lovingly.

"Come, dear little, little sister of mine; eat, little one; little one, Josefina, the friend of you, says eat."

The words, though foreign, were seemingly pure, as also the woman's manner and look, so that Mary was won by the gentle eye and by the voice of sympathy.

Cartwright held the crowd in peace, planning his villainy, and there was much in his boldness which drew his listeners closer as he gabbled a mongrel slang. But soon, as they needed rest, all had stretched themselves under the shelter, save two, who, serving as sentries, played cards while the others slept.

Mary bore up patiently with her new friend, but her head drooped, do what she would to be watchful. At last she gave up and followed Josefina to the cabin, kneeling on the spread prepared for her comfort. Her attitude, as a golden cross on the neck of the woman fell into her hand and remained there, was such as to inspire her comrade, to call back to her a faint remembrance of better days, as Mary's prayer ended and her eyelids closed. Josefina, awed and chastened by the contact, drew the wearied one closer, and pillowed her head, with a kiss.

"Sleep, little gem of the soul of me, in the love of the cross, baby, sleep." She sat for hours awake, revived by the touch of virtue.

Beck made a hasty search around him; glancing at the deserted camp-fire and at the sleeping thieves under the shelter; at Mary, through the open door; at the kidnapper near by, clutching his rifle as he slept; at the card-players on guard. He crawled out of the thicket, to the skirt of brambles; he loosed the picket-pin and girthed the blanket round his sorrel. For a while, leading his horse, he crept along close under the rocky wall, through the brush, and then he mounted.

"They're too many for me now," he said, grasping his rifle, then plying his spurs fast on the flanks, as he madly rode off towards the Divide, where he came upon the boys and called them from their cover.

"Quick, lads; I've tracked 'em to a crib below; she's grabbed by pirates and a tribe of Injins; they'll come a boomin fore we know it." Whack and Jump soon joined him with their horses, saddled. "Now follow me," he said, leading his sorrel back again to the upper limit of the thicket, the boys at his heels with their nags.

From a painful dream Mary waked, and looked

about her dazed and blinded by doubts; she sprang to the cabin-door, was about to pass out, when Cartwright met her. He let her pass, but followed her to the camp-fire; he spoke roughly, — the sleepy, stupid insolence after drink. He told her whither he would take her, — to some low bagnio of the heaven-forsaken haunts of a Mexican town, — and would hold her there till her father ransomed her. She sank down by the smouldering log-heap.

Beck and his boys concealed their horses, and made all safe with the muzzle and picket-pin; after which he crept away to a close-grown cedar bush, nearer the inner circle of the camp, and saw, through the web-like cover, Mary and her captor. What moved him he knew not, but a quick impulse, a gleam of purpose, turned him back to his aides to direct them as his plan was forming. He stationed Whack on the right, Jump on the left, each in his own ambush and in sight, having agreed upon signals.

There came a pause, an endless minute to the spies, in which Beck seemed unnerved, bewildered, as he discovered Kitty near at hand. All at once, as the boys watched him, like a flash his face colored. He whistled very low to the mare, and she pricked her ears; he whistled again and again, in his old, familiar way, and the docile little beast neighed, stamped, pulling hard on the lariat. The scout kept his eye on Cartwright; he saw Mary point to Kitty, and by her motions to tell of the mare's hunger. His heart quivered as he hoped the man would come near the grasp of his hand; he looked and saw instead, Mary rise, and in a rapid walk start towards them; then, with a hopeful, manly smile, his face at once brightened. He signed to the boys, in rapid movements of hands and body, to aim at the thief; they leveled their pieces; he signed again to fire if he followed her; then he knelt by the edge of the bush. Never in all the adventures of his brave life had he felt such a feverish longing; his breath came by starts in the spasms of emotion.

None but a strong, devout woman could have played Mary's part; she played it grandly. As she drew nearer and nearer, almost near enough for Beck's arms to clasp her, he uttered a strong, calm whisper:

"H-s-h!—it's me—John Beck; look at the mare—straight ahead."

She started, drew up to her full height, came on, as a gleam of hope shone in the sweet, young face, flickering like the shade and shine of an April morning.

"H-s-h!—lead Kit behind this bush—I'll save you;" he signed to the boys to join him.

Nearing the mare, Mary turned, motioned to Cartwright that she would lead the animal to graze further on,—the perfection of acting and courage combined. She slowly untied the lariat, made a noose round the nose, turned the hiding-place of the scout; turned and stood at his side.

He grasped her in his arms, seized the rope, and in another moment he was astride the mare, clasping Mary; he whispered to the boys to follow, riding under the thicket shielding them, till they reached the ridge.

"Quick, now; help Mary up behind me on the sorrel; mount and lead the mare; hold tight."

"Look back," cried Whack, riding to the lead. The scout turned his eyes to the far distance.

"It's the Injins Cartwright sent for; spur deep."

The riders spared not, voice nor spur, in that race for life along the Big Backbone.

On the Divide the gang saw far away the tribe approaching in a run; but the delay widened the distance between the scout and the thief, and gave the former's party the chance of a slip.

They had ridden hard for miles when Beck turned in his saddle to call a halt at the top of a hill declining to a creek.

"The beasts can't stand this lightnin, let's down and swap. We must keep Kit fresh; swab out their mouths, Whack, and give em a swallow; how do you stand it, Mary?"

"Well enough, I hope, Mister John," she replied, as she hardly dared to discourage her friends, though almost ready to drop with fatigue.

"That's the way to talk; you'll make a scout yet. We've been a scratchin, boys, I tell *you;*" the horses gave signs of hard work in their drooping heads and foam-covered sides. Just then, looking back along the trailing stretch of the hard, white road to the horizon, Beck's quick eye caught a glimpse of dark objects moving, and he spoke sharply:

"It's them; Cartwright's gang has jined the Injins; and they're a comin, boys, with hoop and yell. I'll dodge em, Mary; trust to me." He took another searching look at the pursuers. "Turn off the road," he said, "so they can't sight us; Jump, help Mary down; lend a hand, Whack, and take the blankets off; be quick." These were spread out in the direction of the creek. "Mary," he continued, "when Whack and I lead the horses to the edge of the spreads, you and Jumper take up the loose ones and lay em out ahead." By following his directions closely, they finally gained the middle of the stream, without leaving any visible trace behind them in the marshy soil. Beck tied a cord to the last blanket, upon which he and his mare stood, and threw it to Whack on his horse. Then he mounted, leaped Kit into the water, and taking the cord from his companion, with a strong jerk he drew the blanket to his saddle bow. They moved on where the bottom was sandy and even, and the water not up to the stirrup.

"It deepens here, boys," Beck said further on; "hold their heads well up, and look to your pieces; here we go."

The horses took the current easily, and after a short swim, landed their riders at the mouth of a canyon. On a bar formed round a jutting rock-shed, they came ashore.

"We're safe now for the night," said their leader, helping Mary to dismount.

"If they miss the trail won't they turn back?" asked his comrade Whack.

"No; Bill's too old a hound; he'll keep up the hunt."

"How can he when the trail is lost?"

"He'll keep straight on, scatter his gang and lay low"

"If he get's off the trail how can he see us?"

"In daylight he can scan the whole country; out of this we strike the prairie."

"So we're only hiding for the night?"

"Jus so; for you see, Whack, the Injins' horses are fresh, and they might have caught us, and at night we can't be seen from the post."

"In daylight, you think, we have got a better chance?"

"Certain; for then our nags will be fresh; and if the gang sight us, so will the Colonel; he'll be in his look-out, sure."

"Couldn't we push on along this creek?" asked Jumper.

"No; this leads out the wrong course, and we might run afoul of em; fightin in the night will do whar there's no women."

"H-s-h!" whispered Mary, whose ear had caught the sound of falling hoofs.

"What do you hear?" queried Whack.

"It's them," said Beck; "stand by your horses' heads."

The sounds grew louder, but suddenly ceased altogether.

"They've lost us;" the scout spoke low, listening.

"What are they doing, Mister John?" asked Mary.

"Thar's jus daylight enough for em to see the trail break off, and it puzzles em."

"Do you think they could find us?" she asked in a womanly way, more timid when comparatively safe than when in imminent danger.

"The Injins might, but they won't."

"Why?"

"A white man's leading em; if an Injin led, I'd feel unsafe."

"What are they doing now?" joined in Jump.

"They've broke up into squads for a search; that's their calls;" shout after shout was repeated. A clear, loud voice rang out, and soon beyond the creek, again was heard the tramp of feet, and gradually the sounds died out.

"He's led off his pack;" exclaimed Beck.

"Have they gone?"

"Yes."

"And we're safe," cried Mary, joyfully.

"Yes; for the night; what's the use for him to hunt a blind trail in the dark; unsaddle, boys."

Mary now urged by her companions to take rest, and feeling its need sorely, consented; she had but touched the blanket spread for her, when she fell into a heavy sleep.

"Whack, why don't you stretch yourself; I'll stand guard; you and Jumper want a snooze."

"Not till she's safe; see, she sleeps as if nothing had happened."

"True grit, boys, I tell *you;* well—Mary; she's got the pluck of a man, with the heart of a true woman."

He left them standing over the prostrate form, and groped his way along the course of the stream.

Coming upon a cove, and near it a pasture waist-deep in grass, he returned for the horses. He found the boys, each seated at Mary's feet, and sound asleep.

"They can't help it," he said to himself, "it takes years to harden the bones and limber the muscles for sich a ride."

Now standing alone in position between the horses and the sleepers, having an eye to both, he weighed well the chances of their escape.

"I've done all a brave man oughter do to get round the use of my weepons," he reasoned, "but if I must, I must, that ends it;" how long he had stood debating with himself, he knew not; but on looking up, he noticed the rising moon.

"Whack! Jump!" he called out.

"What is it?" cried the latter, placing himself at the scout's side.

"Well done, youngster, you take a surprise without a flurry; come, boys, to saddle."

After the horses were brought, he said further:

"Strike a match and see to your guns; Whoa, Kit; you little minx; she's trying to git out er her skin; can you ride, Mary, without a saddle?"

"It wouldn't be the first time."

Beck girthed a blanket round the frisky mare and helped her to a seat.

"Hold your rifles ready; now, Mary, ride between the boys, lean forward and keep her steady; move on."

Striking a road through the valley, the light through a rifted cloud found them in the open country; in the wide, solemn silence, without shelter from the lurking foe. They rode on without a word, mile on mile through the scent of the wild flowers.

"Day'll break on us in sight of the post; let the nags walk," Beck ordered.

"If we can only escape,"—Mary had hardly spoken, when the scout, riding up, motioned quiet.

"I heard em," he said, in a low, firm voice; "it's them on the Divide."

"Shall we spur up?" asked Whack.

"Grab the mare's bridle, both of you; they'll come a bilin soon as they sight us; drive on."

"We can beat em, Mister John," called out Mary.

Beck had fallen to the rear with his rifle cocked and thrown across his left arm. All at once a yell, the wild, shrill scream of the savage nomad, was caught up and flung back by the bloodhounds from their lair.

"Keep a strong hand, boys, and break into a run," shouted Beck. Gazing back into the hazy distance, he saw the gang divided into two parties; the foremost were Indians.

"Now for it, lads; a run for life; Mary, you're safe"— the sentence was broken, but caught up in a higher key; "look thar, to the left."

From behind a mound, not fifty rods away, two Indians dashed at him on their ponies.

"If that's your game, h'yar's mine." Beck halted, raised his rifle quickly, fired, and the savage in the lead reeled and fell. Undaunted, the second redskin held to the chase. Beck had but time to order:

"Give the mare her head and cock your pieces;" he drew his pistol, turning his sorrel to meet the foe. A whizzing tomahawk struck his hat as he raised his weapon and drew the trigger. Another stark and bleeding redskin lay lifeless on the prairie green.

Then shout, and yell and curse, loud ringing oaths and Spanish jargon, mingled with the snort of horses, the stamp of feet were heard.

"They're gaining on us, boys; spur deep for the last heat."

"For the last heat, scout, here goes," cried Whack.

"Here goes," repeated Jumper, riding well.

And Kit, with Mary firmly seated, like a winged speck on the broad expanse, shot ahead.

CHAPTER VI.

SUSPENSE — THE RALLY.

It was true, as Lu had tearfully said of Mary, "Now that she is gone we feel what it is to be without her." Every nook in the lonely dwelling seemed to repeat her words. The long, wide, dreary hall sounded to the tread of feet with a mockery of its former life; even the porch-vines rustled not as when on quick-paced duty she swept by them. The door of her room stood open; within there was a cheerless, wistful hush; the snowy curtains at the window, the patch-work quilt and pillows wore a cold look. More lonesome than all beside, the tuneless throat of the little bird encaged. Scraps of needlework lay just as she had left them, the clippings on the floor; and on the back of a chair a baby's frock, half finished.

Old Chloe, in her morning work, had left the once cheery corner with sobs; while she stood in the door gazing in, she struggled hard against the mute, unspoken sadness of its quietude; against the harsh voice of the Doctor's parrot without, breaking the peace of the vacant hall.

"Mary! M-a-r-y! — gone!" it more than muttered, to the dismay of the old servant.

"I'se dun tole um so," she sighed, wiping her tear-wet face, "dey tinks de ole niggah's got no sense, but I seed de chicken clumb de fens, an scripsher am scripsher." At her cabin, telling her sorrows to Cato, she was not less heart-stricken; she dwelt with love long cherished on the virtues of her lost "honey," — from Mary's childhood, and its little, winning ways, her growth in grace and beauty to the full bloom of womanhood, in which she had been torn away, — at every step her grief grew louder and she mourned like one distracted.

"De Marster keeps her lection shoo, Cato; I'se dun tole yer so."

"An He will fetch things straight," said the voice of Mrs. Garrulson behind her

"You speeks de troof, Ole Miss; indeed yer dus," she answered in an instant change of tone; the words had strengthened faith and banished woe.

The liking of the men for Mary was not a mere formal show of respect; each held to some kind act of hers, as they sat about the camp at odds about her capture and her rescue. Many things were said pro and con; Tim Murphy had more than once leaped to his feet to blame them all for not joining the pursuit, "on their own hook."

"May I niver see daylight agin," he said, excitedly, "but I'll go, if yees will, an foller the scout."

"Beek ees reet, maun," answered Sandy, an older head and a wiser one, "fer what wud ye all go? Gad, eef Cartwright seed yees, deil a onct wud he stap atwix thees an Mexico; yeer speereet's reet, me lad, but tether yeer talk to rason."

"Phat's the good of the loikes of us in camp," replied Tim, "whin the tree of em — an two bys at that — es a fightin a whole tribe, an Mary is ruined by the baste?"

"No, no — no!" answered a score at once, all unwilling to harbor the thought.

"Nuthin kin hinder him."

"Yees, but theer es, tho," said Sandy; "his cowardyce wud keep her safe; I'd jine ye, Tim, to flay him alive weed the snap o' the wheep."

"Och! I don't got some beesnis wid dot boss some more; desh ish dot," joined in Heinrich, whose feelings labored hard with the language.

The coming of Legs to the circle cut short the squabble, and with a message from the trader, who had not been seen in the camp that day, he was listened to closely.

"Boys," he said, as they stood round him, "he'll ax no work till his darter's back agin, an if she ain't h'yar afore to-morrer noon, he's gwyne to mount hisself; he'il want us all to jine him."

"Be jabes, en that's the talk," cried Tim, taking it all as favoring his side.

"Reet fer yees now, Tim; d'yees tak me meenin? By the morrow's noon we'll all gae; but the chiel'll be hame afore that."

"Have your hosses ready, and when he blows his bugle mount an feller him. I'm off to let the Mexeans know," added the boy, and taking his way to the cattle-drove, the men dispersed.

The Judge and the Doctor had urged the Colonel in vain, the previous night, to seek rest, nor could Lu prevail upon him in the least. The strong man, with his stout, fatherly heart, measured off the long hours. His face had grown older since the morning, when, among his people, it was so genial and brave. His life had never known before such a mortal sense of loneliness; his thoughts were in tumult; whether he lived or dreamed he had scarcely sense to know, or consciousness to wonder. At daylight he fled from the thickening gloom of his house and hid himself in his office. Seated in the small wing of the building, he threw his hat upon the floor and turned his eyes upon the walls, where the grim tokens of frontier strife, hung there by his daughter's hand, were shorn of their harsher display. Many hours, on many days, Doctor Tom and Mary had spent together in assorting and grouping these oddities of border-life, which Cheviteau had laid by, in long years, to be placed in this small museum. He scanned the whole collection, as everything in some way gave him a fonder memory of his child, as each and all bore the mark of her tasteful arrangement. But he dwelt too long, as each changing sight but added to his torment. In feverish haste he seized his glass, springing up the ladder to his perch in the outlook.

Lu had shown many very kind attentions to Mary's father. She came to the office to know if she could be of further service in any way, and on going out she locked the door. From the outside she called to him and said:

"Colonel, I've locked you in so that nobody may trouble you; I'll throw the key through the window, and if you want me I'll not be far away."

"Right, child, right," he answered, without turning his eyes from his glass; and Lu returned to Mary's vacant chair under the morning-glories.

Strange to say, Doctor Tom was the most cheerful man in house or camp, and though he paced the porch impatiently, he had an implicit trust that Beck would rescue Mary. In his walk, he was seen to best advantage; a prim, small man with ruddy face, dainty feet and hands, dressed in blue-white cottonade. His shirt-front frilled and starched to the purest gloss, the shine of his boots the wonder of the imp who polished them, and his walk and mien had the air of taste, with a little of fashion's folly.

Lu's grief was most sincere and touching; at times, poignant.

"If you will allow me, my dear," said Doctor Tom, "I would like to talk with you."

"I would like to hear you, Doctor," she replied, drying her eyes.

"I'm not surprised at your distress, but you give up too soon."

"Why?"

"Make yourself more content," he urged, throwing

into his manner every assurance to revive her drooping spirits; "you'll see your friend soon."

"Have you any word? or what hope have you?"

"A strong belief that Mary's now safe, or —"

"Or what?" she asked hastily.

"Or John Beck's a dead man," was the blunt reply. Lu started. "I was about to add," he went on, "that as there's little danger of Cartwright killing John Beck, why, of course, I reason that Mary's safe."

"What is it makes you feel so sure?"

"John Beck is one in a thousand; a fellow, genuine through and through, and what the men call 'squar all round.'"

"Do they fear him, Doctor?"

"No, not that exactly; they trust him, that's it. So now keep heart; just as sure as he pledged his word, he'll bring her back to the old porch, or lose his life. If you want company, call to me in my sanctum sanctorum." He rose, turned away, and entered the hall.

His room, brightened by the vine-sifted sunlight, had the cool airiness of a country-house chamber, and there were many bits and scraps of luxury, caught up from the drift of a fast life, to adorn it. On the window-sill rested a mahogany case, the lid bearing a gold-plate inscription. On a branching rack was perched the parrot, an Italian bird, and a very ill-mannered prattler. Whack and Jump had often placed him in a bush, kneeling by it, to taunt and torment the mimic into a repetition of language neither chaste nor polite.

As a linguist, the parrot was not slow in adopting the vernacular.

The Doctor enjoyed his repose in a lounge-chair, his head thrown back, the white hair lying cold on a passionless brow. The face, at rest, was that of a man whose vices had been restrained by will, but the recollection was surely not without remorse.

Judge Smith, sauntering about the hall, had looked in more than once or twice, with an uneasy desire to impress the inmate with some idea of his, the Judge's, importance.

The Doctor seeing him, said:

"Come in, Judge." The invitation was kind, but formal, but the one addressed seated himself with a lazy sort of indifference, as if constrained to be pleasant, which the other noting, he was at once primed for a cool reception.

"Are the Indians troublesome?" asked the Judge, as one at a loss how to be interesting.

"Troublesome! You ought to know. Were they ever anything else? They're as savage now as ever, and as they will be, always."

"My opinion is," said the other, expanding his proportions, "that they're a great people."

"Great! Is there anything great in a savage? Great! in one that displays all the qualities of an unenlightened people, for ages isolated from the rest of mankind. Great!"

"Well, so I have read."

"Read! What have you read, seh? You may have

read of an ideal Indian, which romance runs mad after; of one who combines all the traits without the inequalities of his race. Read! There are none such. You may have read the poetic conception of him, which as a conception is without a standard, seh; his vices and virtues have been drawn hypothetically, seh; hypothetically from such as belong to the savage state; he differs from other barbarians in the completeness of his savage character, but is he less savage?"

"Well, but we must be kind to them, and tame them."

"Kind! Kind! What kind of kindness are you talking about, Judge? Don't you know we have been kinder to the Indian than any other nation would or could have been under like circumstances? We've been over-kind in a mistaken policy; a policy that will utterly destroy him; or by permission and indulgence he will destroy himself."

"Oh, I reckon not."

"Reckon! There's another mistake. We reckon too much on the supposition that he may be better than he is; we don't face the fact, that he is much worse than we suppose; he is represented generally in his most genial phase, even to palliate his most ferocious acts, by reference to the injustice and oppression of which he has been the victim, as if he had not been a savage at all until the landing of the whites. Now to be consistent, in exact justice, we had better burn down our towns and cities, and start back to where we all came from."

"But he has a good deal of strength of character."

"You don't stop to analyze, and have caught a part of an idea only; what you consider his strength is really his weakness; the contemplation of nature in her primitive, robust form has made him taciturn; he is not meditative; the profound loneliness seems to have terrified all the gentler qualities, smothered all sentiment, and brought out all that is sensuous and selfish."

"Oh, but I know, in a fight he is a hero; he talks like an orator."

"You're wrong again; he never does stand up to an open fight; he is brave enough; so is every wild animal; his motion and action may be that of a fine-mettled biped; his physical attitude and expression are picturesque, nothing more. He is not eloquent; a combination of material objects is his only means of expressing abstract ideas; the barrenness of his language, and not the luxuriance of his imagination, enforces a mode of speech; he is not a natural orator; his mind is a blank in the eloquence of thought; he has no humor, no romance, no poetic feeling."

"But we all see what he is."

"But you don't try to see what he is not; he is not what you make him out to be; he considers everything beneath his notice which is not necessary to his advantage or enjoyment; his wife is a beast of burden; he has neither affection nor piety; the aged and infirm are left to die by the wayside; his attachment to any region depends on its capacity to furnish game;

even his courting is carried on by gifts of good things to eat; he has fear or admiration of another being in so far as he is subdued by superior power, or in degree as another exceeds him in savage traits." *

"Well, what would you do with him?"

"Do with him? What ought to be done is to give him every chance, help him, protect him in being self-dependent; let him learn to be a responsible being, and in contact with civilization he would become civilized; his savage traits, in time, might wear away."

"Oh, that won't do!"

"That's what the politician has said, Judge, for years; he'll keep on saying it for the rest of the century."

The visitor arose, bowed himself out, and a good deal of the starch of his conceit had wilted. "You see, Doctor, it might ruin the party."

"It is a poor party, then, that can't do justice without being ruined."

The absence of Jumper would have left Lu without an attentive admirer had not the Judge, upon sudden reflection, taking in her distress and her income at a single thought, made up his mind to supplant the absent youth. To be smart, or to be thought so, was ever, in his sight, an elevation above an ordinary mortal; he scrupled but little as to the moral or principle of an action, if the action flattered this vanity. He was never alive to consequences, whether his conceit might

---

* The substance of this conversation has been gleaned from "Western Character" — McConnel — *vide* chap. "The Indian," and notes of reference.

lead him to the edge of dishonor or into it, to meanness or incivility, so that he made his mark of credit with such as are so ignorant or coarse as to admire such impudence. He had resolved that in the melting mood a woman's affection is more easily caught, and that to storm her weakened will would be in effect an easy victory. To resolve was to act, and as he had seated himself near her, he said abruptly:

"Wouldn't you like to get away from all this trouble, Miss Lu?"

"Yes," she answered, timidly, for childlike she had been terrified.

"Nothing easier;" he lowered his voice to an insinuating whisper.

"I cannot understand you," she said, unable to catch the drift of his thoughts.

"Nothing easier than to let some one take you out of it."

"That's easy enough, as you say," she answered, still puzzled and uneasy at his manner.

"Some friend, some one that you admire, might take you out of the danger, if you would allow it," he went on in a simpering way, catching at his suggestions by starts. But so far his words were meaningless.

"A friend might do so if I was inclined to go," she answered, with a faint idea that the Judge was halting over some sentimental riddle, and, pained as she was at heart, she smiled at the stupid look and manner of the man. He was seated very near her, and was about to take her hand, perhaps, when a shrill, spiteful voice screamed out:

"Drop it! drop it! drop it!" So sudden, so nearly human was the cry, the Judge fled, and Lu, not less frightened, hastened from the porch. She saw the parrot standing in the doorway. Polly had been looking on, and as the suitor was about to take Lu's hand, had taken her cue; his attitude was the same as that of the boys when training the parrot on the bush, and it had only repeated one of the milder forms of its lessons.

Another night of the most trying unrest had passed, and the trader rose with the light of the second morning to hasten to his outlook. The men had come together — a small army — their nags saddled, and Legs the teamster held the Colonel's horse with his own, at the office-door. When Lu came, bringing a tray with breakfast, she found the old man with his glass levelled on the open country. But he would not be disturbed. For a while he peered through it steadily, only changing position to vary the line of sight. Suddenly he called to Lu to come near him, on the ladder.

"Here, child, be quick," he said, "look due west an tell me what you see," placing the instrument in her hands. She brought her younger eye to bear upon the distance, and had looked but a second, when in a fluttering, broken voice she almost screamed:

"It's them! it's them, — there's Whack and Jump, and there's Mary ahead, riding for life; hold on; it's the scout at their back, fighting a gang, single-handed.

Stop; there goes a redskin from his horse, and look, he has fired again: down goes another; he's free!"

"Quick, chil, get me the bugle!"

Lu turned from the perch, leaped down, and returned in a second. He blew one long, loud blast, and it was answered from the camp. Cheer on cheer was heard, and like a charge in the heat of battle, the men dashed forth; the trader threw himself into the saddle, out-speeding the boy who hung upon his flank.

Cheer on cheer again burst forth as the men formed a barrier against the pirates. The Colonel was the first to reach Mary, nor did he wait to draw rein, but threw himself from his horse. He seized his child, and in a speechless maze, wound his old, fond arms around her.

Just before the bugle's blast, Cartwright bore down on the scout; his throat, neck and arms bared and bronzed, he lent the hideous to the scene, with violent haste. But the bugle's warning checked his headlong race, and turning in his saddle he saw his gang on the retreat; he wheeled and followed.

Pedro the vaquero led the charge from the camp, unequalled in grace as the bells of his spurs tinkled at every motion. He rode close upon the heels of the fleeing boss. Making ready, his right hand held the noose and his left the coil of a lasso. With a swing of his arm it enlarged over his head to a perfect circle, which, as he neared the fugitive, he warily let slip. At the same moment his horse fell back on its haunches to resist the strain. The wily thief kept an eye on the Mexican, and, as the rope left his grasp, Cartwright seized his pony's mane, and stretched himself at length. The noose fell true to its mark, but the boss escaped by dodging.

"Carajo, caramba!" muttered the vaquero, as he quietly re-coiled his lariat.

One of the retreating bandits, unable to control his ire at Pedro's challenge with the lasso, broke away from his party and turned back in a run. He had counted on the other's flight, in which to excel him in throwing the noose, but he mistook the vaquero's temper, as he sat erect in his seat, unmoved. Drawing nearer, there was a glance of recognition in which both were fired to a quickened hate. The cow-boy in haste drew off his poncho, wrapping it round his left arm, dismounted, tied his horse, and with loud threats planted himself in front of his foe. The challenge was hurled with epithet and curse into the face of him who had dashed up to provoke it.

"Down, down, monte-cheat; aha, senor thief; down, down, coward; by the backbone of the padre, I will you smite."

Drawing his knife he kissed the hilt, and threw it trembling through the sunlight, into the earth at his feet.

The other prepared himself in like manner — his tongue more fluent and fiery — the two met face to face, holding their poinards raised. The left fore-arm of each was clad as a shield, and with stab and thrust they fell to their bloody work.

"Hog-driver, peon, bastard, caramba!" hissed the frantic Pedro; he stepped back a pace; recovered, with a quick left-hand flourish of his hat in the face of the bewildered adversary, while the right sunk the steel, and felled him lifeless on the sod. Stripping the dead man's horse, he mounted, driving the riderless beast over the waste.

The joyous party, with laugh and shout, were hastening to the post, while those in retreat were nearly out of sight. At the house, the Colonel bore his daughter from her horse and seated her under the bison's head.

"Boys," he called out, in a firm, familiar greeting, "don't spec me now to thank you, but the day's a comin when I will; that's certin. Come in; we'll drink a health."

They entered the house in squads, and the old man spent with them a brief roystering hour, the jolliest episode of his checkered life. All the lost humor came back to him in redoubled warmth, and Beck, standing by Mary, felt free to laugh aloud for the first time since her capture.

"Well — Mary," he exclaimed, as if in some doubt of what he had done; "I thought I'd get you back to the old porch, and here we are." He had loosened all the restraint of his manner and habit, for once. Doctor Tom, the Judge, Lu, and Mrs. Garrulson, were all of the happy crowd. Whack and Jump recounted to a group their adventures, and Chloe, standing at the door, chuckled and shook her sides.

The men were called to mount by Beck, in the lead, and outside they gave a round, rousing shout. As they rode away, a melodious voice struck up the camp song, and from mellowed throats the chorus, on the sweet summer breeze, was borne away.

>   Crack, snap, whipiti-snap,
>   Whipiti-snap, whipiti-snap;
>   Crack, snap, whipiti-snap,
>   A bullwhacker's life is gay.
>   Whoa-hawr down to your work,
>   Gee Buck, up with a jerk,
>   Crack, snap, bang, jerk,
>   A bullwhacker's life is **gay.**

CHAPTER VII.

THE LONG JOURNEY—THE REAR PORCH.

Just after the cheer at the house, groups of joyous fellows were seen about the camp. Beck walked off to hide himself with his thoughts. When alone, his humor changed, his face lengthened, his eyes were restless; he sat down, played with a twig and broke it into bits. The man was troubled; a heavy weight sat upon his spirit, fears of strange form vexed him. He had seen the packers, with Cartwright leading them; also, the vicious readiness of the Indians to obey his beck and call. He put this and that together, traced their retreat to the crib, and from thence he followed the Mexicans and Cartwright back to where the bandits hailed from. All this was the subject of his unsettled musing; he took up and measured the disjointed outlines of a plot, as his mind foreboded; he knew the actors, and he knew and felt with something like a creeping chill, the cold-blooded enmity of the ringleader.

Suddenly he rose, drew himself to his full height, and gazed with an intent, far-reaching search of the vast expanse. He looked steadily, as if he counted the leagues; he drew his hat down and stared, then he turned, let fall the bits of twig from his raised hand, and said, aloud:

"I can make it; I will if it kills me."

The man had resolved upon making a fearful journey; a long, lone race against the insidious spite of a hated foe. He had settled down to his duty sternly, and walked off with his giant strides let loose.

At the caballada he stood for a short while looking at the drove of fine horses, and singled out, at last, one that his eyes had sought. Legs, the teamster, had given him his morning dash, a daily exercise to tame his mettle, and to harden his muscles. Beck's glance at the thoroughbred was satisfying.

"He'll do," he said; then he moved away to the shade of a tree, threw himself on the ground and slept for hours. It was a giant's rest. For the remainder of the day, and part of the night, he was mending his traps and nerving his heart.

"I'm off, Peter," he said on the morning following that on which Mary was brought back. He spoke as if he was only about to cross the river and return, so easily had his will taken on the discharge of duty

"Whar you boun, John?"

"To head off the pirate."

"Hound him down, an don't let up on him."

"He'll not trouble the camp jest yet, but," he laid his hand on the old man's shoulder, "he will, Peter; he'll never let up till he's dead; I know him. I'll do my best, kase I'm bleeged to."

The trader turned to his iron box and drew forth a

roll of coin, which Beck put away in the folds of his blouse. A few words passed between them as he drew his belt closer about his waist, while Peter continued: "You ken have all you want, pardner; drive out the varmint an I'll not forgit yer sarvice."

But Beck was already busy; he had balanced in his hand the best, long-range rifle from the rack, and to prove it clean and sure he stepped to the doorway and fired; a burr that flecked the taper point of a high top pine, spun splintering through the air.

"Good enough," he said, as he swung the rifle, with pouch and powder-horn, having carefully examined his smaller arms.

He now whistled loudly through his fingers, and soon Legs led up the horse.

"He feels gaily, Mister Beck, an ef he don't take you a bilin, I'll give in."

"What, Tuck; oh, he'll go like lightnin, or like a lamb, jes as I've a mind to."

From a score of the best strain, which the trader had at times imported into his stock from the blue-grass pastures of Kentucky, Beck had long since chosen as a favorite, this fine, blood-bay stallion; the finest of the lot, and one which he had with uncommon pride watched and longed for as his mount, should the time come to need uncommon endurance and speed. The time had come.

Tuck, as Beck called him, was a beauty, a staying speeder, fleet as a greyhound. With the wickedest grace in the world, the horse stood fretting, and the firm muscles twitched under a coat as soft as satin.

Beck stroked the small, lean, racer-like head, fondled the delicate, taper ears traced with veins like a vine-leaf; he patted the high-mettled, fine-strung body, smoothing the broad shoulders, feeling the force of loin and girth, the hard, firm ribs, the clean, slender legs. He clasped the face between his hands, and the man's nature melted, for on earth there are no eyes so spirited as those of a horse.

"Are you ready, Tuck? eh, ole boy?" he spoke as a friend to a friend in good faith. He turned about and looked to his haversack. The provender placed therein was barely enough to last a stout man forty-eight hours. There was a small lump of pemmican, a small bag of coffee, one of salt and pepper, mixed, a dozen or two hard biscuit, a pound or more of flitch, a tin quart-cup. He relied for further subsistence on his gun and the chance meeting of a train on the road.

But this was a light concern of the wayfarer, compared with the exhaustion he must undergo. He went on with his preparations. His hair had been cut close to the scalp, his beard trimmed, he was clad as a ranger, without an ounce of useless weight about him. He strode up to Cheviteau and said:

"So long, Peter; if I'm gone for a spell, don't slack your trust. Jes remember, I'll make it. I'm bleeged to do it."

"Good by, John Beck; I'll wait yer comin till doomsday."

Beck left the office with his blankets, and nothing more was said by either. Standing at the side of his horse, which the lad held, he tightened the girth over the Spanish tree, placed his foot in the hooded stirrup and mounted.

In the blood-boiling vigor of his strength, the horse pranced, reared, then bounded away under a hand as firm as iron. Held to a swinging lope, he bore his rider proudly from the sight of his friends at the post.

In the saddle the man looked his best, and the motion seemed to ennoble his bearing. So much of his life had been given to the wild coursing of the plains, he was never so splendid a figure as now. Sweeping the long, drear wastes, across the wide, green stretches, through forests, over sun-dried rivers, or battling the freshet, he seemed a born rider, and the horse as a thing created for him.

Beck's hazardous scout to the far south-west was full of hidden perils. He would traverse at times the Big Backbone; he might be untouched, unseen, or be tracked, surprised, hemmed in; from bush or clump, the rising prairie swells, from trees skirting the groves or forests, from heights above a ford, from mounds or gorges, a shower of arrows or of whizzing balls might sweep him down; but the man's face was calm; the eyes, with look of daring, stared straight ahead, and beneath him the gray stretches swept by like the passing current of a stream. Along the hard, gravelly road he held his course and the bay his speed, bearing as fierce a rider as ever crossed the plains.

There was much to lend that hard, strong stare to the face of the man. No Bedouin on the sun-stricken, desert sands ever gazed upon a more cheerless expanse than that on which Beck looked, in the almost limitless stretch before him.

One day with another at the start was a pleasant jaunt; he rode freely, but with extreme caution, to spare himself and his horse.

At the crib the Indians rode away, leaving Cartwright alone with the Mexicans. Just before quitting the trader's service he had taken note that contracts had been signed, a route mapped out for an expedition, and it was nearing the time for its departure; he knew further that it would pursue a certain road, and he shaped a plot, at once. He knew the chiefs of hostile bands, who traded in the town from which the pack-train came, and thither he was bent on going, in the lead of the gang.

It was this very design, which Beck surmised and over which he brooded, that had sent him forth.

Cruz, the deposed captain, was ready enough to fall into line as a lieutenant, but before mounting he upbraided the friend of his bosom and laid bare to the amiable Josefina the sin of her fancy for Mary; she meekly, as a matter of course, understood the easy stages by which her spouse reached a climax, and was not disappointed in an after moment, when he thrashed her soundly. Heedless, however, his other pet, in a rear-foot pastime, was playing havoc with packs and saddles, and vehemently threatened the shanty's safety.

The plunder-laden train moved out, taking a secret trail for the territory of the south-west savage and the puebla of the border Mexican. They had many hours start of the scout towards the same destination.

The trader had made known to the Department at Washington the troubles which beset his business, and he had asked for a military escort to guard his trains. Whack was forming a patrol of mounted men, for a skirmish line on the skirt of the camp; the number of teamsters was increased.

Beck had been absent a week. At all hours the snap of the whip was heard; the trader was seen late and early in the camp; the friendship of Miss Lu and the sprightly Jumper grew apace; now and then an ebb in Mrs. Garrulson's talk served to show what the real force of its flood-tide might be, and the laugh of old Chloe was heard, as she sat at her cabin door.

Mary had held up amazingly, but she was not proof against the nervous reaction after so hard a strain. On the day of her return, almost overcome, she gave way, and was not seen for days; she kept her room under Chloe's care. It was at the end of a week when she came again to her accustomed place.

After dinner, on the day of her re-appearance, Cheviteau led the way to the rear porch, followed by Doctor Tom and others of the family. Mary's seat at the side of the Doctor seemed just as it should be, nor was it less as it should be when Lu and Jumper edged away to a corner, nor when Whack was told that two were company. There was something not unlike the fitness of things when Mrs. Garrulson opened fire on the Judge.

The first whispered word in the *tête-à-tête*, which Whack itched to break up, caught his ear.

"None o' that," he called out, to their dismay; "your heads are too nigh."

"Well, Cheviteau, what's up?" began the Doctor; "anybody killed or hurt? The Judge here wouldn't mind having a case, I have no doubt."

"No; somebody might get hurt, if this thing keeps on."

"More trouble?"

"No, it's the same old fuss twix white and red man."

"Yes, and it'll be the same old fuss when we're dead and gone."

"It ought not to be," said the Judge.

"So we all think, but how would you stop it, Judge?"

"Is it the Indian's fault?"

"If you answer by asking, let me ask, is it the white man's fault?"

"Well, then, Doctor, what's your remedy?"

"Treat the bad white man and the bad red man alike; make a law that both shall respect alike, to which both shall be responsible; — then hang them both, if they deserve it; don't make a criminal out of your own kind, and a hero out of a savage, for one and the same offence; that kind of policy is sheer nonsense."

"But the government has been kind to the Indian."

"And has only flattered his vices by being so; it has been generous, but not just."

"How so?"

"With one hand it provides for him, guards him; with the other places him in the path of progress, a scarecrow to enterprise, a hideous fright to the emigrant, to be ultimately stricken down, cast aside and trampled on."

"Jus so, Doctor," said the trader; "he's right across the track of trade with the best land, timber and water in the univarse, which he can't use, which he wouldn't neither, if he could."

"Yes; and trade has no ill will to the red man; it would improve his condition, bring him comforts, if allowed to pass free on the highway, a free highway."

"The government will protect trade," exclaimed the Judge, catching at a chance.

"Will it? That's something new. No, seh, cept its own supplies, it never does," said the trader.

"It couldn't protect it, if it would; the army at its greatest strength ever allowed by law couldn't place a corporal's guard at each of the exposed points along the lines of traffic."

"The Injin knows as well as you do, Jedge, right from wrong; thar's no use talkin bout that."

"True enough, Colonel; philanthropy has spoiled what practical men should have managed. We boast that our land is a refuge for the oppressed; we invite them to come and live on the public domain. We say to the poor settler, go, till the ground and you may have the land, — on this condition: remember, we have a pet tiger at large there, and you must not harm the beast. But, says the poor man, suppose the beast harms me? We have nothing to do with that, is the reply; now, how long will it be before the land is tilled?" asked the Doctor.

"Not till you've killed the tiger," said the old man, with warmth, as he continued:

"We could manage the Injin, if thar was any law; before it can reach us, we have to make a law for ourselves and take it in our own hands. I know we're right."

"It seems a pity, a shame that we can't live in peace. Wouldn't the church and school-house do some good?" asked Mary.

"That's what we strive for, my young friend, — that civilization may come with its church and school. It is not in the love of strife that we fight when we must fight If we were craven enough not to fight, pray who would advance the cause of civilization?"

"I reckon the white man's as much at fault as the Indian; if there wasn't money in it, the cause of civilization wouldn't get on a step." The Judge was rude; his words were too nearly a slur upon the motives of those whose hospitality he enjoyed. The Doctor colored and moved in his chair; Cheviteau sat upright, his face set firmly, and he laid down his pipe.

"Look heah, Jedge," he said quickly, "do you think I'd risk my life as I do for what money I make?"

"No, not you, no;" answered the Judge, beginning to hedge.

The Doctor walked the porch, with quick, short steps.

"Do you think, seh, that a woman who has forsaken all the gentler ways of life, seh, to make her influence the grace of our rough life here, seh, would bring to us her love and her religion, for money,— money, seh! No, seh; you're mistaken; in the whole policy there is a want of law administered righteously; a want of the statesman, seh, in the place of the politician."

It began to dawn upon the Judge that he had stirred a hornet's nest.

"Right, Doctor," joined in the old man; "we mus have law, and the law's officers to hang these skulking half-breed whites; these hounds who lead the pack: these sharks and pirates, without heart or soul, who stir the bad blood and the hate of the redskins, and they go free, always free. Law or no law, we're men with the right to live heah; we'll fight, too, till you law-makers, Jedge, bring us the better day of peace and order."

While her father spoke, Mary rose and stood behind him; she felt almost tempted to pat his back in approval; never before had he spoken so well; never in her sight had he seemed so nearly justified. She spoke out, at last, with much of his own fervor.

"Well said, father; God speed us to the good day."

"What I has made, Jedge," said the trader, more calmly, "has cost a life of hard knocks; ef it war to do over agen, anybody might have my chance."

"They ought to be taught better; made Christians of," the Judge remarked, as an escape.

"Christians, seh!" the Doctor was up again; "why, the Indian says, the white men have so many creeds, he won't believe any of them. He has his own god — a wolf's fang; — if he don't like it, he takes another — a bear's claw; that's his Christianity, seh. Look at the farce of it. They're hemmed in to rot on their own vices, with liberty to slay, with no lawful restraints; treated as a foreign people, a political entity, a moral nonentity; make Christians of them! bah! Christians have lived, worked and died among them, and there are no converts: the Indians slay them, seh, now and then, because they talk too much."

"Can't the army be made stronger?" asked the Judge.

"What's the use? You could not make it strong enough, unless you mean to exterminate the red man. The flower of the army, led by a prince of its bravest phalanx, was decoyed into a trap; a thousand savages swarmed about the little band; not a man lived to tell the story of the fiendish, sulphurous dance of death, wherein drunken squaws beat out the lives of the wounded, or strangled them in their agony. Were they ever punished?"

"But —"

"But, hold on, seh; then there's the men my friend

speaks of, who turn a penny, sch, over the corpse of the settler; who deal in whiskey, sch; in stolen arms and ammunition, sch, and reap a harvest from the bloody spoilage —"

Quoth the parrot:

"Go it! — go it! — go it!"

"D — n that bird!" cried the Doctor, brought to a sudden halt, and feeling his temper rising, he hastily left the porch.

At the request of her father, Mary re-told the story of her capture, from the seizure of her person while stooping over the flowers, to the insult in the camp of the pirates. All were moved at the recital, but her words seemed to strike fire in the kindling rage of Mrs. Garrulson.

"What's that?" "What'd he do?" she cried out, suddenly, as she drew her chair to the side of the speaker; the others gave attention.

"He touched my cheek, insultingly," Mary repeated, and the color came in haste to the spot the rude hand had offended.

"Teched yer cheek! why the copper-cullud sarpent; — ef I'd bin thar — I'd a —"

"Mauled him," suggested Whack.

"Chawed him up," said Jump.

"What would you done to him, old lady?" asked Cheviteau.

"I'd a punched his head, sartin," she answered.

Mary's story warmed the memory of her father, who called up an adventure with the pride of one who travels back into a glowing past. He dwelt, at length, on an escapade with the Sioux in the far-away, fright-haunted days of his youth: how he once, as a bearer of dispatches from one fort to another, rode alone through the wilderness alive with the war-striped foes. He had singled out an untracked course to avoid surprise, and spoke of his riding headlong into danger; how, suddenly, they sprang upon him. Then followed a long, fearful chase; ceaselessly the yells rang in his ears; foodless, and faint with failing sight, he thought his day had come, and that a grave yawned for him on the drear and friendless prairie. Hope was almost gone, when his eye caught a glimpse of a distant river. He rallied his horse, reached its bank, and there his mount gave out; he plunged into the stream, as the arrows fell around him like storm-driven twigs. Now beyond their hate, with succor from the fort speeding towards him, and crazed with a wild delight, he flung back the bewildered words:

"Safe! you devils, safe!"

"It's Lu's turn next, for a scrape," said Whack, thereby bringing the couple to the notice of all; and in the unhappy pause, she not hearing what was said, was heard to say:

"What, Harry, jealous already?"

"She's into it without knowing how she got there," continued the tease laughing, in which the others joined.

"What's the matter?" asked the innocent Jumper, looking up to find all eyes upon him. "Come, Miss

Lu, let's walk; we can't have any peace where that bull-whacker is."

"Miss Lu! why don't you say Mister Harry, Miss Lu?" he railed and teased in his boisterous way, until the two were out of hearing.

The Colonel hastened off to the office and Whack followed him.

Mary was now left alone with Mrs. Garrulson, who had, the moment before, driven the Judge away by the discipline of her talk. Chloe came to the porch with a message, and Mary kept her seat to hear what she knew full well would take place between the two old folks.

"Ah, honey, yuse safe, but deyse musn't shoot no mo squarls," Chloe said to begin with.

"Why not?"

"Kase you see, chile, dat wus de bang o' de rifle an dars ben trubel eber sence."

"That's so," said Mrs. G.; "who'd a thunk it."

"But dat dars nuthin neether; it wus de chicken clumbin de fense; mind I dun tole yer so, afore."

"Oh, sho," sneered the other; "what's ther yuse, all the time er talking bout that ar rooster?"

"Jes yer wait den; jes keep on, ole Miss; wait tell yer seed him climb der fense agin."

"I'se got a game chicken, I reckon; an he climbs a fense all der time."

"Oh — he do, do he? well, ole Miss, dat ar chicken o' mine jes look at me, to take a warnin."

"Thet's nuthink; why, my chicken ken tork."

"Tork!" exclaimed Chloe, with uplifted hands and looking at Mary, who was shocked; "now, ole Miss, not tork I reckon."

"May I never; yes indeed, tork," she replied, not the least abashed; "every time a hawk flewed over thet ar rooster jes spread his wings an cum a runnin."

Here the old woman rose, spread her arms, suiting gesture and voice to the supposed action of the fowl, in close mimicry:

"Runnin to me, Chloe, wid his mouth wide open, an a hollerin, Miss Me-lin-dee! Miss Me-lin-dee! you jes oughter seed him."

"Oh, dat a way," giggled the old darkey, shaking her sides; and Mary joined in the round, wholesome mirth.

CHAPTER VIII.

TIM'S RIDE — NEARING THE END — CATO'S HOLIDAY.

A FORTNIGHT has passed over the head of the dauntless scout and his mount. Cantering down the slopes of the Divide, to cut off the turns of the road, the horse leaped to the green valley-plain. For long days, Beck had ridden a steady, unbroken race. Day in and day out it was an unchanging gallop during the hours he gave to his work; his rule was as strict during the time of rest. At dawn he was astride and away, and slackened speed only when the heat of the day came on. He left the beaten track at every curve to shorten distance; from every rise he took his bearings, sighting afar the greener spots for the noontide halt. At such as afforded water he got down, swabbed his horse's mouth, rubbed down his foaming sides, cooled him in the shade, if there was none other than the mere shadow of a bush. For himself he kept a sharp watch while caring for his beast; he often left him picketed, to hail and join a train on foot, to obtain supplies. He boiled his coffee in the quart-cup, ate sparingly, save when his rifle secured him a feast. Then, in the dew-drenched twilight, he rode forth again, and drew rein at length for the night in the thickening darkness. Again, at daybreak, he bridled his thoroughbred fresh from a bed of daisies, and sped on. But the wear and tear began to show; would show were they made of iron. The man's face, though still sternly set, was drawn down, tanned and scorched by the sun; the horse had thinned in flesh, feeling the strain.

All the while, at the post, the days dragged slowly, and though the trader was busy with his camp and droves, he thought often and anxiously of the distant horseman.

Cheviteau looked about him one morning, weeks after Beck's departure, for a man to fill Pedro's place, who with a wounded arm had been placed in charge of Mary and Chloe, by the Doctor's orders. A blooded colt needed an airing under the saddle, and though kind and well broken, had been running wild for a season. Now full of lusty life, his master thought best to remind him of his training.

The first man the trader met in camp was Tim Murphy, and for whom the old man had a warm regard.

"The tap o' the marnin till yer honor," he cried; "may they all be as bright as yer darter's face."

"Good mornin, Tim."

"Didn't the bys come up to the scratch tho, Colonel, whin we wint arter the pirates?"

"My boys allers do, seh."

"Thrue for you, Colonel."

"Tim, I want a man for the drove, on special duty," the trader said, coming to the point, and his words were caught up by a few idlers standing near. The specialty of the service referred to was to mount a whip on a thoroughbred and to transfer him to the care of stock.

"Fer speeshal dooty, is't? Yees needn't look over me showlder for the loike of him, Colonel."

"Ken you ride a fast horse on a chase?" Many teamsters, while the best of service men with the lash, were poor riders.

"Didn't me fayther ride forninst the Darby afore me, an didn't yees see me forninst the charge of the bys?"

"Well, I'll try you, Tim; come along." The proof of fitness lay in a trial.

The men looked one at the other, as the Colonel and Murphy moved away; they knew that the boasted riding of their comrade was a trifle overdrawn, and that any severe test would upset his vaunt and belittle him with the Colonel; he too had his doubts, but he chose the man as a mark of friendship, for he liked readiness, not less his candor and humor.

The grazing ground was soon reached; it was a wide, green table of level prairie, and the large drove was tended by the best of drovers, the mounted vaqueros. The trader beckoned to one of them, making his wishes known by signs; the dumb by-play mystified Tim.

"An ken yees talk Mexan on yer fingers?" he asked.

"Yes," the old man answered, jokingly.

"It's a pity then yese not tried em on Heinrich's lingo; I'd be sorry for them same, whin yese do."

"When you ken ride like a Mexan, Tim, you'll know sumpin bout a hoss."

While the Colonel was speaking, the drove, at a distance, grew restive, and a steer bolted the line of the range; upon seeing which, the vaqueros dashed after him.

"Watch the boys nab that feller, Tim; they'll lasso his legs an leave him on the ground for punishment." The trader explained these things to his teamster, as his discipline was such he never permitted his whips, unless he was with them, to cross the line of the cattle range; this was done to keep the sets of men apart to prevent feuds.

Just as he had said, one of the Mexicans pursued at full run, throwing his coil as he rode; very soon the fugitive was brought to, lying prone on his back, while the second vaquero caught his heels with his noose. Between the two the runaway was at once in duress.

The horse was now brought up.

"Now, Tim, heah comes the critter; he's a flyer; pure stock, seh, an he knows nothin but bisnis; look at that head, his step, and that ar neck, seh.

"An is't the baste fer me to ride?"

"Yes, seh; an you'll never mount another like him, if I know anything bout horseflesh; but take a caution; don't you let anything come up ahind him, mind; he won't stan that, if he knows it."

"Ef he knows it," repeated the other.

The young, full-fed colt pawed the earth proudly; the eye, soft, open, rolling, in every glance showed his spirit; every pulsing vein his temper, breeding and quality.

"Whoa, Tad, you rowdy," said the owner, patting the horse's face, as the cow-boy saddled him.

"Jes as gentle as a kitten; he was nussed on blue-grass, Tim."

"An that's good for em, is't, Colonel?" He drew nearer, as he spoke, to be friendly with his mount, and helped to bridle him.

The Irishman climbed into the saddle and rode away; the horse stepping off with a keen desire for a free rein and the word "go." One Mexican looked at the other, and both smiled blandly, while the trader turned about for the camp. He had been with his men but a short while, when each ceased speaking and listened.

"What's that?" was said. The sound that came to their ears — a dull, distant thud — was like the first fretful rumble of a storm.

"The drove's stampeded, boys," the old man called out, as he mounted a wagon, to take in a view of the field. What he saw was one of those phenomenal panics, which suddenly seize upon, not only beasts in herds, but regiments in battle; always a fear-stricken madness, without method or restraint.

Murphy had ridden Tad close upon the flank of the grazers at a central point on the line of the immense drove, and there he halted. As luck would have it so, he had but drawn rein, wheeling his horse to face the cattle, when a Texan showed signs of affright. A trifle, perhaps, had scared him, but the loud, angry bellow, the stamp of the hoofs and the snort of rage, filled his fellows at once with terror. On the instant every head was up, the ears pricked, the horns ready, the eyes staring wide; again the mutineer sounded his alarm, and a hundred deep throats echoed it; then, with a bound, the one broke away, his tail whirled like a whip-lash, his head low down, and the panic became general. On the heels of the leader the whole drove, in crazed disorder, broke ranks and fled.

At the first sign of revolt, the vaqueros called to Tim and motioned to him to beat back the rioter into the drove; but Murphy, in truth, had no time for the action. He had tried to wheel his horse across the path of the steer, but a fortunate, as well as unforeseen turn, caused the horse to disobey; had he tarried with the rider both might have been borne down and trampled.

Tad was moved by a single instinct; challenged to speed by the ringleader of the drove in trying to pass him, no hand could now tame the freed and truant spirit. The thoroughbred was, therefore, the foremost in a wild, headlong, heedless race; nor could the most skilful rider have wheeled out of the scrape. There was a break-neck need to forge ahead, as it would have been a deadly chance to cross the track of such a rabble. Cattle, like sheep, hold blindly to the lead, and as the colt warmed to his best leaps, the drove redoubled its speed. The vaqueros on the right and left flank of the mass had screamed themselves hoarse hailing the frightened runaway, but all to no purpose.

Poor Tim. It was the ride of his life, to which the exploit of Gilpin or the scramble of Sheridan would bear but a shady likeness. Tad had caught the bit between his teeth, ducked his head for a hard run, threw his feet into the face of his rivals, and fairly flew over the prairie. Tim held his seat, both hands in the mane, both feet to the heels through the stirrups; he was hatless, his hair on end, the bridle lying loose before him.

"Whoa!" he roared above the loud tramp behind him; "the baste don't know how to shtop."

The horse plunged on.

"Whoa!" he cried again, almost bereft of his senses; "an the Colonel calls him Toad! Whoa, Toad, you laping varmint;" but still the horse ran on; he leaped like a deer and sped like the blast.

"Moses! pfat'll be lift o' me; an this he calls a speeshul sarvice; whoa, Toad, you baste;" he cast a glance backward over his shoulder and turned pale. "Be jabes, an look at that now; the whurld is full of em, an if this horse slips, good-by Misther Tim."

By this time the horse's speed was well spent, as well as that of the drove; but still holding the lead, his movements seemed to indicate a return to camp in a well-directed turn.

Chevitean and his men looked on at the ludicrous plight of Murphy, without being able, until now, to render him aid.

"Get yer whips, all hands," he said, "an be quick about it; if they bolt the bluff I'll lose a hundred head."

Tad had left the drove some distance to rear, and came bounding on. The teamsters stepped aside to let him pass their line; then closing up they lashed and yelled at the cattle coming on. Losing their leader, the drove slackened its pace; at the same time the vaqueros turned it for the tramping ground, where it soon became quieted.

The horse had gone on, until near the spot where Cheviteau was standing, and there he stopped short at his owner's call. Tim leaped down, and struck the ground with a thud.

"Jabbers!" he exclaimed, as the breath escaped him.

"Are you hurt, Tim?" asked the trader.

"Deil a bit ken I tell ye, Colonel."

"Well seh; what do you think of my colt?"

"Yer colt? I'fath, but Toad's a good name for him,—barring the wings."

"He has a splendid spirit, Tim."

"Speerit is't?"

"Yes, seh; good blue-grass breeding."

"Thin ets a good thing, d'ye mind, that he's got down to graen."

Time was never wasted under the trader's management; he kept his men well in hand, and combining his trade with the avocation of a grazer, there were seasons of labor other than these which his expeditions required. So it was that his droves increased, for in his penny-wise foresight the outlying meadows near about his camp were turned into hayfields. He sowed and reaped and laid up against the sweeping blasts and snow-gusts of hard winters. Few of his trade thrived like him; few had the thrift to combine these different pursuits. Stirring as all his daily occupations were he could not lay aside a growing anxiety about Beck; he had been gone six weeks, and Cheviteau often turned from his labor towards the horizon, to strain his eyes in the hope of gladdening them with a sight of the returing rider.

The summer was in its earliest prime and the mowers' blades were seen flashing in the sunlight. Early and late the wide swarths fell under the scythes, and the rakers followed in the track of the swinging blades. Mary was seen again on the path to the hamlet, and Mrs. Garrulson tarried under the hospitable shelter. All the while the Judge was busy; he wrote lengthy scrawls, and waited what the boats might bring in reply, with an air of authority. He was found at odd times, in hidden nooks, conversing low with such as would listen. The Doctor talked much and was fussy, subsiding to a calmer temper on the banks of the creek, watching the bob of his line. In this way days ran into weeks, in the quiet of a far-away settlement.

Beck was nearing the end of the almost endless stretch; horse and rider were worn to the bone. The wear upon the man had left him gaunt and angular;

the skin of his face, neck and hands had peeled; where the sun had scorched deeply there were blisters. He walked with a halt, the muscles of his limbs were crippled. His faithful stallion never failed in pluck or endurance, but the proud neck was limp, held low, the eyes drooping, the ribs could be counted and the gloss of his satin coat had faded; his hoofs were cracked and tender, and when saddling Beck took up much that was to spare in the girth.

There was one stretch more; the horse was equal to it after a more than usual rest. Beck gave him water where they camped, drew the straps tightly in place, and mounted. He had to cross the northern skirt of a small, waterless desert. An angry day had faded out in a brazen sundown, and the scout's trail lay through the white, baked dust; the breeze was heavy and stifling and came fitfully over the drear morass.

The gang led by Cartwright had traveled at a steady jog, — the short quick-step of the prairie ponies, — and the incredible stamina of their wiry frames held out. They hurried on, hiding by day to avoid arrest by whites or attacks from unfriendly Indians. Through the nights and days of long weeks spun out, they had left behind them the wide, green valley lands and softer skies, and rode a path fringed with the sage and thistle, where speary grasses withered in the sun.

Forty miles away, in the twilight of the angry day, where earth and sky were joined in one long gleam, they saw upon the silvery space a silhouette of a horse and rider. The outlines were perfect, though the figure was but a speck; they had seen the forms of Beck and his stallion.

He had distanced the gang, though they knew it not, and by the aid of his rare knowledge in road-craft, he had ridden boldly, and clear of all opposing dangers.

Days rolled on. Chloe, as mistress of certain small matters, had laid down a day's duty for the unruly Cato.

"Now mine, dus yer h'yar; gwy long arter dat cow an caf, out yanner."

"Yes'm;" he answered with quick consent, for to watch the cow called him away from other and more irksome tasks, and made his jaunt a holiday.

"I'se a gwyne — but er — "

"None uv yer foolishtist; gwy long."

"Ain't I a gwyne; kase I knows dar ain't no spooks out dar, is dar?"

"Spooks!" the old woman held counsel with herself as to the boy's misgiving, in which she shared. She gave heed to his words in her own awe of the spirits said to be earth-bound to the space around the haunted cabin.

"I kinder reckon not, Cato; but ef yer sees a spook, h'yar's wat'll fotch him;" a bent horse-shoe nail was the charm she hung round the lad's neck. His doubts took wing from the corn-fed content of his nature, sparkling in a flute-like whistle, which the birds caught up, as one.

Chloe cast a look after him as he went along; a self-reproving look, as if she had doomed him to be the witches' prey, and, perchance, she thought, never again would his form be seen.

"H'yah, boy;" she yelled, as a vagrant hope lent her another talisman, "ef dat ar nail don't do, eat a danjelion; dus yer h'yah me?"

The boy heard her, and called back:

"Danjelion!" He ran on, whistling, out of her sight, into the wide, full gladness of the summer day.

The gray old earth, so gently wild, lay in the beams of the eastern sun, all lonely, lovely; over it swept from the dance of the leaves, a breath of the woodland fragrance, winging the sun-spun mites through the golden vista. The snowy piles of curdled clouds lay low on bars of blue; a silence perfect, moved only by the little singing whispers:

> "The unshorn fields, boundless, beautiful,
> * * * * * * *
> As if the ocean in his gentlest swell
> Stood still, with all his rounded billows fixed
> And motionless forever."

The rich, full voice of the little darkey broke in on the waiting stillness; its notes were like the clarionet's, rising, swelling into a melody of tuneful sounds, a crude cadence, rude, loud, but sweet. He sang a camp-meeting jubilee; the words a pot-pourri of his fears, his hopes and his fun:

> "Gel-o-ree! Gel-o-ree!
> I'se wun ob de Marster's ban,—
> Gel-o-ree! Gel-o-ree!
> Oh-h hap-pee, hap-pee lan;

   Ef yuse git dar, afore I duse,
   Oh, lemme foller in yer shuse,
   Wen I git dar, I'll tell de nuse."
    Oh-h hap-pee, hap-pee lan.
(Clapping hands.)

    Gel-o-ree! Gel-o-ree!
   I'se wun ob de Marster's ban,—
    Gel-o-ree! **Gel-o-ree!**
   Oh-h hap-pee, hap-pee lan;
   De debbil laid awake at nite
   His tail a shakin, was a site,
   He couldn't hide afore the lite,
    Oh-h hap-pee, hap-pee lan.
(Laughing.)

    Gel-o-ree! Gel-o-ree!
   Ise wun ob de Marster's ban,—
    Gel-o-ree! Gel-o-ree!
   Oh-h hap-pee, hap-pee lan;
   Wen Gabril seed de debbil grin,
   His tail a flappin up at him,
   He chop **it** off an druv it in,
    Oh-h **hap-pee,** hap-pee **lan.**
(Dancing.)

    Gel-o-ree! Gel-o-ree!
   Ise wun ob de Marster's ban,—
    Gel-o-ree! Gel-o-ree!
   Oh-h hap-pee, hap-pee **lan;**
   I terry **on** de big, green flo,
   De boat es waitin on de **sho,**
   To lib an laf fer eber mo,
    Oh-h hap-pee, **hap-pee lan.**

All at once the song ceased, and on looking up the singer found himself in the spectral shade of the cabin. He had reached its terrors step by step, as if led by an unseen hand, and from the chill of sudden fright the glory of his jubilee faded.

The bark of a squirrel transfixed him.

All the rounded wrinkles of a merry face were strained and straight; the mouth closed tightly, like the lid of a music-box; the eyes grew larger, larger, until the whites shone pale upon the cheeks, the hands were useless, the knees askew.

Again the squirrel barked; the silence deepened, and like a sheet of brass from the blazing sky, the noon-sheen fell.

"Who dat?" he asked, in a feeble, husky tone.

"Dat!" replied the rotting logs, the hollow chimney.

"Dat you, Misto Johnsing?" he asked again, in a smirkish rally of the nerves, as he edged away, looking over his shoulder.

"I know'd yer," he said, playing off with his fright as his steps widened.

Again the squirrel barked.

The boy broke into a run, and fear lent speed to his strides along the margin of the muddy creek, until his breath came fast, and he threw himself, laughing, into the green, high grass.

"Who's afeerd!" he said, as the wrinkles wreathed about the mouth again; it opened, like a clam, and never a pearl in its sea-shell home shone brighter than the teeth.

Just behind him, in the sunlight, lay a broad, smooth slab; a virgin tablet to be carved by Him who writes with the lightning. To the imp it was an itching temptation; he sprang to the warm, hard surface, and the fall of the bare foot sounded like a smack of the hands. Then his heels flew up, and he sang again, all joyously, the patter of the feet beating time.

Now he crawled down the bank of the stream, and in the glare he seated himself on a flat, unshaded rock, arranging his hook and line.

The creek was an inlet from the bend of the river; it had wormed its way deeply across the plateau by the cabin, down the gorge, to where it met the current again, like the string of a bow. Here it was that Beck rode with fierce leaps, on the eventful night of Mary's capture, and stood sentinel over the pirates' cave. It was a sullen, murky water-course, spreading wide and shallow between high bluffs.

At the first spring of the boy's pole, casting his shotted string far out into the current, a hungry, shovel-headed "cat" swallowed the bait and was drawn up; the fish was soon afloat, strung to a tow.

Now yawning, nodding he gave signs of sleepiness, and bathed in the sunshine, his form was stretched to the undenied beneficence; he tied the fish-line to his toe, nor was his the first inventive genius that made the foot a hitching-post during slumber. The fabled fisherman of "Ole Varginny sho" was whirled to his doom through a like caper. Nor was it ever known,

> "After all their guessing and all their figgerin,
> Whether the nigger a-fishing had gone,
> Or the fish had gone a-niggerin."

Doctor Tom also, with his hook and line, had sauntered forth to the creek's outlet, counting surely that his rod, only less than Aaron's in its virtue, would be the marvel of the sport; his up-stream trudge, over brake and briar and pool, had repaid his toil, with the common luck of his tribe,— scratched limbs and a minnow. Tired truly and well-worn, he found a seat under a sycamore:

> "Its broad, dark bough in solemn repose
> Far over the silent brook."

After a while he stirred himself, and went on, to come upon the dreaming darkey. It was a bright spark of fun that lighted up the Doctor's face as he quietly took the large, fat cat from the boy's line and put his own little chub in the place of it. Passing on, he gave a thought to the bliss of ignorance and the folly of wisdom.

Cato slept like a top, with the healthy snore of a saucy boy; long he slept; the plump, fat face bore no lines save the smooth ones where the laugh comes in; a genuine type he was of "the ebo-shin and gizzard foot," a product of hoe-cake and bacon. He slept on, and not a nibble stirred his sound repose; how long in the calm, sweet day he lay there, he knew not.

"Hal-lo! hal-lo! you boy!"

Presently the hail struck the dull ear of the sleeper; he came to slowly, but as the call was repeated he jumped to his feet:

"Ken I cross the crick? how deep?" asked a horseman on the further marge of the stream.

"Yes, seh!" answered Cato, half awake and scratching his chin.

Kings have been dethroned, and the world set agog through less mistakes than chanced between these two. The boy answered as to the man's right to cross, and the man fixed in his mind the depth of the water by the boy's motion to his chin.

The imp sleepily looked on; he saw the stranger disrobe, but not until he and his horse had reached midstream did the truth make its way to his brain. Then a laugh rang out that startled the silence, and snatching at his luck, with a leap, the boy was gone.

The man, pale with rage, leading his horse, gained dry land; he stamped and swore, bit his lip and swore again; for a gentleman, bare, cuts a most ridiculous figure, to be laughed at, outright, by a little black scamp.

He had crossed the stream, scarcely reaching his knees.

But he rode on, and for years his ire kept warm; in the end:

> "The moral was this, as somebody told him,
> That he had sold negroes, and a negro had sold him."

"Whar's de cow?" said Chloe, as her factotum stood before her.

"Spooks!" he replied, with a face put on for the time.

"Spooks! whar's eny? Wat dese got to do wid de cow, hey?"

"Eat de cow up; heerd um champin."

"Wat! oh, hesh boy; spooks don't eat cow-meat; I knows dat."

"Seed um."

"Go long yer triflin moke; you'd er ruinge der famerly."

It was the chance the fat rascal longed for, and when alone his loud laugh was heard again, as he thought of the stranger's plight. Now, for the first time, he caught sight of the fish, which, as he ran, had dangled behind him.

"Its swunk; laws a massy, how dis nig mus er run'd;" but here a fright came upon him, lest while he slept the spooks had bewitched his catch; the boy laughed no more that day.

CHAPTER IX.

THE CONSPIRACY.

A famished pair were the horse and rider, when they rode out the last long mile. Beck drew up, challenged by a crowd of vaqueros at a ranche not far from the Mexican town. One who spoke English accosted him:

"What you want, caballero?"

"Whar's Ferati?"

The man turned, and raising his voice to a hallo, called out:

"Señor Don Ferati!" The Señor was not afield and came at once to the door of his low, hay-thatched cabin.

"Hi, hi, caramba, man; here am I and not a league off," he said angrily in Spanish; and then speaking to the rider in broken English:

"Americano, will he come down?" he said.

Beck dismounted and, standing face to face with the grazer, the latter knew him on the instant, and in a fervid show of friendship, peculiar to his people, he said:

"Kari, my soul; by the padre's elbow, Capitaine Beck; caramba; in, in, my friend, my companion, carajo; stay with me forever, — Manuela! — Manuela!" He kept on in this strain, calling for some one within, and presently the slender, graceful form, the sweet, olive-tinged face, and the sparkling eyes of his young and very pretty wife were seen in the doorway. "Make ready, child, for my friend, the Americano; a good friend, my Manuela; in, señor;" and Beck entered the dwelling.

"Where from, good friend?" asked the Mexican, eyeing the wearied man before him.

"From sunrise," Beck answered with a cold smile, signing to make himself understood, and naming the far-away river from which he had set out.

The host stared at the speaker, as at a ghost from the grave, crossed himself, and threw up his hands, exclaiming:

"Quien sabe? great saints! Down, down, good, brave horseman; do rest." Then he spread a poncho on the hard floor.

But Beck was still alive and wakeful to his purpose.

After going back through the past of their acquaintance over a meal quickly served by the young senora, Beck turned to the business before them. It was, in brief, to engage Ferati to enter the town and watch for the arrival of the pack-train, to note the movements of the gang and to find out the plans of Cartwright. He paid his host a fair sum to serve him, and when Ferati had seen that his guest was well disposed in a quiet rest, and his horse unsaddled, he gave over his ranche to a trusty dependent. He charged him, on pain of death, to be good to the needs of his visitor, and bidding his wife prepare herself for the fandango in town, he called up his mounts. Very soon thereafter the two rode off, and riding fast were soon out of sight in the darkness.

In the dawn-lighted, sweeter stretches, having crossed the southern rim of the dead waste, the pirates halted. Just beyond their camp the noted Spanish village of the south-west border lay, loosely flecking the plain. Cartwright and Cruz rode away from the camp and into the plaza of the dingy puebla.

Among piles of fruit and vegetables sat the rabble of the market-place. Ill-favored faces peered forth from the hoods of their dirty rebozos, and there was a babel of distracting sounds from a mob of donkeys, yelping, wolf-like curs and swearing muleteers. Intermingling, there were sounds less harsh; the jingle of spurs, the small, soft voice of the child, the bass of the mountaineer, and a note of richest music, swelled in the laugh of a hoydenish poblano.

"*Tortillas! tortillas!*" cried a muchachita.

"*Chile bueno! Chile colorado! Chile caliente!*" screamed a concinera, with his fiery stew.

"*Pan y leche, pan blancho!*" the song of a girl whose sweet notes were overborne by

"*Carbon! carbon!*" from a vendor of charcoal.

"*Aqua! aqua limpia excellente,*" bawled an aquadoré, and the thirsty thief on his horse beckoned for a draught of the excellent, limpid water.

The riders tarried not, but pushed on in the blank glare of the white mud walls, and anon drew up before a squalid abode. The low, thatched roof of the fonda darkened the doorway, which gave poor promise of cheer within. Straightway the two approached the tendejohn and there quaffed a dram of pulque, handed down from the tawdry ornaments of a dusty shelf. Soon thereafter they separated, having arranged for another meeting. Cartwright, after a meal, found a hammock under the eaves outside, and fell asleep among the buzzing gnats.

In the dusk, as he shook himself out of his stupor and sat down on the door-step, a tall savage strode by. The boss knew the Indian's tribe by the long bone bow he carried. There was just light enough to see in the look askant of the swarthy face, a cruel sternness, hard as a statue's visage. The rude dignity of the chief's walk was heightened by the fall of a trailing blanket, lending grace to his form and carriage. Cartwright noted him well; noted also that every passer-by stepped out of his path with a shudder or a curse, and children ran crying, as from the presence of a ghost. They said, with bated breath, that a tyrant, in alliance with these Indians, ruled them; swayed them through their fears of raids, pillage and slaughter, not uncommon; and that this tribe was the police of the tyrant.

The nightly revel had begun, and while the thief danced with a bearish joy among the crowd that thronged the banquette of the tavern, he caught the eye of Cruz; he joined his associate and followed him. As he passed out an old trapper nudged a companion:

"Did you see that land pirate?"

"Whar, Jack?"

"Him as jes went out; that buffler-headed rough that war giving us a bar dance."

"Him, yes; he cavorted round like a hobbled mule."

"Spot him, chum; he's a thief; the biggest on the plains."

Through dark lanes on the skirt of the town, to a tumble-down adobe, Cruz and Cartwright, sneaking like hungry cayotes, found awaiting them in the darkness, the savage who strode by in the twilight. They had met to chaffer over the price of blood with a full flask and clinking gold, and out of the glare of one depravity, the pirate seemed to have found another, and more congenial vice.

Ferati had once been a celebrated matador, but his fall was that of Lucifer,—so he thought,—from the idol of Mexico's capital to an outcast, as he was wont to style himself, in deep chagrin that soured his temper. Not one of the untamed, lion-like bulls, tormented, unfed, infuriated to overcome his prowess, had for years daunted his courage nor escaped his skill. Each had been as a plaything to his two-edged rapier and his blood-red banner. With what a dilettante grace his proud form moved about the arena, — such was his style in deploring his loss, — as with the bow of a courtier he waved aside all other competitors for the honors of the fight, and drove his steel to the hilt.

"Bravo Ferati; bravissima!" cried all. And so it came about, that the mob held him in high esteem, while senoras and senoritas clapped their hands as he entered the ring, or wreathed his brow when he left it.

It was a gala day when he met his fate; a high festival drew the beauty and the chivalry, the dignitaries of church and state, the populace to the amphitheatre. The grandees were in genial humor, the people happy, and the scene within the circular pen, where he stood victor over the slain and mangled bodies of a dozen bulls, turned the head of the vain, though skilful fellow, and raised him to glory's heights. The flaunting handkerchief, the flying bouquet, the wave of the silken scarf, shouts of men, cries of children, the squeaking voices of the old, manifested a greedy delight in the cruel and flagitious sport.

The scene had become commonplace by his repeated triumphs, when the trumpets heralded the coming on of the last surviving beast. Foaming with rage, crazed by the smell of blood and the torturing missiles flung into his corral, in leaped, with a deer-like bound, a shining-coated, coal-black bull. His horns were sharp as spear-points, his roar like an uncaged lion. Pawing the earth, his reddened eyes gleamed, and the thick, white foam covered the breast and flanks.

"Hi, hi, tauro; beautiful bull; at them, beauty!" cried the mob, rising to cheer.

And there was method in the animal's madness which left little to doubt; it was the majesty of frenzy; there was no need of spurs to goad him on, he leaped viciously to the assault. Ferati was unhorsed in the first charge; nothing could divert the onset, for the bull attacked with fell intent; neither flags, explodents, spear-thrusts nor the needle-pointed barbs, could turn aside the straight, full-forced drive of the horns into the vitals of the matador's horse. Gored again and again, the horse fell and expired, ripped open, despite the dexterous handling of the rider. The champion was now afoot, his courage a little shaken, but still he saluted with his sword upraised, as the bull, throwing the earth in fury, made ready. There was one chance, one only, and the man's best. With a spring, he planted his foot between the horns, leaped astride the back, and essayed to drive his sword behind the shoulder. But the bull with a quick dash hurled him to the ground, and tossed him aloft amid the taunts and jeers of the crowd. The ring had been cleared of attendants, several wounded and one slain outright, and there was little help for the bull-fighter, as he struck the earth, and was again hurled high.

But now a sudden sight caused a tremor and a cry of alarm in the brutish multitude.

"Out, out, little one; death to the child; back, baby; go quick; in the love of God, go back!"

The clamor came in an instant of terror on seeing a young, gay girl, dressed like a danseuse, her red scarf floating from the waist, scale the barrier and descend into the arena. The bull glanced angrily at the nymph, and turned furiously, to charge so bold a challenger. But the nimble-footed sprite, with supreme courage, held her way across the ring, and then with a spring, catching a hand-hold on the logs of the inclosure, drew herself up to its rim. Sitting there, she kept the roaring savage at bay. It was this diversion that saved the bull-fighter's life. His body was rescued, while it lasted, and having recovered from his wounds, he married the girl, and hid his defeat and shame in the life of a cattle-raiser.

Beck's acquaintance with the Mexican had been of long duration. Once, when a sergeant of dragoons at a fort near by, he was sent out with a squad to reconnoitre. He came upon Ferati fighting hard with a band of redskins who had stolen his cattle. Beck drove back the thieves, rescued the man's stock, and his friendship had been warm and sincere. He knew nothing of him further than his favors, his gratitude, and those natural, passionate extremes common to his race.

To the overtures of Cartwright, the Indian moodily by signs made answer. He asked a large sum in money and an equal share in spoils as the condition upon which he would agree to plunder the trader's train. It was useless for the plotters to speak of an easy victory and a rich reward, the chief yielded nothing. So the rogues parted to meet again, the night following, at the same place. Cruz and Cartwright, the next morning, were puzzled to devise means with which to bribe the savage. Before evening, the landlord was pressed into service and soon became as zealous as any one of the cabal, enlarged by other free booters from the gang.

As the day wore on, and as they drank and smoked, Ferati entered the place alone. He had not been idle; after his arrival in town he sent his wife to the fandango, while he in the interim of a day had visited many haunts and acquaintances, gathered up what gossip he could concerning the pirate-packers, and had formed a very shrewd opinion from his own knowledge of their leader, Cruz. What remained for him to find out, he trusted to his wits and the keener scent of Manuela.

He was at once noticed as he entered; very much taller than the average Mexican, his fanciful dress seemed to harden the stone-cold sneer on his lips, and the mouth, shaded by an iron-gray moustache, clipped close, gave to the lean nose the outline of a hawk's bill. The eyes, set deeply in the sunken cheeks, sparkled like a serpent's. On his head, bound up in a striped bandanna, rested the glazed sombrero; the calzoneros were velvet, tight-fitting and slashed, below a red, armless jacket, contrasting oddly with the calico shirt beneath. The waist was bound in a rich, silken scarf, above which was seen a stiletto and pistol.

Whenever the chance offered, the man played monte desperately, as he never permitted a challenge to pass at his table. Always ready to break a bank, or to have his own broken, in the parlance of the craft, he was never content with a slow pursuit of his calling; when flushed by success he was a profligate; when penniless he was morose and dangerous.

The landlord whispered to his confederates that the new comer had a fund to be won, and Cartwright took the hint; he saw that under certain conditions this was his opportunity, and he quickly resolved to "tap the bank" of the dealer that night; a term understood to mean that he would challenge the monte player for the amount upon his table, on the turn of a card. It was further agreed that the landlord should manage the crowning shame. Cruz having so worked upon his fears of an Indian raid, and duped him by the show of profits, he pledged himself to manipulate a pack of cards so as to make Cartwright's winning sure.

The lights were ablaze on the rough, white walls, throwing off an ill savor to mix with the smell of garlic, the fumes of tobacco and wine, when Manuela came in and crossed the floor to the card-player. He whispered and she turned away with a serious look, to stroll about the apartment.

The street cries without were growing louder as the night came on, and from the plaza beyond, the jargon of the hucksters was heard in full chorus. A crowd, increased from every house, filled the streets, and young women of almost every hue flocked to the dens near by. The music struck up in the fonda; its first notes reached the ears of the idlers outside, when the tide turned into the room. It was a motley crowd at the height of the revel; mountain-men, trappers, scouts, guides, deserters, negroes, hunters, traders, teamsters, packers, gamblers and land pirates; senoritas, in their trappings of faded velvets and flaunting ribbons; the glazed leather and bell-buttons of the men in accord with the gay jackets and satin slippers of the women; nor was the American's garb out of harmony. His voice was not a note lower than the prevailing discord, from the strumming of the mandolin and the shuffle of the feet on the hard, clay floor.

In a corner sat a penny-pitcher; the lean wretch begged like a mendicant.

"In the name of Saint Peter," he cried, "plank down, plank down; if I lose this bet it'll put me in my cold, cold grave."

Now Ferati took up a guitar, and suddenly his young wife bounded into the center of the room. Flashing, fluttering, circling, bounding like a fawn, skimming like an albatross settling to its ease on the crest of a white wild wave; springing, like the flight of the bird, the dark eyes opening and closing on her burning cheeks, she whirled in a delirium of triumph over the fleetest foot of her sex. She skipped aside and disappeared, as the mountain-men threw coin at her feet.

The dance ended, the gambler seated himself at a table, spread out his cards, placing his gold and silver near him; then he composedly drew his weapons and made them a part of the display.

Cartwright at once challenged him, and as the crowd grew close about them, he said politely:

"Bueno."

"Wayno," repeated Bill; "give us a new pack of kerds."

"As the senor chooses," replied the player; the lowest Spaniard tries to be affable.

The new pack was brought by the landlord; Cruz eyed him closely. Cartwright won the toss and drew the cards; he drew them steadily card after card. The one he wagered on came first; he held it up before the dealer, who, with blanched cheeks, said:

" Bueno, señor."

The winner swept the pile from the table, lighted his cigar, and left the room. He was followed by his confederates.

The danseuse stood in the dark shadow of the house listening to every word that passed between the thief and his pal, Cruz, and as they rode away to the rendezvous with the Indian, she hastened to her partner; he listened, and in sullen humor gathered up his cards, and replaced his weapons.

Soon thereafter a furious row began, provoked by the woman, and as the melee became general, the lights were put out suddenly. In the gloom gliding about, stepping like a cat, guided by a faint shimmer from the street, the maddened player ceaselessly sought one face which his hate had drawn in lines of fire. The riot spent itself, the house was deserted, and the gambler, with his wife, disappeared in the crowd.

In the small hours of the morning Ferati returned to his domicile. Beck was aroused, and to his hasty questions the Mexican answered promptly, bidding him speed back to the post; that Cartwright had conspired with the Indians to attack his train at a certain point, and to start out before these plans could be carried out.

Beck nerved himself to spring back into the saddle; he must outstrip the gang, reach the post, get some rest for his over-wrought frame, and a fair start with his train before the pirates could mature the plot.

He gave over his faithful bay to the Mexican, taking in exchange a strong horse which the grazer thought surpassed in mettle all others of his kind in existence. Beck awaited the break of day, then mounted.

He parted with his host, shaking hands; little he knew that the coin he had placed therein had pensioned a heartless savage to seek his life; that the same hand had driven a poignard through the heart of another, and that the sweet and peaceful light of the dawn, now falling on horse and rider as they sped away, fell alike over the pallid corpse of the landlord on the red-clay floor of the fonda.

CHAPTER X.

THE WAY-WORN RIDER — "ROLL-OUT."

Beck, on his departure from the post, had said in his off-hand way, that he was going to watch the pirate, and the trader was led to believe that this meant the movements of the gang at the crib or their trail thence, when he would return. He supplied Beck with funds to meet any need in seeking information, but he was far from knowing the dauntless errand on which his guide had resolved. The scout's natural reticence, and as a habit of his calling, kept his mouth closed as to the particulars of his mission. His insight into the ways of such an evil-designing rogue as Cartwright, drew him instinctively to the distant nest of the vipers. He trusted his own shrewdness best, feared to disclose his plan, lest they might be over-ruled, and relied upon his physical strength as equal to any trial.

He had been away already over six weeks, and during this lapse of time, the season had advanced into the sun-bright days late in June. The shimmering expanse, lying far to the west beyond the post, seemed to vibrate in the heat of noon. There were no cool spots about the camp; but at the house, a milder ray fell through the morning-glories on Mary, as she sat at her knitting.

"I can't make it out, what keeps John so long," her father said as he stepped on to the porch, from the rear door.

"It seems a long, long time," Mary replied, musingly; but then, with a ready cheer, she added: "I always trust Mister John, father; he'll come."

The trader walked away, and his steps led him straightly to the office-door. He entered and hastily snatched up his glass as he mounted to the outlook. His range on the horizon swept slowly the vast circuit, all deeply blue, but not a line on the curtained space resembled the familiar form of his scout. He drew back and got down from the ladder, much troubled in spirit, for next to his love for his daughter, his friendship for Beck was almost as ardent a passion.

Where was Beck? The question the trader asked himself many times, repeating it to Mary. Where was he?

The scout had ridden away from Feratr's ranche a fortnight before, and had taken a trail to bring him out on a well-known highway, more frequently traversed than any other of the many routes across the plains. He bestrode the grazer's horse, a young, fresh, strong gelding, of Mexican habits, which Beck was not sure he could trust. Trained to the use of the lasso, his mount was tractable, bridlewise and kind; he grazed at the picket-rope without fretting, and thrived on short commons better than his stallion. In build, the horse was high and well-knit; his stride was wide and easy; his natural gait, a lope. The head betokened poor blood; there was not a sign of the thoroughbred about him, but every movement was that of thorough training. Beck did not know his speed, and this stood first in what he would require of his mount; nor did he care to test it lest he might regret the tax upon his strength.

The same routine of lonely camps, the same daily ride and rest, the gallop in the dawn, the halt in the twilight, the sleep under the stars at night in the awful silence. The journey repeated was wearing the man down; his form was bent, overstrained, and he sat his saddle clumsily. In this plight, as a train passed he bargained with the whips to take him up, and he stretched himself, at full length, in one of the covered wagons. The respite from the horseback jar was most delightful, and for days he enjoyed it. His beast was led; for both, it was rest; the horse was lightened of his load, and man's heart lightened by the voices of his fellows. But the drag soon grew to be irksome to one whose bent was to cover distance with all dispatch, whose purpose was to reach a goal within a given time. So, in the first flush of another day, Beck put spurs to his horse and was soon careering beyond the sight of the teamsters. He sped on in a gallop, and now, to test the courage and dash of the Mexican, he spurred deep, raising his voice to a shout, and slackened the rein. The horse leaped, nearly unseating the rider, threw back his ears, and spun like a top along the road. Beck was delighted; he had stirred the latent vigor of a prairie-born flyer. The scout felt now that no fatigue could break down the startling nerve of one of those strange, half-wild, iron-bound breed of horses. The bounding dash waked the man also, when suddenly a foe sprang from the earth before him. He had neared a thicket-grown rise in the land, and was about to draw up, when a band of Indian horsemen, their bow-strung arrows drawn, challenged his advance.

On sight, Beck dropped his rein, seized his pistols, raised both hands, and with a yell, fired.

The freed horse turned sharp at an angle, with every fibre strung, every nerve and sinew strained, and with wondrous power cleared the opposing line, and swept by it. On came the savages, goading their ponies; on sped Beck and his Mexican; he turned in his saddle and bent his rifle on the foremost Indian. The ball fell short, and the arrows aimed at him were out of reach and harmless. He seized the bridle:

"Now, Bones, go it," and, guiding his horse, struck out for a canyon. Hidden away in a cavern of one of these deep-cut gorges, which he had reached out of sight of the foe, there he hid himself and his horse until the dark would shield him.

The wait and watch at the camp for the absent scout had lengthened to a weary, feeble hope. The trader's suspense had grown to be a consuming fear that his friend was a victim of Cartwright's malice. Every hour added to the old man's doubts, and early and late he was seen with his glass leveled in the outlook.

Mary was a silent watcher. Often with shaded eyes she stood in the path to gaze steadily and long, out on the burnished prairie. She would turn away, her face sadder than before, but not to betray her thoughts she cheered her father when they met.

The Doctor never doubted the coming of Beck in his own good time, but many of the men had given him up as lost.

It was a calm summer night, in the later hours, as the guard paced his rounds, when suddenly the tall, gaunt form of a wayfarer, leading a lank, raw-boned horse, appeared before him.

"Who comes thar?" cried the sentry.

"It's me, John Beck; what's left of me;" and the man, reeling in his steps, gave his mount in charge of the guard, and found his way into the house.

Soon, within the dwelling, the lamps were lighted and the sideboard door was opened. There were cheerful voices heard and the smacking of lips; the Doctor's loud salutation, the trader's greeting, Lu's laugh, Whack's banter, and Mary's gleeful tones were heard. But all stood amazed at the man's changed features and attire. His beard and hair were long and matted, the face bronzed to a coppery hue, his form lean and worn; the shoes and leggins were whipped to tatters by the speary grass; his clothes were ragged. He looked up from the meal before him, and with a reassuring smile, he said:

"Never mind, Peter; I made my pint."

"I'll bet you did, John, certin;" he answered.

Very little else than these few words escaped the lips of Beck, but Cheviteau felt that in time he would know the whole story.

The tired giant's return to strength was easy; he hid away in shaded nooks and slept; he ate heartily with his old-fashioned gusto. The morning saw him bathing in the stream; at noon, outstretched from the heat; and night, with its gracious help, built up the strong man to himself.

One day, lying under a grove-tree not far from the rear porch, Mary sought him out. With his blouse for a pillow, he slept healthily, and she stood near him watching his restful repose. Womanlike, she broke a few broad leaves from the weeds near by, and fanned the face of the sleeper.

Suddenly his eyes opened wide and staring.

"Well — Mary," he said, springing up.

"I thought the flies would vex you, Mister John," she replied; then laughing in her old, round, joyous way, "and I found your scalp was whole."

"Is it?" he spoke in a confused way, as if in doubt. "Well, now I've had my stretch, and feel all right; whar's your father?"

"In the office, I reckon."

He took her hand in his, and they walked back to the porch; there Whack met them, and Beck said:

"Come boy, I want you; thar's bisnis on hand."

Together the two went on to the office, where they found the trader.

"Any orders from Washington, Peter?" asked Beck, as the three were seated at the office table.

"Yes, they're pushing me hard, John; an hyar, they've sent me an order for an escort; but it's no yuse, the troop's too far off."

"Are the wagons ready, Whack?"

"Yes, scout; all in good runnin order; the stock's fed up for a long pull."

"Can we camp on the prairie to-morrow night, Peter?"

"Certin; I ken load up by noon."

"Mus have an extra man for each team;" he laid down his demands bluntly.

"What fer?" the trader asked, in surprise.

"Jes this: Bill Cartwright's on the road, at the head of a band of pirates."

"That's bad."

"Bad enough; but wus still, the Spiders ar with him."

"Ken you pull through?"

"Give me that order; put me on the trail to-morrow; I'll fight through, if I send back my bones." Beck's hand fell heavily; he spoke not in boast, for he had measured the danger, but his words were direct and well understood.

"An you," said the trader, turning to the young, full-mettled boy by his side, "will you go? No man is edicated till he's fought his way cross the plains."

"Go!" he answered promptly, "anywhar with John Beck in the lead, don't you know me?"

"That suits," answered the old man, rising; "go now, rouse up the camp."

At the corral Beck called the teamsters around him and chose from the best his guards and whips.

"Be spry, Legs," he said, "bring in the cattle; I'll sort a lead team." As the boy ran off, he turned to Whack, saying:

"Show the men you're training when the team's ready."

"Sort em right; I'll fetch em round."

It was a simple plan agreed upon to put the drivers at ease, for such are always jealous of the knowledge of others placed over them.

The six yokes stood well to the wagon, and as Beck stepped aside, he found a crowd looking on.

"Thar's a team put up as it oughter be," he said, "look at the leaders; jes like prancin ponies, an they're graded, heft an size, down to the vetran at the wheel. Thar's a blaze-face an liver-spots for you, boys; he's built like a steamboat, hoofs out like a regler, the eye like a Kaintuc gal's. That team will get down to work without coaxin; heah, Whack, see how they tend to bisnis."

Whack took up his whip, and standing a few feet from the wheel-ox, he whirled the lash to guide the turn, in a brisk trot. Touching the nose of the veteran, he steadied the movement and brought the team round to the starting place cleverly.

"How'll that do?" he asked of the crowd, as the yokes stood still; "you can measure, and see if the wagon won't stand in the circle." The men cheered him.

"Mary," said her father, at the rear porch, where the old lady amused the girls; "breakfast at five, shure."

Mrs. Garrulson made all the reply needed:

"May I never!—an I hyar wese gwyne at last,—happy land! You shall have yer breakfast, kernel, if I have to cook it misself. See heah though; plenty room for that fedder bed, don't disremember that."

"All right, mam;" he passed on to the office.

Lu and Mary were in the dining-room.

"May I come in?" asked Beck at the window.

"Yes, but through the door, of course."

"He won't leap in, Lu, he's not a jumper," said Mary, teasing her friend.

"I mus see to my traps," said Beck, and after a look at his rifle, he placed it in the corner.

"What's the flurry, Mister Beck?"

"Oh, nothing, Mary; we ought to be on the road, long ago;" as he left the room, she followed him.

"Now, tell me," she questioned again as they stood in the hall, "what about the trip?"

"We're ordered out, and I am making ready, that's all."

"Yes, I know," she said slowly, "making ready with the rifle."

"We can't trade without it; how can we?"

"But what is it?"

"Don't be troubled, Mary, you're safe enough."

Handing him a book,—a pocket companion,—which she had often pressed upon him, she turned back with a serious, unhappy look, and left him standing there, as one in doubt and troubled.

At daylight the teams drew up before the wide, open doors of the storehouses, and stood ready to be freighted.

Breakfast was over; Lu and the scout met on the porch, and she said in her playful, smiling love of fun:

"Leave a lock of hair, won't you?"

"How can I? thar's none left."

"It looks like it was sand-papered."

"That's a way I have to fool an Injin; they can't get a han-holt to scalp by." Beck, in trim, had his hair clipped again.

"Oh, the brutes; but you'll leave Kitty for me; won't you, Mister Beck?"

"If Peter says so."

"Let's go and see him; I'll coax the best I can."

They entered upon a busy scene; the cargoes had been chosen from slips made up, and Whack and Jumper called off to the hands, as the wagons were packed. Lu managed well, for Beck needed a strong, heavy horse.

By noon the train was drawn out in line, loaded. Beck made ready for the start; he looked to the medicine chests, the cooking kits, and stationed his men, a driver and extra man to each team.

"Now, Whack," he said, "I've fixed your traps, your hollerware and cutlery, whar's your pocket knife?"

"All right, scout."

"You can travel without boots, but not without that; the roan's yours, I'll ride the sorrel."

"Move on," called the trader.

"Yes, sir."

"Give the word, lad."

Whack left the house, and in a loud voice gave the order:

"Roll out!"

Up rose a hundred whips, and there was a sound like an enfilade of muskets; sharp and clear was the snap with a ring that echoed on the dull, dead silence of the waste, making the heart glad with its promise, and the faces of the sturdy fellows to brighten.

Beck sprang to his saddle and dashed off to the lead; the mile-length caravan was in motion.

Mrs. Garrulson, against the protest of Beck and the trader, parted from her friends, solemnly in silence, to make her journey to her "ole man" at a distant fort. As she bade adieu to Lu and Mary, she gave them a fold of writing, to be read when she was out of sight. Her bonnet was seen waving far off in the line, and her dismal lament came back to the ears of those who watched her.

"Good-by, vain warld!"

As the lead team moved out upon the road, a half-nude Indian runner stole from behind a tree, and like a deer bounded off on a trail; the sunset lighted the path of a spy. As the darkness set in, the glimmering camp-fires were seen, on the blue horizon.

At night, after the departure of the train, Lu thought of the old woman's written scrap, and calling Mary the two spent an hour at the sitting-room lamp over the scrawl; at length, by dint of a vexed study, they read the ballad of:

MI JON.

jon garrulson es a soger man,
a soger man, es he, es he;
he fyts fer his kullers with his gun,
jon garrulson, mi jon, dus he.

he fyts the injuns onto the planes,
he fyts the injuns, jon dus he,
he gits a myt fer all his panes,
but he fhyts em fer his konteree.

mi soger man is out in a foart,
wah evri soger ort fer to be;
i tak my bed up fer a wark
sterang konterees fer tu see, see, see.

A woyce kauls me in pledin toans,
go du yer jewtee an be tru,
mi bed shal res his akin boans,
no nife ken kut our luv into.

an wen he dys and lyf is did,
ile rap him in ther stars an strype,
ile rite onto his koffen lid,
Melindee wus his darlin wyf.

tak warnin all bi me an jon,
yung gals an boys jes look at me,
an wip yer i as yu jog on
Sterang konterees fer tu see, see, see.

Here the screed might have ended, but through a score of verses it reached a climax in an adventure of John with an Indian:

> jon grabbed his har atwyx his han,
> to grab his har wur all he did,
> that injun squaked at my gude man,
> fer he snached that injun bawlhedded.

"And who in the world is her John?" screamed Lu.

"Her husband, of course; he's a soldier, and the good old soul loves him, Lu," Mary said, trying to be a little grave as a curb to her friend's mirth.

"Well, you may be good riders, good fighters, and all that; but, if that's the way *we* write poetry out here" — she threw down the paper as she ran off, singing:

> "An he snached that injun bawlhedded."

CHAPTER XI.

THE PIRATES — THE ROADSIDE CAMP — YARNS.

Cartwright, in company with Cruz, after leaving the fonda, sought out the Indian in the shadow of the adobe; they found him in waiting. He was easily brought to terms by a sight of the gold the thief had won; so the plot was formed to rob the train, to massacre the teamsters, and that the chief should return to his tribe to band together the most villainous for the deadly mission. The bonus was paid, a promise given of a good share of booty to each savage, and an ambuscade was agreed upon.

As Ferati sneaked away with bloody hands from the melee, Cartwright closed his atrocious bargain with the chief. The pirates were about to return to the scene they had but the hour before quitted, when one of the gang, in haste and in fright from the tumult of the spree, by chance came upon them. The natural bent of his scare added much more to the account of it than really took place, and the knaves who listened changed their course, an incident that hastened their villainy many hours.

"B'wen," said Cruz, with a shrug and a motion to move on.

"Wayno," answered Bill, as they turned to take up the packers.

It was past midnight when the jingling spurs were heard again on the road, ringing right merrily on the silvery silence and keeping time with the song the rascals sang in chorus. Further on Cruz took up his train, to follow close upon their heels, so that when the animals he and Cartwright rode were fagged, they could change to muleback; a slow dog-trot, but an untiring gait.

When Beck rode forth from Ferati's cabin, the thieves had set out with a good start ahead, on a route far away from Beck's, but nearly parallel, towards the post. The form of the scout was still in sight when Ferati and his gang sprang to horse; like bloodhounds they followed Cartwright.

The pirates plodded on. In the shade, when they halted, they ate and drank, gambled, quarreled, drank again, and mounted. Bringing to the long jaunt the steady force and strength of the mule, they gained distance.

Not to follow them on the dreary journey, they rode on without break or accident, covering space with incredible speed. Beck had distanced them some days, as their halts were long and their cups were deep; but theirs was a shorter route, and the scout had counted too trustingly on the time he had himself saved.

The Mexicans and the semi-savage white, stimulated by strong drinks, never tired. Far out on the prairie they fell in with a hunting party of the tribe whose lands verged on the trader's, and hired one as a spy. He was sent on to lie in wait near Cheviteau's, to watch every movement at the post, and when the train started to return with all speed to where they would bivouac on the plain. This ended their journey.

It was while Beck was taking the few days of rest to recruit himself, believing he was so far ahead of the pirates that he could afford the necessity of the respite, and unconscious that Cartwright's shorter route and the ease with which he and his gang changed from a tired mount to a fresh one from the train, gave them great advantage in the race, that the Indian runner started for the post.

Like a panting fox-chaser, he was hiding near Cheviteau's, when he heard the whip-snap of the caravan in motion. The camp-fires died out, when with winged feet, far beyond the train-guard, he fled back to the waiting pirates.

The two trappers who eyed the "bar dance" of Cartwright at the fonda, stood near when he swept the coin from Ferati's table.

"Bill," said the elder, "that war a clean steal."

"I seed it, Jack, an thar'll be a fuss; watch the Mexan, he's white about the gills an his eyes ar afire."

"Come, go long;" Jack moved to leave the place and the other joined him. "That ar skunk es jus in from the road; he's train-boss fer a rich trader an he's workin a big game; them mule drivers is thick bout him as flies; we'll see whar he goes with that ar plunder."

"I'm along, ole hoss; you reckon high on me."

They left the pulquerias, and keeping to the dark side of by-ways and lanes, they followed close upon Cartwright and Cruz. When the cut-throats met, behind a ruin near by, they heard every word of the plot.

As the thieves stole off, Bill drew his pistol and was about to fire. Jack seized his arm, saying:

"Hold on, old boy; none of that; you'll spile some sport."

"I'se itching to pull on him, Jack, plum center."

"He'll fotch up, mind; come hyar an sot down; I'se got a heap to tell about that cuss." Drawing forth his bladder wallet, the other knew what was coming.

The story told by the old trapper was a long one; amplified by many side-scenes, and spun out in his own peculiar drawl. It gave a part of his own history, the early life of Cartwright, referred to the crib, and a passing glance at what was known as the Regulators,—an earlier and ruder organization than that which in later years was known as the Vigilantes.

A pretty girl, of hasty temper, was wooed by two suitors in one of the early settlements of the border. The one was a quiet, peaceful youth, named McQuain; the other, a coarse, wild, reckless fellow, named Roberts, whose manners and morals were corrupt.

The maid Margaret, vain of these attentions, was well pleased enough to have become the wife of either.

The death of Roberts' father called him away, and during his absence McQuain urged his suit; the girl's friends favored it, and in a month she consented to marry him.

An old man in the neighborhood held a commission as justice of the peace, although he had not acted as such, and McQuain was told, and told truly, that any official act of the officer was binding; that he had a right to exercise his functions until a successor was appointed. He was called in, and the girl became McQuain's wife.

The next day, Roberts returned to the settlement; he spoke to no one about the marriage, but quietly sought out the bride. What he said to her no one knew; it was told that she asked her husband "whether he was quite sure that their union was legal."

Roberts brought with him from the east, news of the declaration of war with Great Britain; also, the call of the Governor of the State for the quota of troops. A day or two after his return, when men everywhere were joining the army, he met McQuain in public and taunted him before a crowd. "You're tied to an apron string," he said, "and dare not enlist." Maddened by the sting of this slur, McQuain seized a pen and enrolled his name. Going home to tell his wife of his sudden resolve, she was silent and sullen when she heard it. To be deserted, when married but a week, was little less than cruel, she thought and said; she had little faith in the patriotism of which he boasted.

Both men had enlisted, and before leaving the place, Roberts came to bid good-by to his former sweetheart. It was known that they had a long, earnest, parting talk.

After an absence of several months, McQuain came back, hastening with a rapt heart to his home. He found the door closed. There was not a sign of a living thing about it. No smoke was seen, as of old, curling out of the chimney; there was no one there. Margaret's father met him with a shake of his head; she had been gone more than a month, and none knew whither nor with whom. It was whispered that Roberts had been seen, not far away; but it was a rumor only. The father invited McQuain to live with him, but the man turned away moodily on the path to his deserted cabin, where he was seen to enter. Coming out soon after, he threw his rifle over his shoulder, and without a word, walked away through the forest. In half an hour the dwelling was in flames; in an hour it was a ruin, and McQuain had left the settlement.

Years passed; the war was over, and the country, not far below what was now known as Cheviteau's, began to fill up. A small frontier hamlet was built there, but the treachery of the river suddenly ended its life and its annals. Cartwright had halted on the spot, in his flight with Mary. Among the first to settle there was Roberts, his wife and three children; the wife was Margaret. Her marriage with McQuain was legal, but Roberts had persuaded her that it was not, and her wounded pride at the desertion, as she thought, of her husband, led her astray, which she bitterly repented.

Roberts had changed as much as his victim; a score seemed to have been added to his age; the cheeks were sunken, his figure spare and bent, his glance unsteady and furtive. The evil traits of his character were seen in every action. During the years that had passed he changed his abode many times, frightened away by a fear that the avenger was on his track. For days his wife would lose sight of him: his companions were dissolute outlaws, and among them, none worse than Bill Cartwright. They gave way to drunken excesses, and their intimacy was close. Money was plenty with them, which they spent in riotous living, and the settlers had for a long time watched them, and traced to their crib counterfeits, in notes and coin, which had been freely passed.

The first step to crush this nest of blacklegs was to call a meeting. The people came together, they said, for "law and order," and one was named to state "the object of the meeting." "The chair" said:

"My friends, it is time these rascals were punished; it is our duty to punish them." Then and there was formed a band of Regulators, charged with the duty of "seeing the law administered."

The day appointed to rid the place of the "pirates" arrived, and all were present save one; he the leader. In this fix they were about to disperse to call another meeting, when their circle was entered by a stranger. He was known to a few as a hunter, who led a solitary life; dressed in the garb of his craft, at his belt swung a long knife. He dropped the breech of his heavy rifle on the ground, to lean on the muzzle.

"If you want a captain," he said, through his thin, cold lips, looking wildly about him, "I'm your man; my name's McQuain." He turned away, but they called him back and took him at his word.

At night they set out for the den of the outlaws. It was a log cabin far out in the wilds, from which a road ran to the landing,—the road traveled by Cartwright to the crib, and the crib the self-same haunt from which Mary had been rescued. Roberts lived there with his family; his wife the witness of all the crimes of the gang.

McQuain and his party had now approached within fifty paces, and behind him, as he took the lead, slowly crept the Regulators. A broad light streamed through the cracks across the little clearing. He halted not an instant, but driving in the door with the butt of his gun, he stood before the startled crew.

Roberts sprang to his feet, but the deadly aim of McQuain covered him.

"Your time has come," he said, and fired. His rival fell a corpse at the feet of the deluded woman. Seizing her, a scream rang out even to the further plain, as he threw off his cap and turned his gaze straight into her eyes.

"You're punished enough, go," he said; replacing his knife, he left in the darkness to follow the trail as a trapper.*

* Condensed and adapted from a story called "The First Grave."

The fight was fought out furiously; a savage strife, and only one of the desperate gang escaped. Bill Cartwright fled with a deep knife-wound slitting his cheek, which still marked his savage face from ear to chin.

The old man's story had run on far into the night; long years had passed, leaving him roughened in speech and look.

"I fotched him," he said, "an that ar cuss ain't forgot it; I am the last of the Regulators."

At dawn he was off on the road to the fort; thence to the mountains.

The slow drag of the long, winding train began with the dawn each day, and ended with the dusk. League after league was measured off step by step, to the creak of the wheels and the crack of the whip. Across the endless reach of distance, over the brown, lonely plain, in the still white glare of fiery light, the sunburned men, the panting beasts, plodded on.

"Whack, come up at a steady pull; I've seen hoof-marks of bufflers, and I'll give the boys a treat for supper."

Beck read the road-signs as one would a book; he never tired, and turning his horse's head, he rode away in the pace of a rider who had just begun a journey. The need of the moment he did straightly, without show, without knowing his own value, nor caring for thanks or praise.

An extra man marched abreast of each wagon, with his gun shouldered, the drivers lagging near their oxen, their whips trailing, and the red dust stirred like waves at the prow of a boat. So the dreary, time-serving moil wore on.

Later in the day, Whack saw the scout far away, on a strip of green bottom near a creek. The bloom on its banks sent back its perfume to the hungry and tired toilers, and the cattle pricked their ears as they pulled to the summit of the rise.

Beck had chosen the spot as a camp-ground for the night, and it was soon known that he had killed two cows. He gave orders, in his place again, wheeling the line to park the wagons in a semi-circle, each end of the train to rest upon the bluff sheer to the water below. This done, his camp was fortified, rear and front, against attack. There was fuel at hand in heaps, thrown up by freshets and ready for the match.

The good, old dame was happily far more useful than officious; the wear and worry of the road had tamed her speech, and while she felt a kind regard for the men's hunger, she would now and then sneer aloud in contempt of their cooking.

The meat when brought in, was found to be young, fat and juicy. Beck was not slow to single out the tongues, the fleece, the hump-ribs, as the best parts. He lighted a brisk fire in a hole dug in the earth, and when it had burned down, he hung the tongues therein, and covered the opening with sod. Cutting a score of withes, he skewered a rib-chop, salted and peppered, to the taper end of each. Mrs. Garrulson looked on; she was not willing to admit much, but was, at most, not churlish with her gifts.

"Ef yer gwyne to have a feast, I'll len a han."

Drawing out of the many folds of a white rag wrap, she brought to light a bit of sour dough; this was the leaven of the large lump she was soon kneading; then she seized upon a square tin box, an inch or two in depth, which Beck used for his way-bills. She raised the folding lid and placed her loaves therein; she tilted the box before the fire, sprinkling a few coals under the bottom. Beck laughed, for he saw at once the quick wit of her contrivance; the bright inside of the top reflected the heat upon the rounded loaves, the coals beneath baked the bottom.

He was fairly challenged to do his best; he forced the pointed ends of his sprigs into the ground before the log-heap, and the rods bent over the coal-bed from the weight of the chops at the smaller end; the men copied him, and broiled the tender hump-steaks in like manner.

When all was ready, the bake, as the old woman said, "wus brown as a chesnut, an light as a fedder."

Now the scout removed the cover from his roasted tid-bits, and the matron, outdone, yielded easily.

"May I never," she said, "it smells like a cook-stove in pie-time."

There was naught left for the wolves but the bones, when the supper ended.

"I throw'd a lash, Cappin," said Legs, speaking to Whack, "wen I war only ten, and got my recommen at fifteen."

"How, Legs?"

"Dis a way; my fader sont me out on to the pike a haulin stone, an I hed a one-eyed wheel-ox as cross as a briar-fence. Well, sumpin skeered the team, an that ar ox never stopped till he mired the wagon, hub-down, with a big load. It war in the fall an coolish like, so I didn't mind work with the whip; but it war no yuse; might as leave hev tickled a mountin. Now, Cappin, how would you a got that ar team out?"

"What'd you do, Legs?"

"The fodder was a stannin thick on the hill, and I jes went up to the top of it, on the blind side of that ar ox, an with a hoop an a yell, an these yer arms an legs a spread out, I cum'd a' boomin. It war breakin fodder like a sugar-mill; it sounded like a harricane, an ef you'll bleeve it, Cappin, that ar ox pulled the whole load out hisself."

Beck, in a group of teamsters, was asked by one:

"Wat's the good of all these extra men?"

This broached a subject upon which he had kept quiet not to excite the fears of the men, nor to borrow a danger not yet in sight; but as they seemed eager for an answer, he said:

"Mebbe you'll wish thar were twice as many."

"But we oughter know."

"Jes three things, if you will know: Spiders, Cart-wright and fight; that's the long and short of it, boys, and we'll pull through ef we have to pull over them."

"Spiders?" was repeated by several.

"Yes," said Beck, "the blood-hounds of the sou-west."

"Them's the black-hearts uv the sage-bush," spoke up an old hand.

"An I'se heerd tell," said another, "they can scalp with the throw of a tomerhawk."

"Wat of it," said a burly fellow, "we signed to take the risks, an we'll take em; that's all."

As the camp-fire, without the usual yarn, would have been a feast without viands, the older head who had spoken first, began the spinning. The pipes were puffed at high pressure, when the men, squatting like Arabs, drew round the speaker.

"Well, yer see, boys, them ar Spiders es jes about the wus tan-skinned whelps in this yar univarse; I'se heerd tell about this yar chief we'se a comin on to."

"He's wicked, I knows; kase I'se heerd as how he slayed a party uv emigrents, babes and all," said a chum to warm up the recital.

"Hold on, I'se a comin to him; an yer see this chief is a pooty lively sorter cuss; thar's no white fedder in his top-knot by a long-chalk; he's tall as a pine, squar built, an he wars in hes yeers two scelp-tufts fer yerrings; thar's a bald scar on the top of his head. Dus yer wanter ter know bout them yerrings?"

"Let's have it," said a number; and the old man stretched his limbs, reloaded his pipe, and went on with his yarn.

"Well, they do say he's the wus gambler nor any other black-heart in these yer sou-west tribes. The Spiders an the Bonebows play a game they calls 'Hand.'"

"Yes, I know how it's played," said one; "they puts up all they'se got, down to moccasins, in two piles; then wun shakes a plum or a cherry stone in the hands; then he closes up the hands, an tother wuns guess whar the stone is."

"Well, thesyar chief war out on the war-path by hisself, hungry to raise har an ready for huggin, when he comed to a medicine spring; you all knows wat that ar; ets free ground fer all, one Injin jes as good as tother as frens, all to onct et that. Hyar he met a Bonebow drinkin at the spring; he made a peace-sign an then he drank too; then they smoked their kinnickinnic an sot down to a game of Hand fer all night."

"An they hed a lively ole time, I reckon," spoke up one who took a deep interest in wagers of any kind.

"Jus so, ole hoss, you mine me; thar war nothin else but a high ole time. Bonebow he won clean through; arrer arter arrer, then tother wun's club, hes knife, hes bow, hes robe, an the Spider sot nakit on to the plain."

"Cleaned out;" chimed in the man of chance.

"Sartin; couldn't a bin cleaner; but the Spider hed jus wun more chence."

"How's that? he war cleaned out you sed;" spoke up Legs, to appear smart among his elders.

"Don't throw yersef away, boy; he hed a chence."

"What chence?" said a score taking the cue from Legs.

"His scelp; and he bet it too, boys."

"Did he win?" was quickly asked.

"No sir-ee; he lost agin. He jus bent his head down, jus as if he war going to hev his har brushed, an the Bonebow he lifted it, — jus as pooty, — an it lef him bawlhedded."

"What'd he do?" the story was growing warm and the men excited.

"Well, the Spider war pluck all the time; grit to the last, an he made Bonebow promise to meet him agin at the same place."

"Go on;" said Legs in his boy-like, eager way.

"True as preachin, parduers, they com'd thar agin in anuder yeah, an sot down to gamble on the same spot."

"Which won?" queried an anxious listener.

"Hold on; go slow an shuah like a ox team. Well, Spider had the luck this time; he made Bonebow come every time an sot him nakit on to the plain, an his scelp gone too; but the Bonebow hed jus wun more chence."

"An his scelp gone too? See heah, ole coon, let up;" said the burly fellow, growing a little uneasy as to the truth of the narrative.

"How's that? take keer, ole man;" joined in others.

"But he hed the chence, I tell yer, sartin."

"Out with it, lets heah."

"He had one chence, and boys that wus his life; he played ginst the Spider, life for life; they played, — the Spider an the Bonebow did, — an Bonebow lost. Hardest kind of luck, but it's true, boys, or I'm a saint; an the Bonebow stood up, barred his brest like a man, an the Spider killed him, then an thar, right on the spot. Thet's why the Spider wars two scelps as yerrings, — hissen an tother wun's." *

"Thet'll do for an ole man," said one who had his doubts.

"Thet's nuthin," continued the speaker, "why, boys, thet same Spider stood up in a Sun-dance, — an yer know what thet is, wen they'se cut the flesh in strips, an so on, — an let em drov a knife froo his breast bone."

"An he lived arter that?"

"Lived! why he jus warked with et a stickin thar fer yeahs."

"How'd he git it out?"

"How'd he git it out?" answered the story-teller in amaze; his yarn had run out too long and was tangling; "how'd he git it out?"

"Yes, how'd he git it out?" said several, seeing him flounder; "let's heah, all bout it."

"Don't pester yersefs; he got it out, sartin;" the old man was cornered.

"Let's heah, now."

"Well, he jus let it work itssef out; in course, what else." The laugh went round, in which Beck joined louder than the rest.

"That'll do, ole man;" they all said.

"I don't keer a darn, ef he's got wun yerring or two; ef he crosses our path, boys, we'll make his yer wring,

---

* This incident is gleaned from Ruxton's "Far West;" rendered by the writer into the vernacular of the camp.

fer shuah;" said the burly fellow, shaking the ashes from his pipe.

"An that's the right talk; I'll see you through."

Beck left the crowd, which in small parties soon agreed upon the peril to come; they measured it in their own fearless way, nor was courage needed to meet and defy it.

From some truant thought of home, some influence of the day-like night, perhaps, Mrs. Garrulson's shrill nasal voice burst in upon the slumber of the camp:

> "An my soul it mounted hiah
> In a charyet uv flah,
> An the moon, it war under my feet."

This she kept up until called to order.

But the peace that came again was short-lived; a quick, sharp bark was heard, then again, an echo of the first, then a third and fourth falsetto in the chorus of cayotes, and when Beck relieved Whack, on guard, the discord grew louder.

CHAPTER XII.

THE BAZOUKS — THE BLACK BRIGADE — THE SPIDERS' NEST.

The fleet-footed spy held his pace, with his head up and his arms at rest on his sides. His strides were regular and direct. One foot struck the earth flatly, raising the body with ease, caught it well poised on the other foot, and completed a perfect motion. He ran steadily, and when the stars came out his race had been long, but he kept to it without fagging. Through briar and brush, leaping brooks, wading creeks, out on the glistening tables, down into the bottoms where the grass waved about his waist, he still held his head erect and his arms at ease. A lone tree marked his first goal, and on reaching it he stopped short. Throwing his arms about, he drew a long, healthful breath, dropped to the earth to respite his frame, then sprang to his feet. To feel that no limb had stiffened he put them into play, cast a pebble or two into his mouth, and again sped away. He ran on in easy stages, and when the last flat-footed stride was made, the lad stood upon a knoll, rising above a thicket in the hollow below him. Here he listened long, his hands held as funnels about his ears to catch the remotest sound; with a quick change one hand covered his mouth, like a valve. Then a full-lunged shriek rent the hush of the night and searched the recesses of the silence. It was so sharp, so shrill a warning, so harsh to the solitude, a wolf far away yelped in fright; space caught it up and wasted it round the hiding-place of the thieves. They sprang into the open glade and beckoned to the Indian; he joined them and gave the sign. The train was on the road.

They paid the spy his price; then, mounting, Cartwright with a coarse laugh said:

"Vamo—the Spiders!"

"B'wen," answered the Mexican, giggling; the runner folding his arms, looked after the riders, and with a grunt sat down. He drew from a beaded pocket a piece of dried beef, ate it, lighted a fire, and stretching himself by "the wolf-scaring fagots," he was soon asleep.

It was while Beck sat at the camp-fire chat that the spy signed to Cartwright and Cruz that the train was on the road, and had made good progress towards its destination.

A sudden cry of alarm aroused the camp at daylight:

"Injins! Injins!" shouted the cattle-guard. The stock was driven into the inclosure, the broken wagon-line closed, and the men stood armed, each with his rifle or musket, and waiting:

"Steady where you stand; quiet," ordered their leader, taking up his gun; "it's a hunting band, that's all."

Mrs. Garrulson awaked suddenly from her morning nap, frightened at the horrors of a night-mare.

"Happy Canaan," she screamed, "what's up?"

"The Injins are down on us," answered Sandy.

"Injins!" and she scrambled from her perch; "may I never; ets all my own doins, fer the kurnel did say stay, thet's a fac, an go I would"— after a short pause, "an go I will ef I hev to lick a whole tribe misself." A loud laugh greeted this sudden change of front from a scare to valor, but the men held to their places, looking out on the distance.

Coming up the valley in a hard gallop, the troop of Indian horsemen drew near. They rode at full speed, each rider sitting his horse with graceful ease; when just beyond rifle-range they reined up and held counsel. Their mounts were bare-backed ponies, fat and frolicsome, cousins-german to the wild horse, mustang, with scarcely a shade of difference. In the fitness of things, the little four-footed beast seems created for the Indian, and for nothing else; unfit, as he is, for anything else but the mount of the savage. In habit, form, endurance, he is as much a savage as the Indian, sharing with him all his vicissitudes. He lives through the dreary snow-bound winters on tree bark, a shaggy skeleton. The spring trims his coat and fills his belly. Take him away from his habits and his haunts, feast him on the better fare of better animals, he mopes lazily, a tricky, hateful, sullen cob; he snaps at kindness, and shows his heels to a benefactor. Each rider, nude to the waist, was a picked man for the chase.

The chief, with a wave of the hand, dispersed them, and then began a wild rout. The seat of each rider was held by a girdle, and the dash of each horse was guided by a single thong. On they rushed, helter-skelter, shrieking at every jump; now, one would fall head down to yell under the animal; again, at full length on his back or side; now, the whole band charged *en masse;* on a signal, it was scattered. On another signal, a part wheeled and massed, and during the entire drill not a word was spoken by the chief; a scarcely perceptible motion of the hand directed it. A piece of looking-glass, as the day was sunny, held to catch the rays, threw the signal to any given distance. There are other signs by which the same drill is ordered,—a secret closely kept, as no white man has ever found out the method,—signs which are readily heeded, though the sky be black with clouds, the dust hide the band, or the noise loud enough to drown a human voice.

"That's a good show, boys, but thar ain't the sign of a scalp-knife or paint about em," said Beck.

The chief sat on his horse apart, and with another motion formed the riders on parade near him. They had bows and quivers, and sheath-knives, a few rifles and spears. One, by his orders, rode midway between the two parties, struck a spear into the earth, and rode back.

Beck, mounting a wagon, gun in hand, said to his men:

"Cock your guns and keep your eye on me; I'm

going to meet 'em. If I sign with my right hand, blaze away; I'll take care of number one."

He raised his rifle above his head, then laid it at his feet; signed that his belt was unarmed; then leaping down, he strode up to the spear-staff, and stood there with folded arms.

When Beck had taken his stand, the chief handed his bow to one near him, got down and joined the scout:

"How!"

"How!" A hand-shake and the brief introduction was over.

"Good man—you—Beck," said the Indian.

"Big chief, Little Elk," answered the other, recognizing a noted brave of one of the largest tribes on the plains. The scout was glad to meet him, as he was not only a friendly redskin, but one from whom much valuable information could be had. In the talk that followed, the scout learned that an officer had been sent out to a distant fort to take the Spiders in hand; that they were on the war-path, and that he, Beck, could not, as he hoped, avoid or escape a fight; further, that he might reach the fort in time to deliver the order for an escort, and for such purpose he was kindly offered a guide. In return Beck made many presents, giving them in the name of Colonel Cheviteau.

"Kevochoo! Kevochoo!" exclaimed the chief; "good man, him—Kevochoo; him—heap fren." Then ensued an expressive dumb show, for an Indian is nothing if not dramatic. He touched his breast with his fist, meaning that Cheviteau's heart was big; he stared wide and steadily, meaning the honesty of the trader; he closed his teeth, with reference to his friend's firmness; and that he was truthful, he signed that the tongue was whole and not split. "Kevochoo, he good man; Injin—heap—like him, wagh." He turned aside and was silent.

Presently, Little Elk transferred to the care of the scout an Indian lad and his pony. He was to be the guide, and would lead by a cut-off trail to the lodges of his people, and thence on to the fort. Now mounting, the chief, with his band, galloped away on the hunt of the bison.*

While Beck and the Indians smoked the ceremonial pipe, a teamster who looked on said to Sandy:

"An wat wud they be afther?"

"It's the pipe of peace thee's be doin."

"Pfats 't?" asked another.

"A pace av a pipe they're whiffin," answered the first.

"It's de ould sthock, av coorse."

"Whack," said Beck, a short way further on, "I'm off for the fort in the mornin."

"To be gone how long?"

"Before you get into danger I'll be with you."

"All right. I'll pull slow."

"This boy's a good un; watch him."

Whack glanced at the young redskin, as he moved

---

* The writer adopts this in deference to the naturalist, but the name is never heard on the plains.

about with his pony. He was tall, raw-boned and wiry; his shoulders broad, muscular; a good head, fine face, strong mouth. The coarse, jet hair, plaited, fell upon his copper skin with rich effect; his step was bold and elastic.

Meeting Mrs. Garrulson, who planted herself in dismay at the sight of the Indian, Beck said to her:

"That's your adopted son, mam," pointing to the boy.

"What! that ar sonnerver-gun!" At which the men laughed, and the boy, quick to see that he was the butt of joke, muttered:

"Ugh! squaw!"

"Ef I had yer onct," she was prompt to say, "I'd make yer squak wus nor that."

"What would you do with him?" asked Whack.

"Skin him!" In disgust she turned about and went her way.

The scout and the guide, a little in advance of the train, had ridden to the crest of a knoll, when the latter, getting down from his pony, bent his gaze on certain distant objects. They seemed to the eye a clump of bushes, but when the scout fixed his sight upon them the lad said:

"Bufflers."

Beck, in doubt, watched closely, and as he was able to see dark, moving forms, growing larger, coming nearer, he nodded assent to the Indian.

A dozen stragglers, quietly feeding, were left behind by some passing herd. So thought Beck; but the guide signed to him to wait and they would soon see a stirring spectacle. The truants were now near enough to be seen in the rough sport of a mock battle; the mimic strife was kept up for a time, when it suddenly ceased, and the combatants broke away in a run. In delight the lad threw himself on the ground; then, springing to his feet, he exclaimed:

"Heap!" holding up the fingers of both hands, to denote a great number.

The antics of the Indian and the bison alike might have been confounding to the common eye, but to the scout they were not so. Dismounting, he caught the bit of his young, fractious horse with a firm hold. The fleeing animals, warned by the tramp of a herd not far off, turned out of its path with a quick, instinctive dread, to fall in at the rear or on the flank. They had escaped certain death. On the run, not even for its own kind, is its mad career for an instant turned aside; and knowing this, the Indian read the sign aright, and had fallen to the earth to listen.

Then came to their ears the sound of a mighty tread; vast numbers of the wild cattle were in motion; as they looked, the herd dashed into full view, rounding a grove; its power and bulk combined, compressed, groaned from attrition; its speed, increased from the moving weight, rose and fell, surging like a storm-crossed ocean swell, and black as the clouds above it.

In the lead, a great, royal beast led the charge sternly, his shaggy mane rising like the hump of a camel; his tail, like a baton, waved in the whirl of strife; his deep-throated bellow, the rally-cry to his fellows. Right royally he led; the mass upon his heels pressed him hard. The outer files seemed to bear against the body, compact but moveable, to condense its vim. Therein lay the contrast with the flurried rout of a drove; the one a solid charge, the other a panic; one a stampede, the other an onslaught; one, in motion like a host of veterans, the other a mob; one illustrating Bull Run, the other the phalanx of Marshal Ney. Coming on, it was seen that the band of Little Elk rode close upon the flank, yelling, goading and killing as they rode. The mustangs were fired with the ardor of the chase, and the riders shouted, as they sprung the quivering shaft into the living target. They strewed the broad road with the slain and wounded.

"Hoop-ee!" yelled Beck, wrought up to the wild delight of his boyish nature.

Arrows and spears were plied to spur their horses to the front; the band used every artifice to reach the bull in the lead, and the rivalry grew to be intensely tragic. The speed of hunter and hunted was about equal. Now, with a cry of daring, a young savage came bounding by, and the guide was stirred to frenzy at the sight; running, leaping with a fierce joy, the better to observe him. On he came, goading his mustang to a dash some distance beyond the herd. Then he wheeled, when his first arrow left the bow. The exploit was one to achieve the full glory of the chase, by crossing the path, emptying his quiver into the herd and to reach the opposite flank, unharmed. Nothing but fine strategy could save him from death; again taking a direct, again an oblique, gaining slowly by zigzag turns, the endurance of the horse was cruelly tried. Still the rider urged him on, and as the last arrow sped to its mark, he rallied him with a shriek so shrill the beast leaped from the ground. Wheeling, at last, to escape the rolling wave, all who looked on felt that his triumph was sure.

Just then, rider and horse went down, and the surging, grinding herd stamped into the earth the stricken forms, under their reeking hoofs.

The horse's foot had sunk into the burrow of a prairie-dog, a mischance, from which there was no recall, at the supreme moment of the rider's fate. Beck for a moment closed his eyes, but the stoical boy, pointing to where the hunter and his mount perished, said calmly:

"Brother — me — him;" then turning his back was silent.

The scout, thrilled with manly pity, laid his broad, brotherly hand on the bare shoulder of the lad, and spoke with true feeling.

"Good; — good; him, big, big chief;" the boy smiled, it was enough for his pride; the pity he did not care for. They mounted their horses, striking a trail leading north, riding hard on the road to fort.

The black wave surged on; it swept by like the charge of Balaklava, vaster, grander, — a riderless horde; like Niagara's current on the verge of the fall; like the Mississippi's freshet, the scoria heaved up and flung to the torrent, it surged on and out of sight.

There was not a sign of living verdure on the dark road ploughed by the raid; the sod uprooted was strewn in fragments with the harrowed earth. Of the hunter and his horse there was scarce a vestige to be found; they had gone down to be ground out of all semblance to anything living or dead.

The train halted as the chase came on, and even the mild-eyed cattle stared at the sight. The low, western sun threw back a crimson gleam on the long, silent line, on the startled faces of the men as they leaned on their whips.

But the peaceful glow, lying still, on the green, golden vista, deepened the war-paint of a savage hiding near them; it reddened the "blood-sign" on the Spider's face, and as he stole away, the bald, seared patch on his brow whitened in the fire of hate.

The Spider chief had made a detour from the Mexican town, arriving at the lodges of his people after a long run, and voiced his coming by outcries that aroused the village. His was a bush tribe of the forest haunts which borrows its habits from the beast; stealthy, slow-footed, creeping cravens; sullen from the gloom of their abiding place, conjuring phantoms from the shadows and propitiating them by inhuman cruelties. Every man was robust, of needs must be, for no feeble-born could live through the horrors of a boyhood training.

Young men and old, women and children ran to the outer circle of the wigwams, and sent back an answer to the ear of their leader.

His braves were chosen with regard to their vicious natures, with whom ferocity was a virtue and hate of the whites a fiery passion. Taking breath the chief called them around him, drove the rabble away with frowns, and when the circle was formed, the women, children and dogs dispersed to the prairie.

Then the swarthy crowd crouched, their limbs bent under them, and there never was known a viler horde in the work of death-dealing deviltry. There was a look on all, horror stricken, grinning ghastly in the paint and grime of their faces; some stared fiendishly, — the stare of demons; — other visages in the mask, lean, thin, cold, leered like the false face of a devil; the younger, not less gross, spread their thick-lipped lecherous mouths.

A low, guttural chant was begun, — the distress wail of an animal, — growing louder and wilder till each in his own discord joined in.

The chief was in waiting not far off, and draining a flask which he threw away, he stepped into the circle. His tall form as it rose among them, striped and smirched, was that of a half-nude giant ready for battle. His parti-colored face, black and red, a yellow smear on the upper lip, green, tigerish lines on the forehead, a bald, carious scar from the brow to the scalp-tuft in which an eagle's feather stood stiffly up, and skeins of scalp-hair drooping from the ears, was a hideous picture. He spoke to his band, adroitly firing their malice, anger, greed; he traced the path to revenge and plunder with savage pride, and without much effort was the master of their brutish instincts. He chose his men by lot, a small army, setting a day for the dance and the war-whoop. Then giving orders to await his return, he started forth in the darkness. His race, like that of the spy, through the night and day was the trot of a steady animal; his eyes were feasted on the resting train, and he sped back to his camp as the pirate neared it.

At the camp of the packers, Cruz was left in charge of the gang, and Cartwright hastened forward alone, to the Spiders' town. The fires were seen long before his ears caught the din within its limits; he kept on fearlessly until challenged by the chief in person, who led him into the blazing square.

There was no stop to the dreadful orgy; circling poles that bore as pennants the scalp locks of their victims, the mad mischief grew louder, wilder; a spectacle to be seen but once, and never forgotten; an awful type of the horrible, of creatures writhing, their features all awry, twisting the form of manhood to every grimace, swaying the body to unshapely postures like the stricken or deformed; crawling, leaping, bending, barking like dogs, snapping like wolves, hooting like owls, laughing, crying, yelling, groaning like the damned:

> " A strong adversary, an inhuman wretch
> Incapable of pity, void and empty
> From every drachm of mercy."

The pirate sat there; his game went bravely on; he saw the paint on their faces and naked breasts; he saw the clutch upon the scalping-knives in mimic butchery; he saw weapons of death at every turn of his eye, and the wretch looked on and smiled; the sign of a nature lower than the brute — the painted brutes before him.

The chief waved his hand and there was silence; he spoke of Cartwright and those who would join them on the march. At last, the war-whoop sounded, and from the throats of every living thing in the village, it was echoed back. From hidden nooks each savage brought to light a musket or rifle of army pattern, and laughed aloud as he caressed it.

The chief and Cartwright led, the long, dark line trailing to the rear, the prairie brightening with the glories of the night. Evil could have no apter illustration than the serpent, writhing horridly like this squirming defile, in the most beautiful garden of the earth.

They took up the packers on the path; on their flanks was heard the jingle of the spurs, and often in the light of the stars was seen, the glitter of the cruel knife.

CHAPTER XIII.

TO THE FORT — THE ROUGH-RIDERS.

Beck and his guide in a steady pace were far afield on the route to the fort; the quick dog-trot of the pony hugging close to the horse's easy lope. Away through the timid shadows, soft and feeble in the young moon's light, neck and neck in silence; from hollows where the crickets chirped, over pearl-tipped mounds of wind-sown grasses; through clumps of chapparel, to open glades and far-spread levels.

The mustang came to a sudden halt, looking back at the rider; the Indian leaped down, for his horse was at fault where several trails met and crossed. Near by a few trees formed an arbor over a flowing basin; a desert fountain, where the feet of strolling tribes had beaten down the many paths about it. Turning aside the grass, the Indian pointed to a white boulder, then reaching down his hand, on the stalk of a bush he felt three deep notches; he was sure of his trail and gave the sign to Beck.

Just then the familiar words of a friendly voice, not far distant, caught the ear of the scout, who motioned to his companion to follow.

"Hello, ole hoss," said a gruff speaker, "squat right

down, yuse white; know'd yer more'n a mile off, the way yer sot yer saddle; he's *some*, boys; come jine us."

Beck, without challenge, had come upon a camp of mountaineers, the best type of the semi-savage whites; rough, weather-worn, stone-visaged men, whose clans, cut off from their kind, were ruthless and wild; a grade above their red foe, some stern and rankling cause had made them what they were; the hate of their ancient enemy was to them a second nature, but like all, on sea and land, to whom she is the foster-mother, their social traits were kind, unselfish; their courage without flaw.

The Indian boy held back until one of the trappers, catching sight of his trinkets and the dress of his hair, spoke to him, in his own tongue; then, almost timidly, he kept close to Beck, and was seated near him.

The camp was a beaver party of five from the Platte, who were "making meat;" i. e., killing buffalo for a meat supply of a winter quarter in some more southern valley. Not one stood under six feet height; their garb the hunter's buckskin outfit; their faces shaven clean and burned to a reddish bronze. Their squaws — wives by consent or theft — put on the pots to warm the choice bits of the meat for the strangers' treat; a courtesy of their camps at any hour of night or day.

Each in his turn chatted freely in his own coarse, but hearty way. Off on the grand old prairies; scouting the Cottonwood, the Arkansas, Turkey Creek,

Pawnee-fork; over the fireless route of Coon Creek; through a sea of fat meat without fuel to cook it; trailing to Bent's fort, to Boiling Spring, across the Divide to the Platte; away to the Black Hills, to camp at last with a sound scalp, in the Sweet Water's valley, or in the shadow of Wind River mountain.

The leader ordered the guards to their posts, and two of them drove back the hobbled mules, and mounting a rise, their gaze swept the prairie as they leaned on their rifles; two were left to keep the scout company; one slept.

The sleeper, whose hair was flecked with grey, a much older man than the others, slept soundly. Stretched on a buffalo-robe with his feet to the fire, he had dug with his knife a drain around it, and over him was thrown a Navajo blanket, impervious to rain. A mule, aged and grizzled, was picketed within reach of his hand, its head bent down, the long ears flapping, the back arched and its form tottering as it rested and slept. The trapper was treading the trails of his dreamland among droves of "fat cow," or along streams peopled with beaver, no Indian "sign" to vex him, and in near perspective the sale of his "pelts" at six dollars "the plew." Threading the back trail of his memory, through a hard, hard life, starving one day, feasting the next; now beset by whooping fiends, baying his enemy like a hunted deer, but with all the stern pluck of his tribe; again, all care thrown aside, a welcome guest at the trading-post, or back again, as the trail grows fainter, to his childhood's home, in the brown forests of old Kentuck.

Beck and his guide ate freely, and then the pipes; for the plainsman smokes whenever he wakes, and the smoke of a pipe is never seen without the loose-tongued charm of a story.

"I say, Bill, dus yer mind the time wen we camped with Ole Sam Owins at Independence; — him as got rubbed out at Sacrimenty — dis hoss disremembers which — but he went under; Ole Sam had his train along, ready to hitch up for Mexan country— twenty thunderin big Pittsburgh wagons,— an how his Santa Fee boys took to licker — eh, Bill?"

"*Well*, they did; an Bill Bent,— his boys camped on tother side the trail, an they wus all mountin men, wagh! an Bill Williams, an Bill Tharpe,— the Pawnees took his har on Pawnee-fork,— three Bills, an them three's all gone under; Hatcher, he went out that time, and wasn't Bill Garey long too? Didn't him and Chabonard set in camp for twenty hours at a game of kerds? Them was Bent's Injin traders up on Arkansas; and Bill Bent, them Spaniards made meat of him; lost his top-knot at Taos. He war some, was Bill Bent; as good as ever drove a trade or throwd a buffler; Ole St. Vrain could knock the hind-sights off him though, wen it come to shootin. You went out that time, didn't you?"

"No sir-ee, I went out along with Spiers, wen he lost his animals on Cinnamon; a hunderd an forty mules an oxen war froze that night, wagh! Black

Harris was thar, an he war the darndest liar: did yer ever hyar what he told the landlady down in Liberty?

"This coon hev gone over a sight, marm, ses he; I'se trapped beaver on Platte an Arkansaw; I'se trapped on Columby, Lewis Fork an Green River; I'se trapped, marm, on Gran River an Heely, ses he; I'se fout the Blackfoots; an d—d bad Injins them am, marm, ses he; I'se raised har of more'n wun Pach, an made a Rapaho come afore now, but scalp my ole head, marm, ses he, ef I ain't seen a pewterfyd forest."

"A what! ses she."

"A pewterfyd forest, ses he; I war out on Black Hills the yeah it rained fire, and thar wus no cold doins that winter, or this coon wouldn't say so. Why, the snow war fifty foot deep, ses he, an no meat; me an my ban was livin on our mocksins, leastwise on par flesh, for six weeks, ses he. One day we crossed a divide an got into peraira; green trees an green leaves on the trees, an green grass, an birds a singin in the green leaves, in February, ses he, wagh! Hyar's for meat, ses I, ses he, and I ups ole Ginger at one of em singin birds, an down it comes elegant; its darned head spinned away, but it kep on a singin, oh, yes, ses he, and wen I takes up the meat it war stone; we tried a axe on a tree, out comes a bit of blade; we looks at the animals, an thar they stood a shakin over the grass; I'm dog-goned ef it wasn't stone, too; we takes up the grass an it snaps like pipe-stems."

"La, Mister Harris, ses she, didn't they smell bad?"

"Smell! ses he, an his eyes bulged out as if he war a prayin; h-ll, marm, sez he, how could't wen it war friz to stone. But he's gone under, too; a Vide Poche Frenchman shot him for his bacca an traps."*

Beck and the boy-guide, after a nap, mounted and rode away as day broke over the camp of the trappers. During the morning the far-away lodges of Little Elk's people were seen in the misty distance; the lad, nearing his people, in delight made known that his tribe was about to move their village, and that the hunting party were killing their food for a long journey.

Beck was received kindly, and he and his companion staid long enough to give their horses rest. The redskins were a fine race. They of the plains, in the wider, freer scope for the exercise of their better instincts, were wilder, but less crafty. Their habits and customs were in keeping, their natures broader, more generous; their forms taller, their muscles more flexible in the sunlight life, and their strides stronger. They were horsemen.

Their tepees were all down, save two, kept standing for the final rites. In moving about Beck saw many

---

* In the author's purpose to give a glimpse at the types of life within sound of the whip's snap, this camp scene has been condensed and adapted from "Life in the Far West"—Ruxton. Lieutenant Ruxton was an English officer of distinction in her Majesty's service, who having spent a vacation on the Great Plains, resigned his commission, that he might return to the camps of the trappers. The wild life having so surpassing a delight for the young soldier, he yielded to the charm while confessing a disgust for its associtaions.

sights to revolt his humanity, and one that caused his heart to throb.

An aged patriarch, whose locks were whitened by a hundred years, was set apart under the cruel fiat of "exposing the aged." Crouching by a small fire of a few sticks, a buffalo skin, raised on crotches, was stretched over his head; a few half-picked bones, a dish of water, was his last portion. Without weapons, the miserable remnant of existence, too feeble to march, was to be left to die alone.*

He also witnessed the rite of pohk-hong — the cutting of the flesh — self-torture. The ceremony took place in a large circular lodge. Two men having taken positions for the purpose of inflicting the cruel tests of endurance, — one with a scalping-knife, the other with a bunch of splints, — the young devotees, already emaciated with fasting, thirsting and waking for nearly four days and nights, gave themselves up to the rite. An inch or more of flesh on each shoulder or each breast, was seized upon, and a knife thrust through, followed by the splint or skewer. Then cords were lowered from the top of the lodge by men placed there; these were fastened to the splints, the victim hoisted, while his tormentors hung upon the skewers, his shield, bow and quiver; sometimes, also the skull of a buffalo to the lower arm or leg. All this was borne by each of the dozen or more subjects, with the most unflinching fortitude; at every taunt and jeer of the demons, who seemed to be devising means for their more acute

* See "Catlin's North American Indians."

agony, the look on their faces never betrayed a sign of pain. In this condition they were whirled about, and with the utmost scrutiny to observe a tremor or struggle. There is no escape from the fearful ordeal, until what they called " entirely dead ;" i. e., swooning or fainting from the fearful pain.*

In another lodge he witnessed the " Sun Dance ; " a peace custom of this tribe.

Over fifty braves, — each an Apollo, — painted, and naked to the waist, except a profusion of ornaments, with head-dresses of beautiful feathers. Many had from fifty to two hundred pieces cut out of the flesh of their arms and backs. Men dancing with two, three and four buffalo heads, suspended from holes cut in the flesh. One Indian dragged on the ground eight heads fastened to his back, and in the stooping position he was forced to, they had lacerated or torn the cuts, to the extent of three inches. Some fell faint and exhausted. With screams and shouts in the din of their wild music and of weird songs, there was a Pandemonium.†

Beck and the boy pushed on, and the latter signed to proceed through the grove they had entered after a few hours ride; emerging from its shade they looked down upon a valley, and beheld the fort, a white, clean shelter, in the far-off green expanse. Parting from the

* Catlin, 1832.
† An Army Surgeon, 1879.

The same rite described by Catlin, 1832, and by the other writer, 1879, shows by contrast how little these Indians have progressed towards civilization in a period of forty-two years.

lad, the scout rode into the lowland, and was soon lost to sight among the pale trunks of the cottonwood. About noon he got down under the walls, and hailed the sentry. In answer to the challenge he asked to see Captain Harkness.

"What's your name?"

"John Beck, scout."

"What's your business?"

"That's for your officer; hurry up."

The word was passed to quarters, while he waited, holding his horse. In a little while he was sent for by the Captain.

Harkness was born on the border, and had been graduated at West Point; he was sent upon the plains for training, and there made his mark, being by nature adapted to a soldier's life, with peculiar fitness for this service. Standing six feet two in his stockings, of an iron frame, straight as an arrow, he had the mien of a good officer; nor did he lack the manner of one.

The kidnapping of Mary Cheviteau had reached the War Office, and a very general complaint from the West of raids upon and of plots against lawful trade, had been sent on, in varied forms, to the authorities. Altogether, these offences were too grave to be longer disregarded, and the Captain was ordered to the frontier, as one who would cure these evils by his well-known methods, with courage and justice. He was given a *carte blanche* to recruit and equip his force, and was allowed to conduct the campaign as he thought best. His orders read "to strike hard." The battalion which he commanded was made up from the class who live in the sound of the rifle; fearless fellows, picked for what they could do without being drilled to do it; off duty, he could wrestle, run or shoot with the best men of his troop; he never said "go" in a fight, but always, "Come, boys," and they followed, even unto death.

Beck was directed to the Captain's quarters, where, being seated, in a moment after, a round, rich voice was heard, and a heavy tread, as Harkness entered the room.

"How are you, Beck?" he said.

Beck rose, saluted, and, as he knew he had met an officer of strict habits, he drew forth at once the letter from the War Office and presented it.

From his dress the soldier might have been taken for a ranger; he wore a buckskin blouse and leggins, hickory shirt, a light felt hat with shoestring tie, top-boots and spurs, his sabre, belt and pistols; his hair was cropped close to the scalp, and his fine face was improved by a moustache, the ends of which touched his shoulders. Placing his hat on the table, with a glance at the letter he laid it down.

"Where's your horse, scout?"

"Stabled, sir."

"Have you wet your whistle?"

"Yes, sir."

"And stocked your commissary?"

"Yes, sir."

"Ridden hard?"

"A good brush."

"In a minit you can rest."

"Don't want it, sir."

"As you please."

"Let me know, Captain, what you can do for me."

"What I can do?" he answered, facing the scout; "well, I'm going to knock the spots off of Cartwright and the Spider."

Beck was nonplussed.

"I understand," he went on, "they'll strike your train in The Wedge."

"So I reckon."

"At the Butte."

"Yes, sir; that's whar they'll ambush."

"Then I'll make a bait of your train."

"A bait?"

"Leave that to me. How many men have you?"

The scout gave the number.

"That'll do; all armed?"

"Yes, sir; all armed."

"I'll be with you, to stamp out this hellish game of plunder; this chief is a devil incarnate; all his life an enemy, he has broken every treaty, swears he'll never eat a government ration, has tortured or killed every white man, ravished every white woman he has caught; he has fought every friendly tribe, has attacked every government party, sells himself to do murder, is now sold to slay. Of course, they made a fool of him in Washington,—made fools of themselves also,—and he comes back with a medal! But I'll thrash him, or my name's not Bob Harkness!" His foot came down flatly, rattling his sabre.

Beck thought himself a good scout, but here was an officer who knew all the business he had come upon before he had uttered a word.

"How'd you like to be Sergeant Beck?" It was a weakness of the Captain to ask every fine-looking man he met to join his company.

"Not much, sir; I'm doing well now."

"Don't blame you; I wanted Jack McQuain."

"Is the old man still afoot?"

"Yes, sir; it was he who gave me the dots."

"How? what?" The scout was confused.

"Don't you know? Why, he lay behind a wall and heard all the bargain between Cartwright and the Spider about raiding your train; then he rode night and day till he reached me, gave me all the points, and now he's off for the mountains. He's a lamb, John Beck."

"That's so; he's a stan-by, certain." The scout now felt at ease.

"Where's your train?"

"I reckon, if it has kep up a steady pull, it's in a bee-line south of this."

"At daylight I'll call to saddle."

"We can reach my boys by midnight."

"My boys are brushing up; come and have a look at them."

Captain Harkness led the way to the parade-ground. In groups of a dozen or less, his men were at work.

Some of them burnished their sabres; one took apart his pistol; another mended his bridle, others their saddles. They were a hardy set of nomads, dressed like their chief, and each raised his hand to his hat as he passed, in a fraternal way, with a dare-devil smile. Their mounts were tied near by, and were "in good keep"; each horse, like each rider, had some striking trait or token, and they were not matched in size or color.

"There, scout, are my pets," said the Captain, pointing to two small brass howitzers; "I can take them along, the road is good."

"I reckon they'll talk."

"Yes; I call them Law and Order."

Having looked over the camp and talked with the men, Beck, for the rest of the day, slept off the fatigue of his ride.

With the first bright lines of the dawn, the bugle's note rang out loud and clear, and Captain Harkness, riding a bay stallion, ordered the mount.

"Beck," he called out, "ride ahead, the road is direct; strike your train, then report to me."

The scout put spurs to his horse and rode all day, with few stops; in the night he arrived at the foot of the ridge, and dashing up to its level he saw to the rear of his halting place the twinkling camp-fires of the train. Captain Harkness and his men had followed closely. Beck turned, made up to them, riding back in a run.

"I'll keep you company this side of the range, till

we reach the Butte in the Wedge; now, Beck, keep straight on with your train till I say halt," and Beck, anxious to quiet every fear or doubt, rode off for his camp, at full leap.

"Who goes there!" challenged the teamster on guard.

"Beck," was the answer; "how's all?"

"All's well."

Mrs. Garrulson awoke with a start.

"What's up!" she screamed; "is that you, John Beck, cavortin aroun this time o' night?"

CHAPTER XIV.

"STRUCK HARD" — "WIPED OUT."

In the morning before the "yoke up," every man was armed to the teeth; seeing which, Mrs. Garrulson, in her best vein, said:

"Things begin to look bilious."

The train had camped on the left flank of "The Wedge," — a name given to the land lying between the two lines of hills or ridges, — and from the view at this point they seemed, perspectively, to close in as they descended to the river. This was their conformation, for the lines were not parallel, but gradually neared to a narrow passage, at the exit. The place looked as though a mountain had been riven there, and the small plateau where they dragged along, like a wedge between the divided parts; by some it was called "The Spear-point." A sugar-loaf hill rose from the ridge on the right, topped by a few trees, and bore the landmark title of Butte. Just opposite, on the left and lower range, across the road, was a similar rise of less height, but of a more rugged formation. Its crest was basin-shaped, verged with rocks and brambles. The ascent to the base of the bowl was easy, but from thence, for a few feet, to the rim, precipitous. Herds of bison, with hoof and horn, scooping the saline earth, had at some time made "a lick" there, and the shrubbery not destroyed grew on its skirt. It was a ready-made rifle-pit. The hills fell away to the rear into the valleys. The one to the north overlooked the level gravel road to the fort, that on the south the highway travelled by Cruz and Cartwright.

The pirates and the Spiders kept the trail only at night, but with a forced march in breathless haste. The Indians sprang from sleep, retouched the war-paint, ground their arrow-points, clicked the trigger, flashed the knife; a mania for scalps and pelf crazed them. The chief rode to the front, motioned, and they followed; a long trail, with few stops, brought them in sight of the Butte on the night that the scout rejoined his train. In the moonlight Cartwright and the savage conferred by signs. After the latter had pointed often to the peak, he got down, turned his band to the woods near by, and drew in the sand with his finger a deep, rough sketch of his plan of attack. Now choosing the youngest, a strong-limbed, ill-visaged heathen, with the scars of torture on his breast and blood-signs on his face, he sent him off as a scout, to watch the whites. Within gunshot of their camp's patrol, this young, lithe savage lay until the dawn; he saw the cattle yoked, he heard the snap o' the whip in the start; still staring hard, he saw the train enter "The Wedge." Crawling from brush to bush and hillock, the runner at last rose to his feet, speeding back to his chief. With a frown he was sent off again, and on the top of the hill he stretched himself at full length, glaring down on the train, as a spider watches a fly.

Behind the northern rise, Captain Harkness and his troopers rode at will. Now and then he wheeled in his saddle, spoke to "his boys," rode on, whistled, patted his horse, fanned himself with his hat, renewed his tobacco.

"Ain't you gwyne to let us out, Cappin?" asked the sergeant.

"Well, I won't get a rope to hold you back with; but remember, now, the Spider fights like a catamount; he shows no quarter."

"He's no wus than all the varmints," spoke up a dare-devil on the flank.

"Halt!" The troop drew up to their leader. "Look here. The Spider is a hornet, — he's a — cannibal; do you know that? If one of you fellows are taken alive, you'll be roasted like a chestnut, roasted at a slow fire, roasted by inches. Do you hear me?"

"That's all right, Cappin; don't they have to take us fust?" put in a gruff voice.

"Forward!" He had badgered them with a word to raise the pulse.

"It'll be a dash, with sabre and yell," said one.

"A wipe-out."

"Tom," said another to his file, in a whisper, "he whistles all the time."

"Who?"

"Epylettes."

"All the wus for the redskins."

"Yes," said a third, "wen he's done with em, a train ken pass along this yer road and sleep o' nights without a guard."

Whack and Beck rode side by side in the sweltering heat; the beasts tugged hard at their burdens.

"Mighty close quarters, scout."

"So Cartwright thinks, I reckon."

"Will they strike us, certain?"

"Certain; they're over in the woods yonder, now."

"This is what a feller might call the jaws of death."

"Yes; for the teeth are sharpened."

"How?"

"We'll chaw em up."

"Isn't there another road?"

"No, Whack, and Cartwright knew it; knew jus whar to strike; but he's fooled.

"Thought he'd ketch us in a trap?"

"Yes."

"Looks like he had us, scout."

"I'm ahead of him though, an have set a trap for him; the train is a bait."

"How's that?"

"Wait an see; keep the men in good trim, let em move slow; I am off again," he said, as he rode on.

Mrs. Garrulson had fallen in with Legs, and careless of the rife danger, walked with him at his team.

"What you thinkin bout, Illynys?" she asked.

"Bout the fight."

"What sorter fight, boy?"

"Why, don't yer know wese gwyne ter hev a scrimmage afore we get outer this, granny?"

"No; — may I never — who wants ter fight?"

"Injins."

"Thet's so, es't?" the old woman looked thoughtful.

"Never mine, thar ain't a man that'll let a har of yourn be teched."

"My har; — why, bless you, sonny, I wur a thinkin of yourn. Whar dus yer mother live?"

"Up yanner;" the lad said, pointing to the bright blue sky.

"Dead? An yer farther?"

"Dead too; they moved out to the Meesuree an the Injins slayed em, granny, long ago."

"Too bad, son, sho; I hed kin of mine scelped too. An wese gwyne ter hev a fight?"

"Yes, an afore it's over I'll get even."

"Drot my shoestrings, boy, I'll stan by you," she answered quickly, slapping him on the back.

"An see hyar, granny; spose I'se knocked over?"

"I'll look arter you, son; but yer ain't gwyne to be with me ahind you."

The report of a rifle was heard, which cut short their talk. As Beck rode by, Whack called to him:

"What's up?"

"A chance shot;" he rode on over the northern ridge; as he crossed the hill, Captain Harkness came towards him.

"I heard your shot, Beck."

"I flushed up a Spider, Captain."

"Kill him?"

"No."

"What was he?"

"Spy in war-paint; I was huntin for a sign all day, and found it."

"How near are they, Beck?"

"In the woods below; they'll strike us to-night."

"Pull up in a trot to the foot of the Butte; unyoke and drive your stock over here."

Beck rode back to his train; at sundown they camped between the hills.

The night, midnight and the small hours were of the past, and the scout paced his rounds on guard; he held his rifle ready with his finger on the trigger. Not a whisper was heard behind the wagons; not even a beetle droned in the still, damp air. The men held their breath, and every beat of the heart could be counted in the soundless pause.

"Who's that?" cried Beck sharply, brought to a sudden halt by an apparition, as his eye ranged the barrel of his gun.

The form of the wanderer crept slowly out of the wet, dark shadows; more distraught than ever, when near enough he seized the scout's hand:

"They're coming," he said, in abject terror.

"Who?" asked the scout.

"Cartwright and the Spiders."

"Where?"

"Yonder, behind the hill;" pointing his long, bony finger; "they're creeping on you like a thousand snakes; hissing, too, the vipers; murder, death; they're coming, man; they're coming."

"Get in, then, out of sight;" and Beck forced the poor wretch behind the inclosure.

A feature of the wild man's craze, was his ever-changeful mode of life, and how he lived was a mystery to many. He was an ubiquis springing out of the earth to help those friendly to him, or to foil their enemies. He was fed by passing trains or parties; with these he journeyed hither and thither, with no fixed course or destiny, retracing his route as the mood seized him; taken up again to re-pass; hence his appearance in many places. The Indian looked upon him with awe, but without pity.

The scout called to Whack to stand guard until he came back.

"The devils," he said, "are on us, and they'll strike before daylight."

He crawled up the hillside and disappeared in the foliage; here he came upon Captain Harkness standing in the shadow of a tree, sighting the opposite ridge.

"They're over yonder, Captain," he said.

"I know it," was the quiet reply, "and they'll stay there, Beck."

"Stay there?"

"Yes; not one shall get away, if I can help it."

"What's going to be the signal?"

"They'll open fire; fire back in their teeth, every man, and when these pets" — he went on, pointing to his howitzers masked behind the brush—"stop talking ——"

"What then?"

"Charge that ridge with your men."

"When your pets stop barking, then?"

"Yes, sir; join your train, the ball's going to open."

In the camp the men were put to work upon a ruse to draw the fire, and to foil the foe. Blankets were spread on the slope, and under them bolts of tent-cloth, with here and there a teamster's hat; a good sham of men asleep. An inside breastwork of bales, covering the running-gear of the front wagons, concealed their movements.

It was midnight when the chief signed to his band to move. Spread out singly, a scattered horde, they began the ascent like crouching tigers, lurking and peering above the grass. On the flank, as skirmishers, Cartwright and Cruz led their horses.

In the ambush with his braves strung along its outer rim lying low, the Spider looked upon the camp of the teamsters, in vexed surprise. He stared fixedly at the Butte, opposite, as it frowned down on his meaner site, and was maddened by a mistake that mocked him. In rage he beckoned to the theives; they came to him to be told that he and his tribe must move to the other range. He sent them off to feel the way for a change of ambush, and from thence he would spring down upon the sleepers and destroy them.

Beck drilled his men in whispers; as soon as the savages opened fire they were to fire back; when he gave the command to charge, they were to leap the wagons, form line, follow him and fire advancing. Whack, for the first time was to see a frontier fight, the first lesson which the Colonel thought essential to his success in life; young, hopeful, the youth stood firm and gave his orders calmly.

"Mrs. Garrulson," he said to the good woman who was making bandages in an exposed corner, "get behind cover, you're in danger there."

She turned upon him in wrathful haste:

"Do yer think I'm a coward, boy; thar's grit I tell yer in the ole bones yit, an I'll stan by the boys tell the last wun draps."

If the men had dared so rash a thing, they would have cheered her. She got up, slung a powder-horn over one shoulder, a cartridge-box over the other, and took her stand, from which no entreaty could move her.

The chief strode madly in the rear of his crouching band; now and then he leaped to the front to look forth, and at last, as he looked, day broke in one broad gleam. The savage with a keen, ringing shriek raised his tomahawk. Beck fired on the instant; his rifle's ball clove the Indian's scalp-tuft.

"Great Scott," said Sandy in a low tone, "did yees see the feathers fly."

Just then there was a blaze of light along the ring of the pit; the guns of the painted devils, with a sharp, quick rattle, sent a shower of balls into the camp.

"Steady;" cautioned Whack, showing his mettle.

"All ready!—fire!" cried the scout; the rifles of the teamsters answered.

"Give em goss," cried the old woman, taking up a piece to reload it.

The chief saw at a glance that he was foiled by a vigilant foe, and blind with fury held to the fight, watching his chance to spring from cover. The firing now became general, and in the midst of it granny stood by Legs loading his weapon; he grasped the gun, aimed, fired and returned it to receive another; she never flinched, but stood in her place the picture of frontier pluck; her face begrimed, her hands and arms blackened.

"Goshens," she exclaimed, "the darned thing's hot, sonny; won't it bust?'

The redskins sprung a flight of arrows.

"Saving powder," said Beck, "the devils will stand to it and fight it out;" he had listened long for the hill-top signal.

While he spoke the howitzers opened with whistling grape, and the men stared at each other in wonder, for Beck had kept from them the knowledge of a troop near at hand, that their own courage might be fresh and warm.

"It's all right boys;" then in a sturdy voice he gave the command,—"Forward!"

They leaped the wagons with a loud, Western shout,

forming line; Beck on the right, Whack on the left, they advanced firing and loading in the face of the Spiders. The Indians leaped to the rocky parapet, fired and fell back, and the yell of the chief betokened that the parting shot had been given before he drew off his band, in flight.

All at once, yells like the rally-cries of the trappers, came from behind the ambuscade; a sound of many voices loud in the fiery tones of strife, coming nearer and mingling with the babel of the affrighted savages. The scout cheered; the men took up the battle-note of their leader, crowding close to his manly form; now was heard the jingle of scabbards, the snap of pistols, the snort of horses, and above the din, a voice louder than all rang out:

"Draw sabres!" it said; Bob Harkness was on hand.

John Beck heard it, and all the fervor of his nature, long pent up, burst forth in an answering shout; he scaled the barrier with his men, and joined the vengeful tumult.

Whack, at the left, was the last to come into the pit with his squad; they climbed the rough, sheer rock-front. The chief, surrounded, fought like a wild beast at bay; and, maddened, he furiously fought on. Clubbing his rifle as the last of his band fell about him, he sprang with a bound clear of the victors. Whack, who had just then dragged himself over the basin's rim as the savage planted his foot on the rock, glanced aside and caught the gleam of the upraised rifle, swung to brain him where he lay. Pistol in hand, he fired without aim, but as the smoke raised, the ear-piercing death-scream of the Spider was heard over the cliff, where he fell.

Harkness slapped his thigh at the sight.

"Grit, be gad," he said, aloud.

The savages in setting a trap had entrapped themselves in the meshes of a fearful slaughter. While a few fired the howitzers, the Captain led his men down the Butte on the river side, through the brush to the rear of the Indians, and charged to their ambuscade as Beck advanced in front.

"Call your roll, scout, and count the cost," said the Captain.

On the hillside, as the teamsters drew back from the bloody scene, they came upon the slain and wounded. The Spiders, assailed front and rear, hemmed in, had shot wildly; a score of trainmen had been hurt, and at the foot of the hill, one lay still in death.

"I seed him fall, boys," said the old woman between sobs, in whose lap the head of the dead youth lay; "all the Injins in creation could'nt abeld me back;" she leaned down and kissed the brow of the orphan and her tears fell, a full, sweet flow of pity, as pure as when the angels weep; the men were touched more at her sorrow than by the loss of their comrade, though he had been the lead in the whip's snap, in the rifle's crack. Poor Legs; he lay as one sleeping calmly, his long, brown hair on his shoulders. They took him up with friendly words, and buried him with care, and raising a rude stone-mound, they left him alone on the wild.

"I struck hard, scout," said Harkness.

"Well, it's a mercy; but has Cartwright got off?"

"Yes, like a thief."

"It's bad, bad if he lives."

"Yes, Beck, the breathing devil who lurks behind the savage urging him on, still lives; he always escapes the sword and the law."

The pirate and Mexican had taken a circuit of the ridge, coming up in the rear of the Butte; here they had tied their horses and had crawled up the hill. Cruz, the more wily villain ahead, looked in upon the troopers, from behind a tangled growth. The sight stunned him; quickly, with his finger on his lip, he motioned to Cartwright behind him. The two stood dismayed, as out of a riven cloud a beam of the freed moon played upon the burnished butts of the cannon, upon the sabre-hilts of the soldiers holding their horses; they saw the giant form of their captain and the wave of his hand; they saw the men mount, wheel, ride off.

"The devil;" whispered the copper-colored coward, as they both crouched down. They sneaked to their horses and mounted, for the pirate saw and understood that the Spiders were doomed. The Mexican eyed him.

"Vamo?" he asked timidly.

"Wayno;" answered Bill.

"B'wen."

The scoundrels, in a hard gallop, struck out for the camp of the packers; taking up their train, they sped away out of danger leaving the Indians to their fate. A fate sure as death followed them.

The wounded were cared for and the teams moved on, crossing the river. At the ford Harkness turned off with his troop for the fort.

On looking back at the rifle-pit, Beck saw the dry leaves in flames, and amid the smoke the wild man crazily disporting. He had found a dragoon's pistol, loaded, and hiding it under his rags, he fled with his prize.

CHAPTER XV.

REBUKED BUT NOT REBUFFED.

At the fort the wounded were speedily cared for, and Beck, having unloaded his train, started on the return trip. When John and Melinda came together the camp laughed, but the good old soul was far above the jest; the wifely care which for many years hoarded her little store in some nook of the lonely cabin, the sterling trait which upheld her to bear through strife the homely gift to her spouse, far away in the grim solitude, stamps her sense of duty as something better than impulse, something deeper than emotion. Of such qualities are heroes made, and none better have given fame and ennobled a race.

Fairly under way, homeward bound, Whack turned to Beck for leave to ride on, that he might free himself of the drag of the train and the creak of the wheels.

"Mind your eye," said his cautious leader, "keep the road and open country; if thar's Spiders in the bush they'll spot you, boy."

Whack rode on for hours a heedless truant; he forded the river and spurred away to the Butte, that he might look in upon the rifle-pit or over the cliff where the savage fell.

A few of the Spiders had escaped in the battle's smoke to hide from its rash and fearful vengeance. They had lain in ambush for hours to dress their wounds, or to chant at times their death-songs over the slain. As they lay there they heard the tramp of a rider's horse, and nearer and nearer it came upon them skulking, as closer they crouched to spring. Whack rode round the rocky point on the hillside; his mount shied, when, with yells, they seized his bridle and dragged him from his seat. Before he could fairly realize his danger, they had bound him hand and foot to set about the work of his torture, with devilish devices and with cruel haste. He was stripped to the waist; they singed the quivering flesh with hot arrow-points, scourged him with bow-string and thorn-brush, then bending a sapling with their combined weight, they fastened his feet thereto, and let the tree spring back. His head hanging down, and his body within reach, they stung and bruised it with a hundred blows. The strain on each young, strong fibre — a racking, acute tension as if one and all would snap — knotted the pain-wrought muscles. Moments were told off in long flights of agony; he panted for breath, the veins swelled to bursting, the foam stood on his lips and his eyes grew dim. One last, fainting look into the upper depths, like one sinking in the waves deeper, deeper.

"Get back, back, you painted hell-cats," screamed a voice, and the feeble sight of Whack saw the wild man rushing to his rescue, club in hand, with which he struck down savage after savage. Again he heard another, manlier voice.

"Stand aside," it said, and the sharp crack of the rifle was heard as he swooned.

Beck had followed Whack, giving his horse free rein to seek him out, and he came upon the scene as the wanderer struck down his tormentors. He cut the cords, taking up the body in his arms, and he bore it away to a spring.

Looking about for the wild man, he was seen far off, his arms held high in the flurry of madness.

When the train came up Whack was put to bed in a covered wagon; his wounds were many and sore, and long weeks would come of restless fever before he could again scour the plain.

The book Mary gave the scout was a small copy of the Bible she had taken from the shelf, with the marker between the leaves. It was her law of the household, that it should be read in the long hours of a winter's evening. So little else in print ever found its way to the frontier cabin, the lessons of its text had given strength to many manly hearts. In camp, a few days after Whack's adventure, the scout drew forth the little volume as he sat alone at rest. The marked page was spread before him, and the words which the marker pointed to were these:

"And thy people . . . . " the trite lines in the old Scriptures.

Beck was startled. He drew back as though a blow had been aimed at him, but he did not suspect Mary of design, for she had not, in truth, looked at the page, but still the words stared him in the face boldly. Nor was he tempted to peruse them again, for they troubled him, and he closed the tell-tale chapter, hid the book in his blouse and rose with a sigh.

Whack's was a fine face, the more so as he lay in his wagon-tent half asleep. The tan of his cheeks shaded the glow of health, and the rich brown hair in waves lay on the white roll under his head; the repose of the young, manly features was broken by a smile at some fancy of his thoughts; the smile enriched the picture. While with a lazy content he felt the return of strength, on the rear-porch at the home Mary was seated with Lu. She turned once from her sewing, to glance at the lovely girl sitting near her, as a stray beam stole in to alight on her golden braids.

At dawn the train rolled out, taking a cut-off to reach the Big Backbone, and at noon on the next day Beck called a halt.

"Whack, do you know this yer spot?" he said, as he raised the wagon cover.

"Yes."

"Look down in the valley at the crib."

"I see the same old landmarks."

"Do you see smoke?"

"No; do you?"

"Thar's a way to find out all I want to know."

"How?"

"I'm going to see."

He rode off just as once before he had taken a

sudden flight; as before, he drew up near the pirates' camp, and tying his mount, he began again a search of the grotto. He was about to give it up, when his eye caught sight of a pair of spurs hanging on the doorframe, and at last he saw a pack-saddle. Still not satisfied, grasping his rifle he ventured nearer; as no sound came to his ears, he went on until he stood in the door of the cabin. He sprang back, with a blanched face, and covered his eyes with his hands. On the floor within lay the dead bodies of the packers, each man slain by a stab in the darkness of a night attack. About the door were signs of a hard-fought, hand-to-hand fight, and Beck would have turned away in haste, but he must know if Cartwright was one of the slain. This done, and assured that the thief had escaped, he strode out of the loathsome place. As he did so his foot struck a shining object; he picked it up, to find it a blood-smeared knife; on the handle rudely cut, was the name: FERATI! Beck leaped into his saddle, joined his train, and "rolled out." Cartwright was still at large and he rode far away from the trail, getting down to search for foot-prints, and his search was not in vain.

Jumper had his own way to make in the world, and he had himself to blame if he set about doing so by a bad method. The value of Lu's real estate to the uttermost farthing, her goods and chattels, as well as that in prospect, he had found out, in detail, and as she had not once set him back in his pretensions, as a matter of course, he pressed them upon her. She was a very pretty prey for just such a flatterer. When she left her friends,—the light-headed coterie,—she had vowed in a maidenly way never to come back without having taken a scalp—the border phrase of the day for catching a beau—in some sort of heroic fashion, and Jumper was quick to cross her trail that she might seize upon him as a victim. That two young persons with so much in common should come together often, was only natural. They had been known to each other for a long time as Lu and Harry.

About a dozen miles below the post on the river's bank, was a woodchopper's camp. Jumper had urged Lu to trust herself with him on a visit to this place, and she had consented. They mounted their horses, Lu upon the frisky Kitty, and rode away in the early morning; she, the pretty, blue-eyed, simple little girl, and he, the mannish, over-smart boy, side by side. Just so, through the world they go in pairs, lured on until real life, like a savage in the bush, flies its arrows, and regret mocks them, like the laugh of drunken men. They had ridden a long stretch from the post, and already Jumper began to reckon upon chances.

"Harry dear," said the weak voice at his side, "is there any danger away out here?"

"Can you trust to me?" he replied; "if there's danger ain't I with you?" laying stress upon the ego.

"I do wish so much we were safe on the steamer."

"I'll put you there, Lu; all creation can't stop me."

"How brave you are," she said, with a simpering, childlike trust.

Now in the rapture of an idle day-dream,— the rose-tinted gossamer which veils the sight of youth,— they drew near a thicket. Love's soft nonsense was quickly hushed in fear, for they had, without warning, ridden into a camp of Indians maddened by drink. Lu's horse sprang aside, dashed ahead, and Jumper's followed:

"Dear, dear Harry, what shall we do?"

On looking back he saw that the Indians were pursuing them. They gave chase for sport, and in the muddle of his wits, Jumper said to Lu, almost rudely:

"Run."

The band came on hooting, laughing and springing their arrows into the air, after the fleeing couple.

"Oh, I shall faint; help me, Harry; help me;" cried the girl, in a really pitiable plight.

"Pinch yourself, Lu; stick yourself with a pin;" he said to her, losing what little sense was left to him. Such an answer at such a time was cruelly careless, but it was the spur to her escape, as it proved. She loosed the rein and Kit bounded away. As she looked back at Jumper, there rang in his ears a parting answer.

"You're a coward, Harry Carver," she said, as she swept on, and he saw the graceful form of his sweetheart taking wings and fast fading from his sight.

Jumper was not a coward, for as his flurry calmed, he outwitted the Indians with skill. He was riding an old cob, and as they neared him he quietly let himself down, that his horse might fall into their hands; he knew they would be content with the capture and he would cover his flight by the ruse. And so it happened; catching the mount, they turned and rode back.

Kitty carried Lu out of danger; on the skirt of the wood she heard the sound of the axe and saw the landing on the river; she drew rein thanking her good angel, for the ride of the two was a runaway match. Jumper, by dint of long coaxing, won Lu's consent, and she, to carry back to her friends the trophy she had vowed to seize, had thought the youth not a poor catch. On that day a boat "down stream" and the one coming to Cheviteau's would meet at this camp. In the first they were to sail away to Gretna Green, sending the horses to the post by the other. Jumper planned it all, but the emeute changed Lu from a foolish little maiden to a sensible being in a trice; the good angel's very best whisper.

She returned in the boat, refusing to speak with the crest-fallen hero. How he squared his profit and loss account the Colonel knew best, but Lu, the penitent, threw herself into Mary's arms and told everything.

A few days after, while the captain of the "Pioneer" refreshed himself at the sideboard, he asked to take Carver into his service, and the trader made no serious objections.

The Judge was still a guest at the post; his stay, in his own excuse, was to attend to politics; but the Doctor, a worldly-wise man, let his pretext pass for what it was worth, weighing it against a heavy doubt.

At an earlier hour of the same day, he, the Judge, went forth also, but took some pains to cover his trail from the eyes of the family; he had a written permit from the Colonel to pass the patrol, which he handed to the one he met and rode on.

The Judge knew and felt that there was some danger ahead, but he would take care not to provoke the few Indians left behind from the annual hunt. He was bent upon knowing, with the keen eye of a speculator, the lay of their lands. In taking his bearings, he would keep strict account where best to plant his own stakes, if the future gave him a chance, caring little, though he thought of it, that his rash act might cause a deadly feud. He had framed a petition to have the treaty with these Indians annulled, and to open their reservation to the settler, for sale. The scheme was to be bolstered by a resolution of the State Legislature and then to be hurried through Congress.

The sky was as brass, the earth ashes. The Judge dropped his bridle and his horse walked lazily through the brown grass. The noon blaze scorched; the whirr in the trees, the gleam on the plain were no check to his scheming thoughts. He straightened himself in the stirrups, and was about to coach himself aloud in the cut-and-dried cant of a speech, when a yell paused his hand in mid-air, and he lost his seat in the saddle.

Before he could rise, the band of drunken braves, on their way to their village after their fright to Lu and

Jumper, pounced upon him. They painted his face, twisted his hair into a coil, pinned it with feathers, and tying his arms, they drove him off with laugh and jeer. In this disgraceful fix, late in the evening, the Judge met the trader, who smiled broadly, for he knew that the Indians had taught his guest to mind his own business.

"What kinder chief did them redskins make you, Jedge? You look like a Pache."

"Never mind the looks, Colonel; behavior's everything. I scattered em, seh."

"Oh, you did? Well, if you did, how'd they come to paint your face?"

"Well, they had reinforcements, yes — "

"But whar's your horse?"

"The patrol caught him."

The Judge hurried off to avoid the Doctor, who came up.

The train was on the road skirting the lands of the Colonel's unfriendly neighbors. Beck had good reason for alarm.

Cartwright and the gang, after their desertion of the Spiders, hastened on to the crib. There they had been attacked by Ferati's cow-boys and "wiped out," the thief escaping to the lodges of these Indians, with whom he was then living as a squaw-man. He was in their village when Beck stole upon the crib and came away from the horrid sight with white cheeks.

The pirate had caught a glimpse of the Judge on his ride, and had vowed to the savages that the man was there to survey their lands, and was nearer the mark than he knew; he clothed the Judge with authority to dispossess them; he likened him to a prowling wolf, spoke of him as the trader's agent, and the trader an agent of others in a plot to deprive them of their rights. It was a scheme, they were told, to which the government had given its encouragement.

Even now the speculator was ready to repeat his adventure; in truth, he had need of haste to leave the post, as the Doctor seemed curious about him. His former ride awed his purpose but little, and he now hired two axemen at the camp, a compass and chain, and so soon as he was ready for the work these men would serve him. He felt at ease, that the small band when sober would not molest him, if he guarded his movements. Success required that he should know the area of the timber land, so as to exhibit, in good shape, the best attractions of the steal. He knew the depth by a measurement along the bluff, and now to obtain its length he started out again. He had been careful to hide his plans from the trader and the scout.

His aides were found in waiting, the survey began, and while running his lines through the high grass, he was seen by Cartwright. The night before, the chief had returned from the hunt, and the thief wanted no better evidence than this to convict the trader of bad faith in the eyes of the Indian. He rode fast, concealed by the woods, to find the savage, who was easily led to a hiding-place, where both eyed the shark unseen. In that brief moment the redskin became a bloodthirsty foe.

The Colonel, during the absence of his train, had spare moments to spend with his daughter on the porch. Mary's long formed, most earnest wish was to gain her father's consent to the building of a church and schoolhouse, but he with some indecision had put it aside. He now gave way, willing to yield on condition that she would come round a little to his own crotchet. His age had called to mind that she ought to be settled and cared for.

"So you want to see me married?" She spoke frankly, after he had said as much by hint.

"Shure, child, why not?" he answered.

"So you shall, all in good time, father; wonder what Mister John would think to hear you talk in that way."

She rose, whispering in his ear some secret of her heart, and he turned suddenly.

"Not Charley?" he asked in surprise.

"No, no, father; would you have me marry a brother?"

She saw the Judge standing near, and she hastily entered the house.

While Mary and her father stood on the porch at a later hour, a patrol rode up; gun-firing had been heard, and when he left his line the train was in sight.

"All right," the old man said with a pleased face; "Now, Mary, give the boys the best in the house when they come; call Chloe an have a set-out; I'll tend the sideboard."

Whack was brought in and put to bed in charge of the Doctor and Mary, while Lu, whose sympathy was quickly warmed, fell into the kindly office of nurse, without so much as the asking. Whack, after long, long hours of her tender care, thought he had never seen her look so sweet, as when she came on tiptoe to his bedside. It is more than likely, she had never before taken so much pains to look her best. Mary too, seemed to take an amiable delight in bringing the two together, and as she had once rebuked his fancy for Jane, she seemed to make amends with Lu, and Whack began to wonder.

For her adopted brother Mary had a very lovable respect; she knew his good traits, few faults, and that her father liked him; but she knew and felt too, that his own fancy was for other scenes than those to which her own heart was bound, so long as her father lived. Whack felt a twofold pleasure in being nursed, and in nursing his wonder; he threw aside his banter, for Jumper was long since out of his way, and with the natural humor of youth, gave back to Lu look for look. Never before, in her young, staid life, had Mary felt the luxury of doing good, with such peculiar joy. Lu, in the daily whisperings with Mary, shared her secret with another, and under such restraint became timid in the arts of her sex, and was artless and purely herself. Thus allured, Whack was moved to a frank, open manner; in turn his words moved her heart, and thrilled it with a music even her dreams had never heard. Little blue-eyes was in love.

Mary may have heard some stray note of the rhapsody, at least she felt it, and she caught Lu at times and held her. She talked to her often of a true wife's life as her own rare faith believed it should be. Her friend was happy as her love grew deeper, stronger, and trustingly Lu felt the pride of her sex, in the counsel of one among the truest.

Even the old man began to suspect, and he would tease Lu, and beg her to tell him exactly what she thought of Charley; the scout too looked askant at Whack.

Sitting by his cot the Colonel said:

"Charley, thar's nuthen in the warehouses."

"I know, and fall trade's open in New York."

"Will you go back thar?"

"Right off, as soon as I'm well."

"If thar's anything in the way, you ken say to the girl for me, that I'll give you both a fair start in life; now git well soon."

The young man's emotion kept him still, and the trader went on:

"Lu has got sumpin of her own, but let her reckon it all up, boy, an I'll kiver it all for you, do you hyar."

The lad who had always shown to him a ready obedience, harsh as the order sometimes was; who had fought his way across the plains, and was thereby "edicated," had claims upon him he was ready to meet. Whack was about to speak, but the old man had his say without allowing his thanks:

"Sparking is a good enuf sort of thing in its way, but bisnis is bisnis, seh;" he turned back from the door to add, with a twinkle in his eye: "An she's pooty, Charley, an a very good sorter girl."

What passed between the young people after this was theirs to keep, but one evening, as time sped on, the light and shade flung from the vine lay golden on her head; she heard the cool, fresh ripple of the stream, and his words were like it, so delicious are love's first minutes. She sprang up from the cotside, and her kiss-warmed cheek was as bright as a fleck of the sunset.

Mary heard Lu's quick step in the hall; she turned and saw her standing in the doorway, her eyes all deeply blue. Her words were spoken over the form she drew close to her breast, and Lu's whispered answer was:

"He's mine; he's mine."

Whack was easily captured, bound down as he was by plaster and splint. The little trapper, in whose heart love lighted its camp-fire, took the young man's scalp with a glance of her eyes.

CHAPTER XVI.

IN THE WING.

After breakfast the Judge made his appearance, taking a seat near the trader, on the porch.

"You look kinder tired, Jedge," said the old man; "jine me in a smoke."

"I don't mind," he replied, as he drew up his chair.

"What about my horse?"

"I gave him to the patrol."

"So they stripped you, did they, Jedge?"

"Well, yes; you see, Colonel, they rallied after being routed." And he whipped round to the first subject his wits caught at, and said: "How has trade prospered with you?"

"Well enuf."

"Before long you'll be a millionaire?"

"No, seh; not half, an it's cost blood and sweat enuf for the other half, an no thanks neether. How do you get on, Jedge?"

"I've done well, but it was shrewdness, nothing else; we've got to be smart, you know. Why, you see, Colonel, I buy land grants, and lend money, and when a settler comes to squat on a hundred and sixty acre tract, at one dollar twenty-five cents an acre, I let him have the money to pay for it, on credit; now, you see, I take his note for twelve months, at two per cent. interest a month, and a mortgage for security. You know, Colonel, no settler can make it up in a yeah, on raw prairie; they break the sod, grow sick from malaria, die or move away. Well, I foreclose; get land, improvements and all; first cost to me, next to nothing. The law only 'lows me one tract, as a settler, but in this way, Colonel, — why, I own whole townships;" and the Judge's air was that of one well pleased with himself, but the Colonel bit his tongue to keep the word "shark" from slipping. He made excuse, at once, to part with the Judge's company and hastened off.

Whack was ordered to New York; Lu was to go with him, and with her aunt's consent they were to be married at her own home. As the boat was expected he sought Mary in her retreat, and found her sewing on a piece of needle finery, a souvenir for Lu. Now and then she held it up in the light and smiled at the witchery of each stitch, and on the lovable little things entwined in its meshes. Looking up she saw Whack standing near. He was no longer a dread for womanly caution to hold at arm's length; he was no longer to be feared, when he was the captive of another, so she dropped her work, and laid her hand on his shoulders:

"Ain't you happy, Whack, old fellow? and your scalp is clean gone; well, now in our happiest hour you will let Mary say to you, with all her heart, God bless you."

What followed the veriest spinster might guess; they kissed of course.

Lu was packing her trunk, and having closed the lid she sat musing. She had come to the post a fickle little being with views of life childlike and vain, but the friendship of Mary had so gained upon her, she had grown stronger and better every day, and now with a truer spirit she found a happier heart.

Whack had a parting talk with the trader in his office, and he remembered it gratefully all his after life. The old man believed in early marriage; it gave a young man, he thought, a purpose in life, raised his ambition and trained him for serious work. Whack, in his, the trader's belief, was the beau ideal of a candidate.

Beck met Whack as he came away from the office, and with warmth of feeling he said:

"I'm sorry you're going; come back as soon as you can, this yeah's the best place for you."

When the whistle was heard the old man took Lu in his arms, Mary and she embraced in tears and Chloe cast the shoe as they all went down to the landing. Whack and Lu were seen far away side by side on the deck of the boat, and as they in turn looked back, they saw the form of the scout; he leaned on his rifle.

"Come Mary, let's go to work," said Doctor Tom after her friends had gone; he saw that she longed for them and was lonesome.

"Where will we go, Doctor?"

"Into the wing; we can assort and arrange your father's collection; and make the place a sort of museum."

Together they went to the little room stored with the odds and ends of savage customs and warfare, of the border garb and weapons, and the Doctor sat down in a chair. Above his head, the steel-pointed spear and arrows and a Navajo's battle club, hung on a quaintly woven blanket.

"Just see, Mary, with what labor these savages work to destroy; those weapon-points are beaten into shape with stones; what must their hate be?" he said, looking up.

"I've just read a book written in the East; it throws all the blame for all the strife on us; that's not right," she answered, taking up a reed whistle of the Seminole, and a long, sinew-bound bow of the Apache, which she hung up side by side; the one listless, the other unstrung.

"Eastern people are educated by reading novels, to a romantic admiration of the red man; their philanthropy is safe because it is distant; they're sincere because they are ignorant, but we know; we have had our goods and children stolen, our houses burned, our wives and people murdered."

The Doctor was hanging, on a scalping knife driven into the plaster, the feathered head-gear of a Sioux warrior, and with it his tomahawk, pipe, moccasins, wampum and bullet-pouch; they were laid on a dressed fawn skin embroidered with stained quills;

these he circled with a hide thong, the bridle of these horsemen.

"Now, this is the dress and outfit of what they call a brave," he said, as he finished the group; "he was a warrior, and the best that can be said of him is, that he was enduring, self-reliant, cunning; a lazy loafer about his camp one day, he was a swooping demon the next; an abject beggar or a daring thief as circumstances warrant; lying to him was one of the fine arts; licentious without generosity, treacherous in all his acts and dealings, most cold-blooded, and full of inventions in the refinements of cruelty, he was a most dangerous and terrible animal; he fought to the death when cornered, but it is as the wolf fights, who neither gives nor expects mercy; there is a total lack of that courage which prompts men to fight from a sense of duty; craft with him was better than courage." The Doctor was standing on a chair as he warmed up to his subject, and he resembled an auctioneer crying down the things before him. "Hand me up the lot to your right, Mary, which I have assorted."

One by one she gave him the outfit of the Mexican; calzoneros trimmed with round plated buttons; large roweled spurs like those the vaqueros wore, with little bells that tinkled at every motion; the faded poncho, the scarlet sash, the horse-hair cord bridle, the cruel bit, the black, glazed sombrero of brigandish cut; these the Doctor set in the coil of a split hide lasso, flexible as a whip-lash.

"Well, then, Doctor, why should these people write

and talk this way? I have great sympathy for the Indian children and women," said Mary, taking up the thread of the conversation.

"Well, Mary, it is just this: a man surrounded by the influence of a moral, cultivated society has no conception of the Indian character; the truth is simply too shocking, and the revolted mind takes refuge in disbelief; as to the children, take the Indian as a boy; his models are men great and renowned in degree as they are ferocious from the number of scalps they have taken, or the thefts they have committed; there is no right or wrong to him, his own will is law; his only instruction is to fit him best to act a part in the chase, in theft, and in murder; he is taught all that is necessary to savage life, nothing more; privation teaches endurance; when he has food he eats to repletion, when he has none he hunts for it; if he has clothing he wears it, if not, he is happy in leggins and paint; he is patient, for time is nothing to him; he is never homesick, because all places are equally his home; virtue, morality, generosity, honor are words not only absolutely without significance to him, but are not accurately translatable into an Indian language of the plains."

"I hope you don't do them injustice, Doctor," said Mary.

"Oh, no, my young friend, not injustice. I wish my voice could be heard all over the land, for it is only by knowing what the Indian really is, that ever he will be pitied; if he is left as he is, he'll be annihilated.

No, Mary, it is a mistake that will prove most cruel to the Indian; he must be known as he is; the grandest exploits, and the noblest virtues to the Indian are comprehended in the English words, theft, pillage, rapine, murder; he can expect no honor from man or love from woman, until he has taken a scalp or stolen a horse, and he who crawls upon a sleeping enemy and kills him before he can awaken, is a better warrior and entitled to more praise, than he who kills his enemy in a fair fight; a scalp is a scalp with him; the tender cuticle of an infant, the "long, fair hair" of a helpless woman, are as dearly prized as the grizzled scalp-lock of the veteran of a hundred fights.*

"Now hand me that collection, Mary, near you; that's the rig of the fellows who have tried to open the way for civilization; what blood it has cost."

Piece by piece she gave him the costume of the American frontiersman; the deerskin hunting-shirt with fringed skirt and leggins alike, shoes of parflèche, the coon-skin cap with fox-tail drooping from it; the long-stocked Kentucky rifle, the hunting-knife, from which the Bowie was a copy, and other things of the outfit.

"How I wish the strife was over;" she said with a sigh, "this has been my wish all these long years, but you give me little hope."

* The substance of this conversation, wherein the Doctor speaks of the Indian, is borrowed almost *verbatim* from "The Plains of the Great West;" Lieut.-Col. R. I. Dodge, U. S. A, and the introduction to the same, by *William Blackmore*. The author has taken the broad liberty to appropriate and adapt, so that his own opinion of the Indian, which coincides, may not stand unsupported.

"Well, child, it's only the story of the world, of the race of mankind; it has been written, you know, in blood; heroes and martyrs, the strong to slay, the weak to perish; man to be great must dare and suffer so long as there is cruelty or wrong; when there is none then comes the millenium."

Mary had come to her father simply taught in the principles of duty, by those to whom the sense of it was inherent; she had taken her place scarce knowing what she did beyond the impulse of that duty; it was a part whose trials she little knew, and would have shrunk from them as little, had she known. Her presence was the first sign of social form through which has come the after rule of church and school, the after peace of law and order; and whatever her trials be, though floodlike they come, there is another tide to bear to her a blessing for every tear.

She and the Doctor were now assorting the minor curios; the wide-spreading horns of a Texan, the antlers of a moose, the twisted butters of a mountain-goat, the hoof of a lead-ox, labelled "Blaze," a grizzly bear's claws, the tail of a stallion, the wicker cradle of a papoose, the guarache of a peon, rifles, short and long, of scout and trapper; and the Doctor hung up an antelope's head, *vis-à-vis* with a grinning catamount's. They kept at their work steadily, for it seemed to please Mary to hear the Doctor talk.

The redskins near by were "showing their teeth," and the scout knew that the pirate's malice was working the mischief. Stray cattle and horses were stolen, the vaqueros and patrols were shot at, a hay-stack was set on fire; the men were growing restive. It was these alarms that had taken him away so often. Beck had tried to bring about a parley to pacify the few, and, by presents, to win them to friendliness; but he found them cross and hateful, and, in degree as they became more and more so, he measured the infamy of the thief. The scout also thought he might put danger aside by seeking the chief on the plains, to arouse against Cartwright a counter feeling, and he was about to take the trail when the patrol sent word of the tribes' return.

All this wore upon the man's manner, and Mary saw under an unreal cheer, his trouble of mind; her eyes followed and haunted him with a thousand ugly fears. Happily for those who sped the glad hours under the trader's roof, the chief was slow to act; he let his temper grow hot by degrees, kept his own counsel and waited.

"Good bye, Mary," said Beck, as he rode up on his horse to the window of the wing.

"Where are you going, Mister John?"

"To look about for pirates; mus go;" and he spoke wearily, as one needing peace and rest.

She gave him an anxious glance. "Must go?" she asked, "when will the time come to say you won't go?"

"Jus when the law says so, and the government sees that the law is carried out; then we won't have to take the law in our hands, and it'll hunt and hang a thief like Cartwright."

"That'll be a long time, John Beck; it has been put off up to our time, and the children of to-day, out here, will say the same thing when they are grown."

"Will we never have peace?" asked Mary.

"Not till we make it by fighting down its foe," said the Doctor.

"If your father and me, Mary, hold back, they'd come like wolves and chaw us up;" the scout added.

"Who, the Indians?" she asked.

"Not allers the Injins, they're bad enough; but the sharks and pirates."

"Beck means the squaw-men, the Indian name for what we whites call the pirates," said the Doctor.

"What's a squaw-man?" she asked.

"Bill Cartwright;" answered the speaker. "Living among these tribes are outcasts, — American, French, Mexican, — the lowest refuse spewed out by the society in which they were born; they bring with them horses, sufficient not only to make friends, but to buy one or more squaws and a tepee, to enable them to set up housekeeping; the squaws draw rations from the Agencies for themselves and their children. Having more natural shrewdness than the Indian, they soon gain ascendancy. These are the men who furnish arms, and supply whiskey. At his own best game, in lying, stealing, drinking, and debauchery, the squaw-man is so far superior to the Indian, as to gain admiration; it is from these men that the Indians get their ideas of the character, capacity, morality, and religion of white men. These ruffians, with their half-breed children, are fed and fostered by the government; they are adepts in the Indian language, and all the intercourse between the government and the Indians is filtered through them, and partakes of their character; **full of duplicity, treachery, and evasion."** *

"Good by, Mister John," Mary said, as Beck turned his horse to ride off, " a better day will come."

"May be," he answered, as a sudden shade passed over his face; he turned and rode away. Mary sat down, and over her own fair features a shadow swept, from the strong man's mood. The talk of the Doctor and the scout had chilled her spirits; suddenly she seemed to take in the wider scope of the dangers about them. She knew, as all on the border knew, that the braver pioneers fought the battles and were swept away; passed away from the memory of a thankless government. It was a solemn truth for a young woman to think upon; hate was burning in the heart of the white and the red man, a consuming fire, like the gust-flames of the prairie. How soon would her fair dream vanish, her hopes to blackened cinders turn, and the scene so dear to her, withered and scorched, be scattered to the winds?

"I am sorry, Doctor, for all you have said about the Indian; and I wonder where Mister John is gone?" the thought of him raised a spirit of womanly courage, and she caught a gleam of the brighter side. "I reckon," she added, "we'll fight it through." This was a new phase of faith; hitherto her prayer had been

* *" The Plains of the Great West."*

that peace would come, to spring like early flowers around a church and school; now had dawned upon her an idea of a struggle; it found her armed in soul for the bitterest moment, and all that courage needed lay deep and warm.

While the Doctor and Mary were still at work, Judge Smith, sauntering by, came into the room. To the Doctor his appearance was always a provocation; not that he hated the man, but he mistrusted him, and the Judge always managed in some unhappy way to wake the other's ire by touching upon some unpleasant subject; he was prone to take the part of the Indian, in order, as the Doctor believed, to cover up some hidden scheme wherein the Indian was concerned.

"Hello, Doctor," he said, in a manner to irritate, "you're at work among your friends."

"Who do you mean by my friends?"

"The Indians."

"I'm a better friend of the Indian, Judge, than you. I'm not an intermeddler, seh, trying to break up what the law and treaty have established; what little law we have and whatever sense there may be in a treaty with a savage."

The Judge winced, for the Doctor, perhaps without knowing, was treading heavily on his corns.

"Well, the Indian feels that he is being crowded and pushed back; that's only human nature."

"I tell you there's very little of human nature about him, seh; its all inhuman. Trade is a pioneer, and while it seeks to open a way for civilization, it has not been hard on the Indian. Its motive has always been to conciliate; it would have profited by friendly alliance with him."

"Oh, he don't understand these things."

"He understands only too well the law of his own rights; can't he be made to feel the law that values human life and sets a penalty on murder? If the white man was not a brave, patient enemy, and should he rise to resent in force, he would reform the evils with the snap o' the whip and the crack o' the rifle; he would reform them altogether."

"You expect too much of the Indian, and not enough of the white man."

"I don't consider a man white who tampers with the passions of a savage, or in any way incites him to revenge." The Doctor was growing warm. "There are too many Cartwrights on the highways of our progress, seh; we want scouts, honest, fearless guides on the open plain of action; sentinels to cry the hour and the "all's well" of peaceful pursuits; that's what we want, seh."

Just then the voice of Chloe was heard screaming, which at once broke up the squabble between the Doctor and the Judge, and brought them to the door. Mary was there first.

"What's the matter?" she asked.

"He's begunned agin, honey."

"Who?"

"Dat chicken; dar now, foh de lah chile, he's gone

an done it agin." She was watching the rooster, and he had climbed the fence to the mystical number of three times; each time he had crowed lustily, and she was in a sore strait of mind.

CHAPTER XVII.

THE OUTBREAK.

Cheviteau had striven through all his life to keep alive good feeling and good faith with the Indian; not alone from prudence but from a really generous nature; he was sure to punish those under him for an infraction of this rule. There had been many vicious, spiteful tricks played upon him by the redskins near the post, but with a manly disregard he let them pass. He was not blind, and he knew that his gifts to them were received, not as gratuities, but as tributes he was bound to pay to placate a secret foe. In degree as success helped him on, as his trade and thrift grew to a blooming bay-tree, the jealousy of the savage warmed, his hate deepened, and he stared with eyes full of fire. It was by the strictest cautions that the trader lived in peace; it was in waiting a chance that the Indian permitted this peace by sufferance, and the old man felt that there was a spark burning low, anon to burst into flame.

On the morning after Lu and Charley had departed, Mary was seated under the vines, and saw Beck mount his horse, ride off, and she watched him until he was seen to take a trail to the prairie.

Cartwright dogged the steps of the chief whispering his venemous and deadly lies; he urged, he plead, and at last he saw the lines in the face of the savage fixed for revenge. What he would do was soon known. He smeared his breast that his band might behold a mark true to their own malice. He folded a blanket over his shoulders, snatched up his rifle and tomahawk, and strode away. They looked after him on the trail he had taken to the post.

Later in the day, while Mary and her father stood on the porch, a patrol rode up to say, that a chief had been halted on their line; he wanted to have "a big talk" with the white man, — "the man with the whip." A guard was sent for, and as the patrol rode away, Mary spoke to her father, quickly:

"I don't like this."

"Why, child?"

"I don't like it; something tells me that this Indian means no good."

"You're kinder outer sorts, Mary, that's all."

"I hope so, father, indeed."

"Go in then; he won't come nigh you."

The chief was well known to the trader; known to be taciturn, and suspected of being a thief. He was crafty; a little more so than most of his kind, which passed for a better trait; he kept hidden but hot the antipathies of his race. The patrol came with him and stayed near at hand with the guard.

"How!" was the blunt greeting of the trader. He felt sore at the thought, that by the aid of this tribe

Mary had been stolen, and the scout knew that it was now in collusion with the pirate. Hence the old man was civil, nothing more.

To the white man's words the chief was cold and stiff, and turned his eyes away, fixed on the cabins in the distance. He walked to the rear of the dwelling, and then spoke to the Colonel in broken English:

"Heap house," he said, pointing to those in the circle.

The trader nodded.

"Heap blanket?"

"No."

"Me—he—see—um."

"No."

"Me—him—no—see—um."

A shake of the head was the answer; the chief eyed the other and paused.

"Heap ox?" he went on.

"Yes."

"Heap mens — you?"

"Yes."

"How much—heap mens you?"

"Heap;" said the Colonel, not caring to give him an inch, as the Indian would be sure to grasp at an ell.

Mary brought some food, and her father, in the hope that it might move the visitor to a better temper, said she might offer it; Mary motioned the Indian to the shade of a tree, but to the surprise of both he drew himself up, refolded his blanket, and turned his back.

Cheviteau was quick to see and to speak, almost angrily:

"Take it away;" then turning his steps towards the office, the Indian followed him. The quick, bold glance of the one, was much at variance with the calm manner of the other as he offered a pipe; it was refused.

"Big — lan — you — heap?"

The old man rose from his seat to point through the open window to the far-off line of his estate, miles away, where it lay close upon the timber of the tribe.

"Injin's — you — steal um," said the chief, looking over the trader's shoulder, and hissing his words.

"No;" answered the other firmly.

"No steal um — you."

"No, me heap lan."

"Injin, he — no — go."

"No."

"Big father, — you — tell — um."

"What?"

"Injin — go — way."

"No," the trader said, with a glimpse at the evil lodged in the other's mind, "No; me Injin's fren; good fren, — me no lie."

"Good," was the reply given with a grunt.

The savage was about to leave the office with a more friendly disposition, when his eye searched out in a corner near the door, the compass and chain which the Judge, in the trader's absence, had placed there.

Cheviteau, much surprised, not knowing that these

harmless tools were fraught with cruel evils, treated the matter lightly; but on sight a fiend entered the soul of his foe. As the trader stooped to look at them, the savage clutched his tomahawk; he would have dealt a death-blow, but the guard looked in at the window. When the Colonel raised up, the chief had stepped aside, and casting back upon him a look of fierce enmity he strode out of the room. The old man shook his head.

While this "talk" took place at the post, the patrol at a distant point had caught thieves with cattle belonging to the drove, and in trying to reclaim them shots were fired and an Indian killed.

It was the chief's son.

The trader closed his office to seek his daughter, to whom he always came when in trouble, to borrow a little of her calm courage.

"I don't like the looks of that chief, father," she said, "but then, we have nothing to fear, for we've tried to be just to them."

"Oh, he's like all of em; they hate the whites."

A commotion in the camp drew their eyes in that direction, and they saw the scout on Kitty turn away, riding with mad haste towards the house.

"Sumpin's gone wrong," the Colonel said. Beck drew up before them, and getting down, he said to his employer:

"Has the chief been heah?"

"Yes."

"Tell me all about it; quick, Peter."

Mary stepped down from the porch, and alarmed at the scout's manner, she laid her hand on his arm, as if about to speak. He looked into the pale face at his side and said:

"Thar's no great danger now, Mary."

"But what is it?" she asked.

"You'll know as we go on; how was it, Peter?"

"Well, the redskin wanted to see inside the warehouses."

"Didn't you let him?"

"No."

"Wrong, wrong, Peter; thar's nothin in em, and he'd seen thar was nothin to steal."

"You know my rule, John."

"Go on."

"I brought him something to eat," said Mary.

"Didn't he take it?"

"No; he refused it with scorn."

"Bad."

"I saw," Mary added, "as he unfolded his blanket, the black and red stripes on his breast."

"Bad; — war-paint."

"He axed me," said her father, "if I wanted his lans."

"Go on, I see."

"I said no."

"Well."

"He was moving off, when he seed in a corner that ar compass and chain."

"What! Who put em thar?"

"That's what kinder puzzles me; the Jedge, I reckon."

"The cold-blooded idiot! Whar is he?"

"Gone!" said the voice of Doctor Tom, who had come up unnoticed and stood before them. "Yes, seh, the shark is gone. What have I told you all along? You've been feeding and feasting a scoundrel in disguise, Peter; a heartless sneak, who, having stirred the hate of these Indians by an act of treachery and a mean, secret scheme, has left us to bear the brunt." He strode off in a bad humor.

They all remembered now that for a day or two the Judge had not been seen about the place. He had, after months of waiting, accomplished his purpose and had taken the first boat to steal away from the hospitable house.

"If the shark was heah, I'd hang him," said the scout, stamping the earth in anger. "What did the chief say and do?"

"All at once, with a face as black as a cloud, he left the office, John."

"And he's raised the war-whoop and will fight us, Peter."

"Is that so?"

"True as you live."

"What do yer know, John? Tell me all."

"Twix the shark and the pirate it has been brought about."

"I treated these Injins well."

"So you did. Even Cartwright couldn't stir em up, till this pinch-faced shyster took a hand."

"What has the Jedge been doin?"

"Surveyin their lans, and the thief made em believe it was meant to steal them away."

"The Judge is a fool."

"A fool! that Judge is as bad as a pirate."

"Can't we parley with em?"

"No, it's too late; while you and the chief were talking, his son was shot by the patrol."

"Shot! I told the patrol never to fire less they was fired on."

"Jus so; they were fired on, and they fired back; I was on the plains when all this was going on, and when I came in sight they had jes brought in the body, and thar was a big rumpus. You could heah em, Peter, for a mile. I saw the chief when he came back. I saw him raise his tomahawk before the tribe, and I fled. Now, Peter," — he added slowly, — "they'll be down on us like h—ll broke loose."

If the scout had thought of Mary's presence, he would have held back his words. She was still standing near him as he spoke, biting her almost bloodless lips.

"What must I do, Mister John? Show me what I must do, I won't flinch."

"Well, Mary," he answered, and taking her hand in his, he led her to the door of the house, "I'll see that you're safe." She called Chloe, and went about her work, looking sad, but calm.

"John Beck," said the old man, as the scout joined him, "this hyar's my fight, an we'll give no quarter. The hound fus stole my chile, then he struck my trains, slayed the men; now he's comin down on us with them panthers. I'se got no marcy in my heart.'

"Fight we must, Peter, and fight our best, for they're more'n five to one of us."

"Before mornin we ken hold our own; they'll have their pow-wow an war-dance."

"That'll give us time to choke em off. I'll yoke up the teams." The scout leaped to his horse's back and rode away.

The old man entered his house, and he, who but an hour before had shown in his step the slow but sure failing of age, now moved with a firmer tread; the eyes, that now and then drooped aweary, shone with the sparkle of his youth; changed, as by magic, the face of the man was of iron; the lips closed tightly over the jutting chin. Throwing down his coat on the porch, he hurried through the hall in search of his daughter. The heavy, riveted shutters were closed and barred, and a dim light struggled through the round loop-holes, pierced at the top. He found Mary and Chloe; in every corner they had placed muskets brought from the attic arsenal. They had provisions at hand, and candlesticks and candles in handy places.

Mary saw the change in her parent's face; she threw her arms about his neck, saying:

"Let us trust in God, father; that's best."

He drew her close to him, with a fond look; then he spoke to Chloe:

"You're a good soul, old woman, an I won't forget you, neither."

"Oh, sah," she answered, with a shake of her head, "ets dat chicken, nuffin else; I dun tole yer so."

On going out again he met Beck coming from the camp with a number of men, and his horse was standing ready for him.

"Scout, I'll start the drove down country, an let the drivers give the alarm as they go."

"Right, Peter."

"Have you yoked up?"

"Yes, I'll send the stock after the drove."

"Good."

"Whar's the axes, Peter?"

"In number three, an muskets an powder enuf fer a rigiment," he answered, mounting his horse, and then galloped off.

Loud were the whip-snaps as the train came up in line; Beck's commands were heard above the din, and the sound of the axe broke in upon the babel of voices. Standing in position to direct its movements, with his sleeves rolled to the elbows, his glossy beard filling his open collar, and his form drawn to its full height, John Beck looked his best.

"Lively," he called out; "every minit counts."

Again the whips snapped fiercely. The lead team had neared the space between the office and adjoining house, when he again called out:

"Wheel in on the run."

The first wagon grazed the side of the house, the cattle coming into the circle, and when on line with its front, he ordered:

"Halt."

They were then filed in, one after the other, locking wheels, until the space between the two houses, beginning at the office, was compactly closed; all the spaces were shut up in this way, completing a circular and strong barricade around the dwelling.

While this was in progress the drive of the cattle was heard; the vaqueros spurring hither thither, on the road to the river, and thick clouds of dust rose and darkened the scene. Cheviteau was seen on his horse, and when the drove took the stream, rising the opposite bank, he rode back to the post. Beck pushed his work, and each team was taking its place, closing up the spaces.

"Now Peter," he said, in haste, "look to the wagons, I'll go to work with the axes; heah, come on a dozen of you; fall to, an let the chips fly."

Beck planted his heels where he stood; he raised his arms and his frame swayed, with his weight and strength combined; his body moving on a pivot, the axe was driven to the eye in the yielding fibre, and blocks of the green, juicy wood, flew about him.

All but one of the open spaces were closed, and Beck now hitched his teams to the fallen timber, dragging it to the barricade. Long and strong poles were trimmed, drawn up and thrust between the spokes of the front wheels, the ends resting against the storehouse fronts, holding each wagon from being drawn back; then crotches were cut, driven into the ground and set against the front axles to prevent their being forced forward; they were thus locked and blocked. This done, the tree-tops were also trimmed; poles were propped against the houses across the spaces by longer crotches, planted; then the brush was piled above the beds, interlapped between the poles and forced into a twisted mass; the abattis of sharp points reaching to the roofs.

The trader had ordered his patrol forward on the plain as skirmishers, to fall back upon a sign of the enemy. He now looked about to every need of the garrison, and with a squad drove to the river. Filling his casks, on his return two oxen were slaughtered.

Beck had thrown open the warehouses and made openings between the logs for the muskets, to drive back the savage with his torch. He found an old, but good-sized cannon, which had been bought from a wreck, and had been used on its deck as a swivel. Thrown aside as junk, Beck now put it to use.

The road to the house from the river was deeply cut into the bank, a wide defile, and led into the inclosure. Beck thought it the weakest spot of his defiance to the foe. He had crossed it with timbers and tree-tops, still it would require many men to defend it, so he masked the swivel in the brush, and having loaded it, he felt sure of its terrible aid.

Wagons were ranged inside of the barricade, from

one point to another across the space, in front of and to the rear of the dwelling, in two lines, between which the men would be stationed, and where their muskets were now stacked.

Cato and Chloe worked with a good will at the oven, and Mary overlooked the baking. She came now and then to the door of the cabin to gaze about her with restless eyes, and her father and the scout saw the look with doubt and pain.

At last, as the work was done, Beck mounted a wagon, and casting down his hat as he wiped his brow, he said, with a brave, proud smile:

"Now, d—n em, they can come; — boys, take rest."

CHAPTER XVIII.

THE ATTACK — THE BUGLE-BLAST.

As Beck threw down his hat, ordering his men to take rest, Mary rushed from the cabin kitchen, to make her way, in haste, to the mare.

"We've forgotten the women and children; come along, Mister John."

In another moment she mounted Kitty, and rode off through the one opening in the barricade. The scout on the trader's horse, rode after her.

Arriving at the hamlet she soon stilled the fears of the camp-folk, and taking up a babe from a mother who had a number of little ones clinging about her, she placed the young rogue on the saddle-bow with its smiling face turned wonderingly up to her own. She led the crowd to the house within the safer limits of the fortified inclosure, and found that her father had served to the wearied men a substantial meal. They loaded their guns as they ate. The use of buckshot and slugs was a sign of close, hot work at short range.

In the dwelling Mary looked to the comfort and needs of her small colony; the rooms were turned into a camp. In her dread, that the house might finally be made — as the fight grew to be desperate and the numbers of the foe overpowering — a place of retreat or last resort, she put the women to work, and cleared away every convenient space for full, free action. This done, they sat down in silence, listening for the yell of the foe, and the crack of the rifle.

Leading a few of the feebler children to her own room, Mary placed them on the bed to be cared for by their mothers. In a corner of the room, on a stand, rested the old family Bible. She had brought with her a musket, which she took up and held to the dim flame of the candle. Handling it firmly the light flared and threw a fitful gleam on the features of the heroic girl.

"An wat wud ye be doin wid the gun, chile?" asked a tremulous voice in the darkness.

"Heaven only grant that I need not do anything; but, if I must defend these babes from the knife, with God's help, I'll use it."

She placed the gun near the Bible stand, and passed out into the hall. The Doctor's parrot followed her; the patter of its feet on the bare hall-floor and the screech of its broken voice were dismal sounds in the solemn peace of the place.

All the day long, at the Indian village, the worst excess of the savage orgies was kept to the height of fury. The dead brave was borne from the cattle foray on the shoulders of his fellows. They strode into the dark, damp, leaf-covered abode stealthily, through lines of wailing squaws, stared at by eyes "snapping fire." Hours were given to the wild, weird rites over the slain; the chant of a few old women was caught up in the shouts of the crazed wretches. Fires high-heaped flamed aloft, and the furies leaped about them, blackening their bodies with cinders. Through it all, now and again, was heard the shriller war-whoop; the wolf-growl of the beasts. The chief sat apart, a moody ringleader of the blood-thisting crew; he was silent, conning the cruelest wiles to slay. The corpse was given up, and as the stars came out one by one, the embers of the pyre grew gray.

The savage rose, motioned to form a council of his braves, and they came together squatting in an inner circle of the wider one of the tribe beyond. The chosen few were ranged near him, to whom he drew the picture of a midnight slaughter; his appeal drew them closer, standing on their feet, to join the onset, knife in hand. The thief looked on; each painted ruffian held the best improved fire-arm of the pirate's traffic. The hour of his vengeance drew nigh.

Beck and the trader had mounted to the outlook, and watched during the long hours after dark. Just at midnight patrol-firing was heard; the scout leaped from his post, stepped into the camp and ordered the men in place. The old man followed him, standing near the opening to be ready to close it up as the mounted men rode in, and as they passed in a squad fell to work and blocked the gap.

"All heah?" asked Beck.

"All," they answered.

"Down and tie up behind the wagons," he ordered.

"Is the redskin near?" asked the trader.

"Right on us," they said.

"Light the beacon," commanded the scout, and soon the flames flashed upon the black curtain of the darkness.

In the house, the watchers waited with beating hearts.

"Hark," whispered a voice, "did yees hear the guns?"

In the dim, restless light of the candle, Mary rose and listened; listened till her face by the awful stillness paled, grew sadder, whiter, as she stood intent and breathless. Calmly she knelt down, saying:

"We will pray;" and about her they knelt, even the little ones, turning their eyes in awe upon her form, her gentle features, as upon one sent to shield them.

Save in the snapping of a twig the cat-like step of the foe was unheard; there was a spell-bound hush in the pause of caution. Through the screen of the wagons the eyes of the men were bent upon the barricade. The savages had crept from the council-fire, and they lay in sight of the white man's magic reared to foil them. Vexed to madness at what he saw, the chief gnashed his teeth, for, fearing his tribe, who would turn and rend him on the least sign of cowardice, he was compelled to fight. Whispering the signal, he took his stand on a knoll, that his voice might reach each section of the tribe. Then in the silence that dwelt around the low-breathing camps, broke in the challenge; three shrieks sped by an infernal chorus. And now the barriers swayed to the wild tiger-like assault; the devils let loose sprang to the wagons; they tugged at the wheels, leaped to the abattis, strained at the twisted tree-tops; through every gap and crevice whizzed their balls and arrows; they yelled like hungry demons, snarled like wolves, and heaped and pent upon the outer circle, they swarmed like ants.

Now was heard the sturdy voice of Beck:

"Ready — fire!" Every gun replied; the rattling shot, the singing slugs tore through the squirming mass; they fell in scores.

Outside there was a scurry of many feet, and the tribe drew back; then after a brief halt, with shrill and flurried shrieks, the redskins threw themselves again upon the barricade; they rushed to the attack through the blood-wet grass, they climbed on the bodies of the slain, scaled the housetops, hurled the tomahawk, and sent a shower of arrows; some crept under the wagons and fired; they fired from the roofs.

Once more, the calm, loud voice:

"Ready — fire!" Again the guns of the white men rattled; it was a deadly chorus; a summons of awful meaning, and the balls cut through with a singing hiss; the foe fell until all about the outer side of the defense they lay in heaps. The chief forced the fight, hurling his bands in reckless haste upon the barricade, only to be slaughtered. It was hot, close, mortal work, such as the Indian knew little about, save that in his madness he fought like a wild beast, and fearing that some agency of the daylight might bring succor to the whites, he fought on. They strained with desperate strength to tear away the twisted, web-woven lattices of green boughs; they were bent and borne down in many places by the weight hurled upon them, but they would not break, and as they leaped in bands to the wagons, Beck's voice rang out:

"Ready — fire!"

Foiled with heavy losses, driven back at every assault, the chief drew away his stricken tribe.

"Stand fast, men, thar's more to come," said Beck, as he placed his men under the trader's orders, and hastened to the house. Here he put guards at the doors, that they might be kept open, in case he had need to fall back and take shelter behind them.

The sounds of the struggle had gone out far beyond the post; every surge of the angry river caught up the crash of the guns, mingling with the yells of the horde, and bore them away for miles. They were heard by the "Pioneer's" captain, who stood still and listened long. Again he heard the crack of the muskets louder than before, and he ordered silence on deck. Now the far-away volley came clearly to his ears.

"Did you hear that, Carver?" he said to his clerk.

"I heard it, captain."

"What do you make it out to be?"

"Don't know, sir, but I fear—"

"Well, your fears; quick."

"Then Cheviteau's post is struck by the Indians; that's my belief."

The d—l," he answered, in his rude, off-hand manner, "we must take a hand."

On the lower deck he said to his mate:

"Send the gang aft."

"Who, Captain?"

"The roustabouts, be quick."

When they came to him, and he had drawn the rough crowd around him, he first warmed up their courage with a friendly grog, and had stirred their mettle with an oath or two, when he told them that the savage was at his hellish trade, and the defenseless trader at his mercy. He was answered by a shout. The captain steamed up till the boiler hummed, and dropped his landing plank on the wharf. Under the bluff he had moved along unseen by the Indians, unheard in the clamor of the fight.

"Go, young man," he said to Carver, who had volunteered to lead, "you owe this to your old employer; go, and you'll never need a friend while I live."

Jumper led noiselessly up the roadway at the head of the crew. The captain stayed by his craft, as he was in honor bound. Tim Murphy, with a lighted torch, stood at the swivel, and catching a glimpse of the steamer's lights, and hearing the English of those who drew near, he let them pass under the logs.

"Who's this?" cried Beck, as the young man stood before him.

"It's me, — Jumper."

"Jumper; well done, boy."

"Where's the Colonel?"

"Come here." The scout went with him to the trader.

"Here I am, sir," he said to the old man; "I've come, and have brought help with me to do what I can in the fight."

"An I like you for it, Harry; it's right manly in you to come; put him to work, scout; but mind, lad, it's death work."

"Come heah, Jumper; bring your men," said Beck.

Carver had jumped at the chance to regain the good-will of the trader; he had felt abashed from the day he left the post, and the scout now stationed him at the swivel, with his men filed behind in the brush, on guard over the road. As Beck turned away, the sudden alarm of the crowd stayed his steps.

"Look there," said one. A bright red flame-flare fell upon the camp; it lighted the wide expanse, and a stream of light, thrown back from the hamlet of cabins, disclosed them all ablaze. In the glow of their burning homes the men saw the red foe, a countless swarm, ten to one of them they seemed, piling the fagots and leaping from house to house. The keen sight of the scout singled out the chief; at his side was Cartwright, the evil spirit of this terrible, hell-bred madness, who urged him on. And now as the flames rolled up out of the darkness, they drew from gray-capped clouds the gleams of day; morning burst upon a scene of blood, of smoke and ruin.

The dawn-light turned the savages to another onslaught; the scout saw that the pirate had planned it.

One section of the tribe, led by the chief, moved along to the front of the inclosure. They came on in a run, and the raking fire ordered by Beck checked them but an instant; they passed on at safe distance, around to the left of the barricade, to crouch behind a building, which the scout had found locked.

"See, Peter," he said, "they'll burn that storehouse to make a breach."

"They ken do it, John; but jes look out."

"For what?"

The trader bent his head to the other's ear and whispered; his face grew dark as he spoke:

"It's full of powder, man."

"But the men —"

He strode off to each armed group of his brave fellows, cautioned them in haste, and moved the wagons in readiness to bar the gap.

The Indians clung close about the house; a few ran off, and the scout said:

"They've gone for wood to light the fire."

Creeping back from cover to cover, those who bore the fuel for the fated building stole from bush to bush under a galling fire; a few fell, some fled, but a number reached the powder-house. Soon the roaring of the flames was heard, and on the margin of the black, close cloud of smoke, the pirate and the chief were seen. The lingering climax of the fight was the slow burning fire.

On the floor of the magazine grains of powder lay scattered, by careless handling, much like a bait to a hidden trap, and as the blaze lapped the bark and crept through each chink and crevice, a lighted coal dropped down. There was a sound of thunder, a cloud-burst tremble of the air, earthquake and storm, and through the battle-smoke and the sunshine a thousand flaming splinters fell, like a miracle; the rent frame reeled and came down, the barrier was broken. Clan after clan sprang on the blackened ruin in the teeth of an enfilade of slug and buck-shot; files aimed and fired; others toiled with amazing strength and closed the break with wagons; the Colonel cheered "his boys," his white head seen above their line.

Now a yell rang through the swivel-guarded defile, and Carver saw a horde leap into the roadway, coming on with knife and tomahawk — along the bluff line from right and left — to tear away his ambush and strike him down. He had but time to snatch a coal and fire the cannon; a stern, terrific sweep it was, hurled by the rusty piece. The pass was choked with the dead and dying; still another band leaped into the gorge, while the whites with frantic haste reloaded, as the Indians, crowding close, came on again. Carver touched the match and, boy-like, cheered; his men once more seized the swivel to repeat; the foe in crowds gained ground, firing as their numbers doubled; they pressed hard. Torch in hand, in the flush of youthful pride, the young man fired his gun again, leaping to the front to see the havoc of its loud-mouthed vengeance. He waved his hat — rash fellow! A dozen rifles covered his form, and in an instant stricken down, he fell into the arms of the scout, who reposed the lifeless body and covered it with his blouse.

The swarm bore down the tree tops, but the deck-hands were an ugly lot to handle. Caught at large on the wharves of the western cities, they were no mean hand-to-hand fighters; they fought with sheath-knives, clubs and musket-butts, and one, a buffer, struck out from the shoulder, felling his man at every blow. Beck was in the thick of it; he had borne the brunt all day, and hemmed in, his form rose up like a giant's, his voice calm, but his strength prodigious. Once he was seen to seize a savage bodily, and dash him with a deadly force back into the pass.

Loud screams were now heard coming from the house, the cry of the little ones and the shrill, pleading voices of the women. Beck's grip relaxed, the brave man's heart was stilled; breaking through the lines of hate-hot men, he ran wildly to the door of the dwelling.

A few of the red dare-devils stole to the porch, climbed it, passed through the windows and down to the floor below, and as the scout forced his form into the hall he helped the guards to fight back the intruders; he saw them driven to the field; all but one. At the door of Mary's room a long-remembered sight thrilled him; a tall, fear-stricken savage drew back amazed; within the darkened place, where the low light of the candle flared, Beck saw a group of babes behind the form of Mary; she stood still, poised like a marble image, her long black hair uncoiled and her dark eyes fixed upon the lean, cold steel of the musket. Not a tremor of her little white hands, not a twitch in the sad, rigid face, not a muscle moved; a death-like, daring moment; the travail of a woman's strength, the acme of human courage.

The Indian leaped through the door and was gone; Beck, speaking fast, said:

"Well Mary! — good God; stand fast, you're worth a hundred men; it'll soon be over;" he, too, was gone, for the fight lagged without him.

At the garret window, during all this fatal turmoil, the parrot looked on, and in a loud, cross screech, cried out:

"Stop't — Mary — stop't — stop't."

In a corner near by the imp had crept behind a bed, the space that held him smaller than his proper self, and never before had spook or witch so paled the color of his skin.

Doctor Tom was busy; many were wounded, many slain; he turned the storerooms into hospitals, as they brought the brave fellows to him, one by one. He was seen here and there with lint and bandage, and now and then his face grew almost black with rage; they heard his whispered wrath.

"D — n shark; curse him."

At the gap where the trader fought there was desperate fighting; there the thief skulked, watched with eager eyes, and as the Colonel's "boys" fell back to load their guns, he made a dash, tripped the old man's feet and fell upon him heavily. As he raised his knife a hundred hands seized him; they lashed him to a wheel, and but for the scout they would have shot him to death. Hurt deeply, the Colonel on rising reeled like a drunken man; helped on by Tim, he dragged his feet to the house. Mary saw him coming:

"Father, father, are you shot?" As she spoke, her cheek was paler than when the savage came upon her.

"No, chile," he said, feebly; "in here, in here," and entering a door, he fell upon a bed in a faint.

The redskins drew back for the final rally, and were divided as before, into two bands. The sleuth-hounds sprang from cover, with the cry of a hungry pack. Again they tugged at the abattis; again they choked the narrow channel, and the larger band, led by the chief, made a last and furious onset. The tug had come; the odds against the whites began to tell in the hoarse cries of the infuriated men, as they fell, and the scout began to feel the cold chill of doubt:

"Ready! ——"

Hark! Like a voice from heaven, a bugle's note was heard faintly in the far bright distance; louder and louder on the air it sped its challenge.

Mary heard it; she ran to the porch and in an ecstasy of hope she climbed upon a wagon, her hair the sport of the wind; she clapped her hands, waved them over the head of Cartwright.

The savages broke away; Beck drew himself up to the tree tops, and the men saw a troop of horsemen swooping down upon them.

"Thank God," he cried, as he threw up his hat; "Hoop-ee, Bob Harkness is on hand."

On came the furious riders, sweeping the plain, tearing down upon the fleeing redskins, firing their pistols with shouts, their horses leaping to the charge with snort and kick, unreined. The men within the barricade laid down their arms to listen.

And now Beck heard the old familiar war-cry, "Draw — sabres!" and he knew that the agony was over.

CHAPTER XIX.

TWO DEATHS — BECK'S DUTY.

Captain Harkness rode up to meet the scout.
" Who sent you to us ? "
" Good luck, I reckon, Beck."
" What brought you in from the fort, Captain ? "
"They say I have slaughtered women and children ; " the rich, round laugh was tinged with scorn.

"They lie, I'll swear," said Beck, and while he thought upon the recall of so good an officer, he knew that some confederate of the Judge had aided it, and that the charge against him was an old slander of the sharks and pirates.

"I'll camp my men, Beck."
" Down and let 'em shake the kinks out."
" Not now." As the troop moved away one of the riders said to his file :
"They'se had a high old time, them boys."

Beck with his doubts alive as to the trader's condition, wrote a line to Whack, and sent it with the Captain's despatches by the "Pioneer."

The worn-out men had stretched themselves to rest about the barricade, and Beck borne down alike, threw himself on the ground ; as the stars shed a pale light on the camp where the day had seen the flames of strife, sleep enthralled him where he lay. Late in the night Mary came to the door to catch the sweet, cool breeze from the plain, and saw the huge form lying at full length; she went out to look upon the brave giant as he slept like a big, overgrown boy; she turned about hastily and came again with a robe, which she spread over the sleeper with gentle care. She sat for the rest of the night, with the Doctor, at her father's bedside.

Just after the fight, the threats of the men, overheard by Beck, cautioned him that the thief might be lynched, and fearing it, he laid hold on Cartwright, saying:

"Come with me; you'll swing for this business, if I have to ride a hundred miles."

Forcing the pirate ahead of him to the haunted cabin, he there bound him to the logs inside, and placed an armed teamster on guard.

The night to the wretch had been one of sore trial; in the ghastliness of his guilt his fears of the supernatural took strange and hideous forms, and the dying out of an unnatural strength from strong drink, left him in the throes of a fevered brain. Every sound that came to his ears resembled the tramp of some one he feared; he raved with deadly blasphemy, and endured the ferocity of suffering. The scout's strong hands had tied his arms and fettered his ankles. What might rise in judgment before his captive, Beck had not thought of, but the darkest dungeon never conjured spectres such as came to haunt the prisoner's vision; sights which only the besotted ever see. Out of the ruined chimney-place came an accusing spirit in the grave-shroud, and Cartwright cowered like a shrinking dog. Throwing up his arms in piteous fright, great drops of sweat fell from him; he dragged at his cords.

In the summer storm a poor, drenched outcast crept from bush to bush. The troopers had met him far out on the prairie, as they rode in a slow trot coming East, but he was then so common a sight to all who travelled the road, they would have passed him by but for his pitiful pleading. When they gave ear to his words, they heard that the post was attacked, and throwing him bread from their haversacks, with a shout they sprang forward on the run. Fast as his limbs could move he followed them.

Far aloft in gloomy grandeur the storm-clouds rose; curve sweeping curve to towering peak darkening deeper and blacker; the lightning glared on the shadowy cloud-cliffs and sharp-lined slopes, and now its hot floods rolled like lava; the winds came and a howling chaos of rain and flame caught up the wanderer like one consumed in fire. From its fury he had stolen near the cabin, and when the shower was spent he stood near enough to be heard in his muttering:

"Just sixteen years to-day," — he paused; "and she was just sixteen," — he paused again; "and then that viper came. Come down, come down, give me strength to smite — to slay." Now tugging at his girdle he drew forth the trooper's pistol, looked at it closely as time and time again he had done, since he found it.

Now the sun shone brightly and the scout had called the prison guard to breakfast; he was about to take the man's place when the trader sent for him.

Among the ruins of his former home lurked the crazy tramp. He gazed upon them, his sight resting on the form of Cartwright, and in imagination he saw the demon of his long years of misery. For the moment it was an insane vagary, for the thief's silence fed the delusion. The wanderer fell to work to dispel it by lighting a fire.

Every chance meeting of the thief with his fright had been such as to increase his fears, and to strengthen his belief in a ghost; he had crossed the lunatic's path suddenly at all times, in places lonely and obscure, and was halted by him with startling threats. Now the dread presence that he feared the most had come upon him, and he was held by thongs that would not yield; it glared at him and seemed to gloat upon his plight. Where he stood he seemed drawn to the horror; then with all his strength he tugged and strained again, like an animal entrapped; worn down, his head fell like a bull's; he swore aloud. The fire was kindled at the log to which the rope that held him was fastened, but his tongue let slip his only chance of escape.

While the scout stayed with her father, Mary made up her mind to visit the prisoner; she had filled her basket, and under the napkin, resting on ripe fruit, was laid the Bible; she was near the ruin, when, looking up, she saw the smoke and heard high words.

The curses of the pirate, his voice, his manner and his face awakened the wild man's wits; in a lucid instant he saw writhing before his eyes the living, actual thing his hate had held to for long, long years; he snatched his pistol and leaped to the cabin door. Just then the rope that held the prisoner parted; he sprang up, loosed his toils, and drew one free breath, — one only. There was a snap, a flash; the dull thud of a fallen body. Strengthless and bloody it lay stricken in its full force; the limbs flexed, an outstretched arm; dead as one before the flood — dead as a stone. In the smoke of his weapon stood the unhappiest among the living; the fire of his passion out, the ashes cold and gray on his heart.

Mary cried for help, and turned from the sight, shading her face; the scout soon joined her, he glanced at the victim and the slayer.

"Bad as the worst may be, Mister John," said the voice at his side, "He pitied and forgave."

"As you say, Mary," he answered, then turning and taking her hand, he led her away.

The crowd seized and bound the lunatic, and hardly a word was spoken, for the majesty of death was terribly enthroned on the lifeless trunk.

> "Thou dost avenge,
> In thy good time, the wrongs of those who know
> No other friend;
>
> The wicked but for Thee
> Had been too strong for the good of earth."

Captain Harkness and his men left the post, taking with them the wild man, to be placed in an asylum at Saint Louis.

Some weeks further on Lu and Whack — Mr. and Mrs. Charles Marshall — arrived by boat.

Mary's looks had altered much during the little while they had been absent, and care had worn deeply into her spirit.

"So much strife and misery, Lu, since you left us," she said; "and the worst is yet to come," turning her streaming eyes to the bed where her father lay.

"You will let me be nurse now, Mary, won't you?" her friend asked, throwing her arms about Mary's neck.

Doctor Tom came in, and feeling the patient's pulse, he said as he withdrew:

"You need not repeat the medicine, Mary."

The scout followed him from the room, where he had taken his turn in watching.

"He may not last through the day," the Doctor answered gravely to the question put to him; "he has internal injuries, Beck, which cannot be reached."

"And thar's no chance for his life?" asked the latter, with much feeling in his voice.

"None; and Beck, you must tell his poor child; I've not the nerve to do so."

In a few moments after this conversation Beck met Whack.

"The Doctor has jus told me that Peter can't live."

"I feared so," Whack replied in a spasm of grief,

and his friend left him in sorrow so keen he would not disturb it.

"Come, Mary,"— he said, in his straightforward way when prompted by a sense of duty — as he entered the room, and his voice was very kind; "come out for a breath of air, Lu will stay till you come;" he took her hand in his, leading her to the porch. There they were seated, and raising her head her face was so purely pale, the scout, who was about to speak, faltered.

"Do you think that father is better or worse, Mister John?" she asked, with a searching glance into her friend's face.

Taking her hand again in his, he said slowly, as if each word was a pain:

"He never can be better, Mary."

The long suspense was broken by the touch of the simplest words; for a brief second the blackness of despair seemed to hold her eyelids down; again the manly tones of his voice were heard, and she felt the tight-drawn misery of her heart relax; she wept aloud.

Beck rose, and suddenly he laid his big, broad, tender hand, with a touch as gentle as the girl's, on her brown hair, and pressed it down; again and again he pressed it, as if the touch drew to his heart some of her sorrow, and he said:

"You'll never want a friend, Mary, while John lives."

She turned her tear-wet face with a look that sank

into his sight to be held there always; and she answered him:

"I know it, Mister John; God bless you."

When the two went back to the room the sick man lay in an easy sleep; the pain had passed away, and had left an eager innocence on the aged features, the stamp of a frank, single-hearted nature. His form was the remnant of an athletic life, sinewy and strong even now; all was calm, there was no passion to throb the heart; in truth he had but two passions through all his life, a love for his child, a pride in his trade; the first had tamed the sharp points of his character; the latter had given him a method to do the best at once; with both he seemed to have grown lighter hearted as he became older headed. His thoughts were far away from his people; he spoke to his horse in his dream, the horse on which he was again crossing the plain; he urged him on with feeble voice. His friends stood about his bed, and outside on the green, groups from the camp sat and waited with downcast looks.

Still the sleeper sped on over the waste, the howling savage at his heels; he raised his form suddenly from the bed, waving his hand, and falling back, he murmured:

" Safe; safe.'

"The Indians were after him in his vision," said Mary, in a whisper; "he has crossed the river again."

"True, my child," replied Doctor Tom, touching the patient's forehead, "he has crossed the river of Life."

With a low, choking sob, and with a tearless face growing fixed, Mary stood up:

"I know he's safe on the other side," she faltered, when Beck with manly haste caught her up in his arms, as he would a child, and bore her from the room.

"She's my baby now," said old Chloe, following them.

The crowds from the camp came and stood about the place, with every token of a deep respect, and on the morning of another day, in line they moved away from the house, passing out under the bison's head to the prairie. They rested the bier where in life he had wished to lie. Each man, in turn, cast a handful of earth on the coffin, and from the silence of the sleep eternal they moved away. In the sunset glowing with rich, warm beauty on the mound their hands had raised, they left the aged sleeper.

> "And greatly would their hearts rejoice
> To hear again, his living voice."

Far away from the sick man's couch, while he lay in pain; from the wretch's hell while he writhed in toils; from the cots of the wounded, the Judge and his fellows feasted. The lobby's scheme lay before them; they laughed and drank and were merry. The plot on the table was a demand for the Indians' land, drawn by the Judge; he considered it the cleverest effort of his smartness. Whether he knew that graves had been filled to pay for a sharper's folly, or that the kind host whose friendship he had trifled with, had been snatched away by Death, matters little; would matter but little to him. Type of the trickster, all the world over a trickster is a sneak; a sneak, the meanest thing on earth.

There were legal as well as business needs that the will should be opened; Beck and Whack felt that it must be attended to.

"Jus say what we shall do, Mary," said the scout.

"I believe father has named some of the men in the will, and it ought to be read aloud before all."

"If you say so, to-morrow morning I'll bring em here."

When they had come together, Beck unfolded the brown paper envelope, and read:

THE LAST WILL AND TESTAMENT OF PIERRE CHEVITEAU, TRADER. It had been written by some careful agent, and very little that had ever moved his respect was left out. First, his beloved daughter claimed "his whole heart," and to her he willed the bulk of his property; to Beck and Marshall, equal shares in the trade with Mary, and large sums of money. The will set apart a tract, upon which stood the post and camp, for a town site to be called MARYSVILLE; also sums in trust for the building of the school-house and the church. To old Chloe he gave a house and a small dowry; to the imp his freedom; to each of his faithful men who had served him a given time, he gave a tract of land with money, and when it was the wish of one or all to work the soil on their own account, a team of cattle to each, "to begin as he had done, in the snap o' the whip."

At the last clause Beck folded the paper without reading further, and placed it in his blouse; his face changed and his hands were unsteady, but Whack said:

"I think that the will should be sent below, at once, and I should be in New York; don't you think Mary ought to go with us, as far as Saint Louis, to stay there with her friends till her troubles are over?"

"Jus so; I wanted to say that; get your wife to tell her."

He left Whack hurriedly, entered the office and closed the door behind him; he locked it, placing a chair at the table, and laid the paper before him as he sat down; he read the last sentence aloud:

"Before bidding farewell to those so dearly beloved in life, it is the long-cherished wish of my heart that John Beck and Mary, my daughter, should become man and wife, as I believe it to be the wish of their own hearts."

He read the words again and again, then turning down the sheet, he laid his head on it and groaned.

It was agreed that Mary would go with her friends to Saint Louis, and remain there some time, and the Doctor, seized with what they all thought to be a whim, joined the party.

"Beck," he said, "when I'm gone, open that mahogany case of mine, and read what you find there. If I don't turn up soon, you are at liberty to keep the papers, or burn them, as you please."

"Why are you going; what's the matter?" asked Beck.

"I don't mind saying to you, old fellow, that I'm going to find the Judge."

"What for, Doctor? he ain't worth looking for."

"Ain't he? He'll think so when we meet, seh; I'm going to call him out; call him out, do you understand me?"

No persuasion of the other to cool the fire in the veins of the little, old man, availed the least. The next boat bore them away, and the scout stood gazing after them until the steamer dwindled to a speck on the shining surface of the river. Beck turned about, and with strange emotion he said:

"I must do my duty; when it's done and she knows all, I'll take to the road again."

Through the long winter he toiled late and early to carry out every project or purpose expressed by his former patron. He tore down the abattis; the storehouses were moved away and turned into dwellings; rebuilt and whitened, they dotted the green outlying knolls. The camp was moved beyond the thickets, and where the corral stood was now an open common. A saw-mill on the river bank was kept busy; the wharf was widened by cutting into the bluff; the school and the church were begun, and the arch over the portal of the latter bore Mary's chosen inscription:

"*Where the spirit of the Lord is, there is liberty.*"

Tim Murphy turned an eye to the main chance, and drawing on his legacy, he laid out some of it, in material for "*The Bullwhacker's Inn.*" In time it was completed, — hastened on by the personal labor and care of the owner, — with a swinging sign the wonder of the village, and its two stories the marvel of the rustics. Then a farmer started a line of road-wagons, called stages, and noised his coming through a tin horn to the alarm of the urchins and the colored folk; next, a barn was needed. One of the larger log-houses was furnished with rude store fixtures; a large storehouse at the landing finally bore on its broad, white front, in deep, black letters:

Beck, Marshall & Co.

with Mary as the silent partner.

Beck never wearied; the labor he had set about to perform, and what he believed would have been his old friend's wish, had requited but little the pain he seemed to suffer. The man was worn to a shadow and the smile from his fine face was gone. He had tugged on, holding his course without a word of complaint, not caring for praise, nor for censure. He had earnestness, and his strength was untamable, but the trial seemed almost deadly in the traces it left on his form and features. Coolness and restraint, the habit of a life full of peril, were still his, but his lips seemed to be sealed, by as strong a clasp as honor. He toiled on with a strength he never felt before through a wild, strange longing; it was neither the lash of self-rebuke nor self-hate; no sign of remorse tinged his unhappiness.

In the brighter, warmer days of the early spring, he put the painters to work on the house and brightened the old place in and out. Then he sat down, wrote a line to Mary, saying:

"Come."

She started for home in company with Marshall and his wife, and Mr. Foster, a preacher, came with them on an errand to consecrate the new church. Beck led Mary from the boat. What he said was, as of old, the frank greeting of a companion, a little grave but still hearty. He went with her to a seat on the rear porch in the purple light strained through the morning-glories, and left her there, charmed with her surprise, and in the arms of old Chloe.

He found Whack — for such he would ever be to Beck — and showed everything new, and dwelt upon, as they passed along, the future wants of the trade.

"It's all just as it ought to be," said Whack, "I could almost manage things myself."

"Could you?" asked the other quickly, and when his partner started at the sudden answer, and turned his face to his friend's, he was forced to say:

"You've worked too hard, scout, you show the strain."

CHAPTER XX.

THE MAHOGANY CASE.

Doctor Tom was put ashore at a little village and taking a stage from thence, soon reached the capital of the State.

Bad news travels fast, but it had not been swift enough to outrun the Doctor. He would have been the first messenger to deliver the ill-tidings of the disaster at the post, had he not thought best to keep silent.

Judge Smith, and the combination of which he was the moving spirit, had heard good news from Washington. They had been assured by a letter received on the day of the Doctor's arrival, that steps would be taken in the near future, to remove the Indians from the reservation which adjoined Cheviteau's. The subject, it went on to say, had received the attention of the Department, and it was thought expedient, owing to the too close proximity of the savages to the whites, to remove them to a less exposed location. Such was the pompous phrasing of an extract from an official letter received by one of their friends from the Indian office.

The knot of speculators came together in a back room of the town tavern and held council. At such a conference, the prerequisite to formulate their proceedings was a liberal supply of "corn-juice."

Judge Smith was particularly happy, in fact delighted, and showed his satisfaction by an eager claim of leadership, and an over allowance of credit for "working the thing through."

"It's the finest piece of wild land in the West," he said, "and I've been all over it; the soil is a black, rich loam, ten feet in depth, and as for the timber, gentlemen, there ain't a wood that grows but can be found there."

"There won't be much trouble with Injins, I reckon," suggested one of the cabal.

"Not much," said the Judge with a knowing look; "you know the army has to carry out the order."

"Is there any good town sites?" queried a third.

"Town sites!" laughed his honor; "why, the first thing I intend to do is to run opposition to old Cheviteau; set up a post against his, work him out of his landing and build up a town right under his nose."

"Yes, he's too old and slow for these times; have you staked your claim, Judge?"

"Certainly, and I reckon you'll all admit my claim to the best as just."

"Thar's jes one thing I don't like about this move," said a gruff speaker, and a man who, by his manner, seemed a little cautious.

"What's that?" asked one near him.

"Why, jus this; if them Injins get an inkling of this, they'll like as not get red hot and then—"

"Well, what then?" spoke up the Judge.

"They'll murder every man, woman and child at the post."

The speaker's words were cut short, for without so much as a knock, an officious waiter threw open the door, and in walked the small, well-knit form of Doctor Tom.

Glancing about him restlessly, as some of the party rose from their chairs, he singled out the Judge and made up to him with short, quick steps.

"Hello, Doctor Tom, is that you?" said the Judge in a free flow of humor, as he offered his hand.

"Drop your hand, seh," said the Doctor, halting; "it is stained with blood; it's the hand of a coward. Gentlemen," he said, turning to the crowd, "the Indians on the border have risen and they have attacked Cheviteau's post. This man I charge with being the prime cause of the massacre. Don't you believe me?" he continued, turning round; "go out then, the mail-stage is at the door; it brings the news." This was a ruse of the Doctor to clear the room, and hardly a moment elapsed, even while he spoke, when they all hurried off. The Judge was about to follow, forgetful of the affront put upon him in his haste to learn the worst, but with a spring the Doctor reached the door, closed it, locked it and placed the key in his pocket. He had shut out all except himself and the Judge.

"Now, seh," he said, turning to the other, "we can have it out alone. Peter Cheviteau is dead, and scores of his brave men have been slaughtered through your infernal trickery. You enjoyed the hospitality of my friend's house to betray him to the fiendish malice of the savage. You knew the evil your secret scheme might bring upon him, upon the heads of helpless women, upon babes and children. I repeat, seh, you're a coward."

The Judge had been so suddenly confronted with the irate little man, and his announcement of so startling a nature, he was slow to recover. But the Doctor while he spoke had drawn from the inside pockets of his coat a pair of pistols, and laid them on the table before him.

Now a rap was heard at the door.

"Take the choice of these weapons, seh. I am the friend of Peter Cheviteau, and over his grave I demand satisfaction of you."

The noise at the door of voices and confusion increased.

"Take one," said the Doctor, "I'll give you a chance for your life; if you don't, I'll shoot you down like a dog."

A voice outside cried:

"Let us in or we'll break down the door."

Whether it was the nearness of his companions, or the fear of showing cowardice, which even they would not brook, the Judge plucked up courage, and at last found voice to say:

"If nothing else will do, take your place." He spoke loudly, and taking up one of the pistols he turned towards the end of the table.

The door was pounded heavily, and a number of men without talked in an excited manner.

"Are you ready?" asked the Doctor, in a steady voice.

Just then the door gave way, and the crowd rushed in to seize the Doctor's upraised arm with the finger on the trigger. Both men were disarmed, and pocketing his weapons the excited old man hastened from the room.

At the door he turned and said:

"Judge Smith, I here publicly challenge you to fight this out, and leave you with your friends to decide upon the time and place. If you do not accept, seh, you are what I have denounced you for, a trickster and a poltroon;" and he walked away.

"Oh, I would have shot him," said the Judge boastingly to the group; "in another minute, gentlemen, he would have been a dead man. Immediately after he locked the door and offered the pistols, I seized one, covered him, and made him take back his insult; if he hadn't he would have been slain."

The end of the affair was inglorious. Doctor Tom waited several days for the satisfaction he had so rashly sought, but the friends of the Judge, upon due consideration, with his ready acquiescence, declined the meeting.

The Doctor was also kindly persuaded by some of the wiser heads of the place to forego a duel with a man who was not in any sense his equal, and to whom he gave an equal chance for life with himself as the party aggrieved. Not entirely satisfied with the logic of such advice, the Doctor was, nevertheless, content to post the Judge in a weekly paper, and shaking the dust of a place he contemned from his feet, he soundly abused his adversary and departed. The next seen of the fiery little champion, he was on his way to the post.

On entering the house Beck called to mind the last words of Doctor Tom, and going into the deserted chamber he found the mahogany case on the window sill. It was unlocked and he raised the lid. Two compartments which from their shape he knew had held a pair of duelling pistols, were empty; in another a closely folded manuscript, which showed its age in the brown tinge of the paper, caught his eye; as this, he supposed, was what his old friend desired that he should read, he took it out to peruse it.

It was a document of some length, written in a round, legible hand, and began, without preface, the recital of an episode in the fitful career of the writer.

"My father," the writing began, "inherited a very comfortable income which he spent early in life through the temptations of youth and a love of display. He had just entered manhood, and a fortune misspent at such a time clouds the future and dampens the ardor of the bravest. At this trying time to be deeply, madly in love with a very poor but a very pretty woman was unfortunate, and his infatuation carried him into wedlock with scarcely enough between the two to set the pot boiling. The match was sneered at by his friends and relatives, and truth to say he found little in common with the partner of his bosom. She was illiterate, coarse, and their married life, though of short duration, was not happy. The wife died and left a son. My father's fortunes improved but little during the infancy of the child, and through boyhood his education was sadly neglected. The lad was bright and apt, and not to grow up a dolt, he taught himself much of what he knew; not a little, for he was a close reader.

"It was said of my parent that he was a handsome man, of winning manners, and some accomplishments, and with such, in those days when beaux were few, was to be much admired.

"Some years further on, he ceased to be a widower. Having met a lady, between whom and himself there sprung up a mutual and decided admiration, he paid her his devoirs with the most assiduous gallantry. She possessed a very large estate; he literally nothing, with the incumbrance of the boy aforesaid. But they were married in good time, and in the further course of events I was the fruit of that union.

"To pass over much that belongs to a truthful history it will suffice to reach the purpose of this memorandum to say, that both my parents died leaving me in possession of a fortune. I pass over also the intervening years of my college training.

"Meanwhile my half brother, Tobias, had grown up to be a quiet, inoffensive sort of fellow, but like his father before him, had taken hold on matrimony, with the same disregard of proprieties, and with the same penniless risks. My own remonstrance was all in vain, and besides we became in a measure estranged. The woman he married was by no means his equal in any respect, but he married; that was the long and short of it.

"There was a large barbacue near by the town in which we lived, and very distinguished men were invited to address the people. The best people of that section were there also, and altogether it was the most notable event of the year. My brother was there with his wife; my mother's relations were present also, and while he was kindly and courteously received he made little progress in helping himself to their better acquaintance. It was while we were both standing in the group of happy faces, he with a bashful hesitancy of manner, that the young sprig of a wealthy lawyer, much the worse for his libations, rudely broke in upon our company. Tobias, who until then had given but little sign of interest in what was passing, now rose to his feet, and in a very respectful way tried to persuade the intruder to pass on. What was my surprise, and not less that of the entire assemblage whose notice had been drawn to the loud voice of the tipsy upstart, when he turned suddenly and in a violent rage struck my brother full in the face. Not content with this gross affront, he coupled it with language the most vile, insulting the name of my brother's mother, and heaping upon him the rudest abuse. Friends interfered, the men were separated, but not before I had gone to a brother of the rowdy and said:

"'So soon as he is sober he must apologize or fight.'

"Days passed and the town talk, as well as the whispers which passed from the lips of the men of note who had seen the insult, all agreed that there was nothing my brother could do, but to demand from his assailant the proper satisfaction. To learn how far he was prepared for this just demand in the vindication of his honor, I went to see him.

"I had not known until told by others that Tobias was a member of a church, and a strict conformist to the morals of his faith. This, however, made no impression on my well conceived ideas of his duty as a man.

"On meeting him he made no hesitation in saying that he should let the matter pass, and that he forgave the rudeness in the belief that the man was not himself. I urged in vain, that he had no right to evade the responsibility; that the affront was an open insult to the family name; that his alternative would drive him from the community branded as a coward, and that if he did not himself challenge the offender forthwith, I would myself do so, and take upon myself the sole charge of the affair But, I added, it would cause, of course, a severance of all affectionate relations between us.

"He begged to be allowed to consider, and I left him with the conviction that I would have to fight the fellow myself. In station he was my equal, and fully equal to the mischief he could make out of it. Time passed and my brother was fast becoming a butt, sneered at and shunned by his associates, and publicly avoided as one disgraced. But the crisis came in a most unexpected way, and put an end to the strain and fever I endured.

"My brother's insulter was a born bully, and without provocation and only to gain notoriety had he committed the assault. Now to gain a little more bad eminence, and to flaunt another feather of the bravado with his like, to prove the cowardice which he said belonged to us, he challenged my brother, making a pretense of some fancied wrong.

"On the instant, much to my surprise, Tobias accepted the challenge, and by right of what had passed between us he insisted that I should second him in the field. We went out, and on the first fire he shot his antagonist dead." *

At this point of the reading, Beck impatiently spoke his thoughts aloud.

"That's all stuff," he said, "brave men know better; every time that bully showed up he oughter been put down; I'd a lammed him outer his boots."

The scout gave a long-drawn sigh, either in disgust of his surroundings, or in his contempt of the wingless Florimel, which the Doctor spoke of as honor. His thoughts ran astray, and the old sore seemed to

---

* The writer prefers to interpret the feeling of the time, in regard to the duel, as near as may be in the words of one who favored the barbarous practice That one professing religion could engage in mortal combat of the kind, persuaded to it by his own brother, and return to the fold after slaying his adversary, is not an overdrawn picture, and is founded on a fact. It needs no garnishing.

bleed afresh; his eyes were set upon the floor before him, but arousing from the reverie, he turned to the paper and read on.

"Tobias Shorter after this became a changed man. His soul seemed to have been moved deeply. He became a schoolmaster, and it was his habit to read the Bible to his pupils, and this so often repeated, with ponderings upon the text, he laid by in memory the best of its traditions and in his heart all of its lessons. It happened, at this time, that a religious panic seized the minds of the people, wherein masses were swayed by an unwonted fervor, and he, a sensitive and profound believer, was swept into the frenzy. At large musters, in camps and meeting-houses, none exhorted with the fiery vehemence of Tobias; none so ardently besought to repentance, or prayed with the same intense and frantic ecstasy of faith. He went about from house to house; along the roads he was seen at unseemly hours, halting the traveller to warn or to upbraid him; in class and church he led in praise and protestation. His school was closed; he was really already mad, but induced to seek the wilderness, with the promise of work in the vineyard, he left the town, and it is said that his reason failed. I never saw him after this." Here the manuscript ended.

As Beck refolded the screed and was about to replace it in its place, he kept repeating the name of the Doctor's brother as one he had surely heard before.

"Tobias; Tobias Shorter; I've heard that somewhar; let me see;" then suddenly he remembered to have heard the Colonel tell the story of the haunted cabin, wherein he spoke of one Tobias, and weighing the coincidence he followed out the trace to the wild man of the plains, and further to the lunatic in the asylum. "Sure enuf that's him I reckon, an the Doctor doesn't know it, neither. Well, well," he said, as he was about to close the case. But his eye discovered another manuscript, and taking it out he read what seemed to be the Doctor's suggestions as to the proper mode of treating the Indians. Without heading or a word of comment, the unexplained notes laid down certain ideas which were those which he often expressed openly:

"Put the tribes so far apart that they can't form combinations.

"What's the use or sense of a treaty with a savage?

"No more treaties should be made with the Indians; those now binding should be abrogated.

"The system should be changed, and the Indians brought directly and individually under the laws.

"Magistrates should be appointed* to enforce in each tribe, or on each reservation, the criminal laws of the United States, with power to call upon the army at any and all times to carry out their decisions and orders.

"The squaw-men (pirates), whites, Mexicans and negroes, should be put away from the reservations and not be permitted to live with or go among the Indians.

---

* The Indian boys now being educated, if trustworthy.

"Cohabitation, miscalled marriage, with Indian women should be punished.

"Liquors, arms, ammunition and property of any kind, taken without authority into the Indian country, for traffic with the Indians, should be destroyed on the spot; the owner, if captured, should be punished by imprisonment and fine.

"Congress should pass laws making it penal to sell or give arms or ammunition to Indians, even by agents, and thus gradually disarm the Indians.

"Give an Indian enough to live on, (lands in severalty) and see that he gets it.

"When a marauding party is trailed to a reservation, force the tribe to deliver up the individuals composing it for punishment.

"Punish murder, pillage and other similar crimes exactly as they would be punished among the whites." *

Having read the last slip hastily, Beck took from his pocket a pencil, and scrawling on the back of the Doctor's advice the letters "O. K.," he returned the papers and closed the lid. For the first time he read the inscription on the gold plate: "*Shoot folly as it flies;*" then he left the room. He glanced at Mary, from the rear door, in her place at her knitting, and then as if rebuked for his weakness, he turned about and strode off to the office.

* Taken in part from a code laid down in "The Great Plains"—Col. Dodge, U. S. A. Very much the same opinions were held by intelligent Western men, at the date of the story, and borrowing from this very comprehensive work, to be used in this connection and way, will not be much out of place.

CHAPTER XXI.

THE STRONG MAN'S TROUBLE — HIS REWARD.

The men for a long time had noticed the changed appearance of Beck; they asked him if he was ill, but with a shake of the head he passed on, annoyed; Mary saw in his looks, in his silence, his awkward way of avoiding her, at times, and more than all, in the feeling he so often threw into his words, that an old, deep sorrow lay behind his manner. It was to her a vexed mystery, such as she could not solve and dare not probe.

Taking up a pen at the office table, Beck sat down and wrote rapidly; pausing now and then to wipe his brow, he wrote on as if each word pained him to trace it, and then raising the paper to the light, he read it.

It was a letter written to Mary and told the secret of his life, and ran thus, in a free-hand plain English:

DEAR MARY: —When you receive this I will be far away. I would have come to you to say what I have to say, but that would only make things worse, and I want to take all the trouble to myself and take it away with me. You have had trouble enough. I send your father's will along with this, and you will see what I did not read, and what I cannot carry out. It almost kills me to say so.

Now I must tell you why. You will not think less of me when you know all, I hope. When I was jus of age, I had a good farm well stocked down in Kentucky, and was comfortable. Thar was no young man of my inches could hold a rifle, swing a whip or ride a horse alongside of me. They tried it often and was beaten, and that's how it all come about.

There was a young girl in our parts, and she was called the belle of the neighborhood. All the boys took a shine to her, I among the rest; and among so many she hardly knew how to choose. At a shooting match she gave me an open preference after I had won the prize.

Well, we was married and I was a happy man, too happy, mebbe, for I loved her well; but I soon found that I had let my heart run away with my head. She was not a good wife; no, not even a true wife, Mary. You have known me long, and you know it was only my wrongs that could drive me away, so I left her. I left everything jus as it stood, after I had told her we could never live together, and I journeyed West, become a soldier and a scout.

She still lives, and you know I am in duty bound, so long as she bears my name, to live as I am. You will say that never by word or sign have I ever said a word against her. And now that everything is jus as your good father would have liked it, all but this, you will see that it cannot be. Sooner than deceive you,

Mary, I would take my own life, — the little that is left that is worth taking. God bless you and goodbye. From your friend in life and death,

JOHN BECK.

There were moments to the lonely writer of acute and cruel misery. He loved Mary with a love as pure as the purest, but there was not a word nor line of his letter that disclosed it. In all his long and brotherly intercourse with her, there had never been a look or sign to warm or awaken in her an attachment stronger than friendship. And yet through all these long, manly years, the smothered passion burned like a slow, consuming fire; it had nearly destroyed him. By the gentle instinct of woman, Mary was guarded in her liking for Mister John, and never but once had a spoken word, by any one who knew them, touched the chord that lay so deeply hidden. The Colonel, in his friendly, familiar way, said just before the attack on the barricade:

"John, sumthin or nuther tells me that this fight may put me outer ther way; we can't none of us tell, but thar's my darter, John; I bleeve that she loves you, John, leastwise I think so, and I kinder bleeve you love her —"

His speech was cut short by the yell of the savage, and never finished, but his words "I bleeve that she loves you" rang in Beck's ears night and day; these coupled with the lines of the will which Mary must, in time, see, drew from his honor the cruel sacrifice which he had begun. He read his letter several times, folded it and placed it in his blouse pocket.

He went about quietly taking a last look; at the cabins he took up the little ones and talked to them; he spoke good wishes to the men that each might remember; he stroked the face of a favorite ox; he stood by the grave of his patron and tore himself away to find Kitty, and saddled her.

The guard who came on his rounds in the evening was Sandy.

The teamster at Beck's call joined him.

"I'll be off on a long scout pooty soon, Sandy, and when I'm gone, hand these papers to Miss Mary;" here he drew from his breast the will and the letter, and placing them in the hand of the messenger, he went on: "Bout an hour from now she'll come into the dining-room and you'll see the light thar; go in and hand them to her; that's all. Good-bye, Sandy."

They shook hands; in a moment more the clatter of the mare's hoofs was heard out on the road, and the guard surprised peered after the rider into the blackness of night.

"He's not afeerd o' the deil hissef; but it's mesel that dinna loike the looks of things nor of him nyther: shure and the lassie has worrit a bit too much, and if it be to worrit more I'll wait a bit."

The scout gave free play to his spurs, with a reckless dash into the dark, but his limbs fell out of the stirrups, he dropped his rein, and his head sank low on his breast. The vigor of his free, open nature was gone; never before in the sweep of the wild gallop had he come to so sudden a halt. He sat on his horse in the darkened solitude as one stricken; never before had he dreamed with his eyes open, and never had his strong pulse grown feeble at the touch of a sudden chill. He felt something dearer to him than he had ever known, something more bitter than his heart had ever felt. In the stillness, heavy upon him, he listened; a sound far away had caught his ear, and somehow it cheered him like the whisper of a better fate; again he heard it, now louder and nearer, like a blast of the harvest-horn heard over the meadows. He turned his horse's head, he knew not why, and rode back to the landing. The boat tied up and he stepped aboard.

"Any letters for the post?" he asked quickly.

"Yes," said the clerk, "here's one for '*John Beck, Cheviteau's Landing.*'"

"That's me; let's have it." Taking the missive he tore it open.

It read as follows:

"LOUISVILLE, KY.

"Mr. JOHN BECK:

"*Dear Sir*,— After a long search I have found out your present abode, and this is to inform you of the death of Mrs. Beck, which took place six years ago. She left all the property unencumbered and subject to your disposal.

"Will you please send me word, in what way you

wish the estate attended to; whether to be held in trust for you, or sold?

"Very truly yours,

"Geo. Thatcher, *Attorney.*"

Not even a word of regret as a dying legacy from the woman who had embittered his youth; only a formal notice; only this, as cold as the slab that covered her.

Beck sprang to the wharf, leaped to his mare's back and dashed forward; as he came in sight of the house he saw Sandy on the porch, and the light in the window.

"Stop," he cried as he jumped down; "come heah, Sandy, quick."

The man turned and came to him.

"Whar's the papers?" he asked in trembling haste.

"It's me wat has em, shure."

The scout snatched them almost rudely.

"Take the mare to the corral, Sandy," he said; "I'll be guard to-night."

As the man rode away Beck tore up his letter to Mary, and with the open will in his hand he entered the house. Mary glancing at him, as he came to her through the dining-room door she asked:

"What's the matter, Mister John, you're so very pale?"

"Am I pale? Well, Mary, a word from you will bring me right."

"Come, sit down, do," she said, with a tremulous voice; "I fear you're ill."

He sat down at her side as he placed the will in her hand, laying his finger on the final clause.

"Read, Mary," he said, "the last words of your father; answer me, as you would answer him if he said these words to you."

She glanced at the sentence and conned each word as the color came to the sweet, sad face; in the light from the shaded lamp, to Beck's eyes it changed to that of a seraph's, purely beautiful; she raised her gaze and softly it fell upon his own, and her speech was gentle and calm:

"No voice, not even the dead's, Mister John, can command my love for you; it's yours,"—she paused but an instant,—"and you know it, don't you?"

Like a little saint's her arms were folded on her bosom as his girdled her form.

"For better, for worse, as my wife?—Well, Mary;" and suddenly she wreathed her arms about his neck.

He drew forth from his pocket the Bible that had lain there many days, and opening it on the page where the marker pointed to the old, trite lines, he read them aloud; he closed the book and kissed her; and the man's pent-up nature was forever freed by the one she gave back from her soul.

On a sunny morning, John Beck and Mary Cheviteau joined hands in the village church, and passed out to begin life's errand.

Peter Cheviteau had served his day and purpose,

and had served them well, somewhat in the fashion of all who needed caution more than prowess to get round the perils that beset them. The savage was too stern a foe at first to face and resist, so Peter and his like with prudent steps moved slowly. They endured much, and bore up under bloody provocations in the hopeful belief that time would strengthen the whites.

They were not disappointed. From the seaboard striding westward, with an impulse that knew no pause, trade crossed the mountains of the Middle States, and where the snap of the wagon-whip grew faint, the louder snap of the ox-train began; trade pushed its agents to the front to widen the road; bolder men were sent or came to beat down and override, to break away the barriers, to "pull through" straightly. Beck, a born captain, was found in the lead; and now, with the way clear, at once sprang up the thrift of a new era; under the ægis of safety, scattered groups in waiting far away came together, settled down in content, and began the town.

A few years rolled by; Tim Murphy with busy feet waited on all comers to his inn. Looking in on his guests at a table where "a squar meal" was served, he turned about to wait on a stranger who stood at his bar. The man's high beaver was a day's wonder thereabout, and his speech was that of the East.

"A cocktail," he said to Tim, as he stroked his beard.

"A pfat?"

"A cocktail," repeated the other.

Not to be outdone by any show of genius in his line, which the East might claim, Murphy made up a drink, known in those remote corners as an "eye-opener,"— a cross between aquafortis and "Thompson, No. 6,"— and placed it on the counter.

"Jabers, an is't that ye'd be afther, me boy," he said with a show of triumph, "it'll raise the feders of a paycock;" and truth to say it satisfied.

Tim had lived well and had prospered; the path which the villagers called a street, wormed its crooked length past his door, and Mary Beck, as of old, walked daily over it by the inn. If Tim caught a glimpse of her as she came, nothing could stay him, not even the profits of his house. He said he was in duty bound, and his bow was low. He bade her good morning as one would thank a princess, and if there were few or many to notice him he never failed to add:

"Whist, d'ye mind; that's the lady, an may she live a tousen yeahs."

An aged pilgrim came one day from the "sterang kontree;" with her came also the "gude man jon," and the savings of years in his pocket. In a little while thereafter they rented the store, and with Mary's help carried on a brisk sale of trifles. It was John's rule not to allow his gifts to droop, so at odd times he managed all the rough jobs that were needed. He painted the logs in plain white, and in shining contrast touched up the chinking between with a blazing red. It was something near a marvel to the eyes of those who gazed on the old fellow's art, and he spoke of it proudly, as a conceit to hand down his reverence for the flag, which, at a distance, the colors resembled.

In his useful way, to fetch and carry, and to lend a ready hand in all things, he once set about to make the place look new; to brighten the shelving and to scrub the floor. It was during his wife's absence that he fell to work with soap and brush. Her pencil marks against certain of their creditors, were kept in hidden spots on the white surface. All unknown he wiped out the "p's" and "q's," and settled accounts without striking a balance. On Melinda's return, her first concern was to look up these debits, and her scream brought John to "about face" standing at present.

"Yuse gone and spyled us," she cried.

"How?" he answered, bringing his hands to his side, the little fingers touching the seams of his pants.

"We'se busted, John, sho," she said, speaking fast like one with a peck of trouble, and was about to berate him when voices were heard at the door. It was the talk of the men in her debt who came to pass an hour over their mugs. To one she said at once, with easy wit and tact:

"Them chalks of yourn run up to twenty, arn't that right?" It was a venture near the mark, not under it.

"Yes," each in turn replied, to hold on to her favor. She put back the scores as debts acknowledged, without causing a doubt.

Months before one of the boats had set Tobias on shore at the landing. Sent home to his friends as a harmless simpleton, and as all things have their uses, in time the poor wreck found much for his hands to do. He ran errands for the store; was stableman on shares with Cato, the jockey; a companion of the school-boys in their games. Under his care the vines grew greener about the porch, and the flowers, more deeply tinted, shut out the heat where Mary sat. One freak, fashioned out of a mental chaos, he held to always as a link with his former misery. He dug a grave and covered it with a slab, a tomb in miniature, wherein he said his lost child slept. At times, he delved in the debris of the old cabin and carried a spadeful to his cave and buried it. A pitiful sight, that of a mortal bending over the ashes of a ruined past entombed in the remorse of the present, and a truth might have been written on the stone; the pursuit of so low a passion as revenge never elevates, but degrades even as low as the helpless idiot.

Doctor Tom returned to the post; at Beck's request he became an inmate again of the house, and one of the shutters bore the rude "shingle" of the physician.

At first sight of him, the parrot cried:

"Hello!" and skipping from its perch with an expression almost human, stroked its wings and face on the Doctor's feet.

Beck had said on meeting him:

"I've read the papers in the mahogany case, and I've found your long-lost brother."

It was not hard to trace the resemblance between the Tobias Shorter of the Doctor's notes and the poor simpleton, and when this and that were put together, the old man felt the force of each coincident. He had not seen the wanderer for many years, but when brought face to face with him, the recognition was complete. Ever after it was touching to see the meeting of the two, as there seemed to be a glimmer of some past episode that caused the feeble-minded man to smile. And the Doctor strove hard to arouse some recollection through which he might be better known, but he dropped the hand of the other with a sigh.

Doctor Tom Shorter had always been judge in the disputes among the men, and the umpire of their wagers. When the ruder forms of meting out justice had passed away and the first steps of political government were taken, it seemed the proper thing that he should be made a magistrate. There were many perplexing "ifs and buts" to be squared in knotty questions that came before him, but he managed well and kept the peace.

Two men in the town fell out about a small debt. On the day of trial before his honor he proposed to them a basis of settlement to which they agreed *on condition* that there should be no costs, to which the Doctor, in his official capacity, consented. But a difficulty arose. Heinrich, who had been duly appointed a constable, and who had a right to his fees, was unwilling to give them up. The Doctor tried to prevail with him, but in vain. Finally growing impatient, as he considered the constable a mere attaché, he gave a *peremptory order* to consent, and on his refusal *fined him* the exact amount of his fees *for contempt*, entered up the judgment on the basis of the compromise and adjourned the court! *

Beck dropped in at the school very often.

"Schoolmaster," he said, one day, "I'll bet these boys a pony they can't tell the duties of a citizen."

One lad looked up with a cheerful face and seemed to wrestle with the question.

"If you know speak out, sir," said the teacher.

"First," he answered, "is to fear God."

"Spoken like a man; what next?"

"To love his country."

"Right, sir; look out, Mister Beck, your pony's in danger; go on, little man."

The lad faltered; it was an idea of his own at which he halted.

"Go on," said Beck, "you shall have the pony; what's the next duty of a citizen?"

"To shoot an Injin;" the boy answered boldly, and believed what he said.

"That's not exactly it," the teacher said, but Beck was pleased and gave up.

"He can have the pony," he added, laughing.

On the fourth of July following the little horse was presented as a gift from John Beck, and during the holiday the recipient and his chums put the pony to use, boy fashion, and bantered Mrs. Garrulson to a mount. They helped her to her seat, and one went so far as to kneel,

* Adapted from "Western Character — McConnell."

that she might step from his back to the saddle, while another applied a match to an explosive which hung from the pony's tail. What followed belongs to the chronicles of the town; a legend in after years told the story of a horse flying by, its tail on fire, and puffing smoke from its nostrils. The old woman, it was said, waited her turn with patience, but before the year was over she had thrashed every boy in that school.

Charles Marshall — the Whack of other days — and his charming wife Lu made their home at the old place; the trade called him away often, and she travelled with him. The baptismal name of the blessing which heaven sent them was Mary Cheviteau Marshall; a blue-eyed baby beauty.

Tim Murphy, not once or twice, but many times to many strangers, as he stood on the village street, called up its history; it was over this path, he would say, that Mary came to visit the sick, and near it she sang, when the infant was buried; along it she sped to the help of the women and children; over it ran the savage with his torch, and about it glared the rash, red flames of that terrible midnight; here rode the rough riders to the bugle's note, and madly in pursuit drove the invader back.

"Ah, be jabes, me boy, yees may look at me, what's lift av coorse; an yander's the stone-pile, whar under it slapes a score of me frens; an we fout like tigers, do ye mind; rest to their sowls."

"John,' said Mary, in the early morning, as she sat on the old porch, "look there!"

He came and stood at her side, looking down the walk; a broad, bright flood of the summer sunrise-light, in broken glints through the foliage, fell on the porch of the inn, on the steps of the cabin-store; it gleamed on the little mound, stole into the school-house window; it shone all radiant on the poplars, and glanced to the grave of the trader; in one lone ray, golden and glad, it clung to the church's spire.

"It is beautiful, John," she said.

"Yes, Mary," he answered, as one who had found his content, for his face was young again and full of hope; "the sun seems to think it good what the law has made; and the law calls it Marysville."

Just then their baby boy came running to outstretched arms; she raised him to her shoulder, turning the fresh, fair face to the beams of the morning; every feature was his mother's. Type of a new generation, the little fellow gazed out on the wide, green wonder and clapped his hands; looked long on the waste whose spectres his father had felled, that he, of a race to come, might live and be happy.

Near enough to please him with the whirl of the whip, Beck stood, a proud, true, sturdy man, as he sprung the lash with the old, sharp snap; the signal of after years, when the Pathfinder and the Goldseeker led the way, which was heard in one commingling sound from lines of trains continuous, beginning at the river to halt by "the deep sounding sea."

www.ingramcontent.com/pod-product-compliance
Lightning Source LLC
Chambersburg PA
CBHW022025240426
43667CB00042B/1188